IRISH AND AFRICAN AMERICAN CINEMA

THE **SUNY** SERIES

CULTURAL STUDIES IN CINEMA/VIDEO

WHEELER WINSTON DIXON | EDITOR

IRISH AND AFRICAN AMERICAN CINEMA

Identifying Others and Performing Identities, 1980–2000

MARIA PRAMAGGIORE

STATE UNIVERSITY OF NEW YORK PRESS

Published by
State University of New York Press, Albany

Printed in the United States of America

For information, contact State University of New York Press, Albany, NY
www.sunypress.edu

Production by Marilyn P. Semerad
Marketing by Anne M. Valentine

Library of Congress Cataloging-in-Publication Data

Pramaggiore, Maria, 1960–
Irish and African American cinema : identifying others and performing identities, 1980–2000 / Maria Pramaggiore.
p. cm. — (SUNY series, cultural studies in cinema/video)
Includes bibliographical references and index.
ISBN-13: 978-0-7914-7095-4 (hardcover : alk. paper)
ISBN-13: 978-0-7914-7096-1 (pbk. : alk. paper)
1. Motion pictures—Ireland. 2. African Americans in motion pictures.
3. African Americans in the motion picture industry. I. Title.

PN1993.5.I85P73 2007
791.4309417—dc22

2006020755

10 9 8 7 6 5 4 3 2 1

CONTENTS

ILLUSTRATIONS

ACKNOWLEDGMENTS

A number of people have provided me with intellectual and material sustenance as I worked on this book. Foremost are my colleagues at North Carolina State University, who were there from the beginning. Without your encouragement, this project would not have come to fruition: Joe Gomez, Jim Morrison, Jon Thompson, Tom Wallis, Elaine Orr, Dawn Keetley, Deb Wyrick, Sharon Setzer, Leila May, and Cat Warren. Colleagues elsewhere have provided me with ideas, suggestions, and encouragement through their own scholarship and their generosity; they include Krin Gabbard, Luke Gibbons, Diane Negra, Martin McLoone, and Brian McIlroy. The annual Earth Day gathering not only provided a benchmark with which to measure progress, but it also gave me a reason to work toward it, and I am indebted to Kim Loudermilk, Ellen Garrett, Annie Ingram, and Martha McCormack for that. Thanks to Jans Wager for her unflappable optimism.

Sunniva O'Flynn and Manus McManus at the Irish Film Archive in Dublin were tremendously gracious to a jet-lagged Yank with a long list of films to see. My research needs at home in North Carolina were ably attended to by the crack reference librarians at NC State's D. H. Hill Library.

Several anonymous readers offered extremely useful comments and suggestions that strengthened the manuscript. I offer sincere thanks to Wheeler Winston Dixon, series editor, and, especially, to James Peltz, Interim Director at SUNY Press, who has been an extremely supportive editor at all points along the journey.

INTRODUCTION

> The danger is in the neatness of identifications.
>
> —Samuel Beckett, *Disjecta*

Taking its cue from Samuel Beckett, this book examines the disorderly identifications of screen characters in twenty-five Irish and African American films made between 1980 and 2000. In these films, character identification functions as a politically charged act that ruptures the boundary between self and other. These moments when characters suspend themselves and explore what it means to be an other are linked to experiences of social disenfranchisement and psychological self-estrangement.

As screen characters explore otherness, they explicitly question paradigms of identity founded upon exclusion and hierarchy. In contemporary African American and Irish films, these paradigms are associated with colonialist and racist power dynamics that are based on essentialist notions of identity. Yet the same essentialist frameworks are shown to underlie anti-colonial nationalisms that can mirror the colonizer-native binary and merely reverse its terms. Thus, in these films, acts of identification reflect a profound skepticism toward monolithic identities and emphasize the diversity that disrupts national, racial, and gender identities. They also reveal an interest in exploring Irishness and blackness as performances rather than ontological imperatives.

The porous sense of self that these films depict is a cinematic counterpart to W. E. B. DuBois's potent concept of double consciousness, an epistemological standpoint from which the self is perceived as subject and object that is derived from experiences of racialization and internal colonization. Irish and African American histories and experiences of colonization differ in critically important ways. To study these two contemporary film cultures alongside one another is neither to compare nor to equate those histories. Instead, I consider these emerging cinemas of the 1980s and 1990s in terms of their common metaphor for addressing the dilemma of postmodern but not-yet-postcolonial identities. What this book proposes is that, during the 1980s and 1990s, a common interest in rejecting lingering colonial stereotypes, and the rigid racial, gender, and national identities that inform them, was expressed in Irish and African American cinemas through an emphasis on character identification. The films posit that acts of identification offer a means of moving beyond the terminology of *self* and *other* to explore the constructed, relational, and performative aspects of identity.

The films I examine are not radical countercinema manifestos but conventional narrative films addressed to general audiences. In fact, many of them are Irish and African American "themed" films that represent the mainstreaming of indigenous Irish and black independent film traditions. In terms of their production histories and their textual address, the films embody contradictory desires to create distinctive Irish and African American visual cultures, to counter lingering colonialist stereotypes, and to stage an encounter between essentialist and postmodern concepts of identity. Those desires are expressed through characters who identify with others across boundaries of race, gender, class, and nation and discover new ways of defining self, other, and self as other.

The popular yet political character of these films reflects the material circumstances of filmmaking outside Hollywood in the late twentieth century. Government subsidies, the Eurimages Fund, television and cable networks, and private investors funded low-budget African American and Irish films such as *Daughters of the Dust* (Dash 1990) and *The Disappearance of Finbar* (Clayton 1996). Others, such as *In the Name of the Father* (Sheridan 1993) and *He Got Game* (Lee 1998), were co-financed and distributed by major studios: the former was a collaboration between Sheridan's Hell's Kitchen Films and Universal, and the latter was a joint project of Lee's production company, 40 Acres & a Mule Filmworks, and Touchstone pictures, a division of Disney. Despite their somewhat marginal status within an industry increasingly dominated by Hollywood conglomerates, these cinemas garnered international recognition during the 1980s and 1990s. This attention was partly the result of the prominence of several directors, including Neil Jordan, Spike Lee, Jim Sheridan, and John Singleton.[1]

The emergence of these quasi-national cinemas might seem paradoxical, given the period in question: two decades during which the stability of national designations and the fixity of racial identities were increasingly called into question. During the 1980s and 1990s, a number of events and trends seemed to confirm the nation-state's demise as an economic, cultural, and political entity. Those events included the dissolution of the Soviet Union, the movement toward freer trade, and the increasing importance of international capital flows. Ethnic nationalism as a model of political organization was discredited, not only amidst the "ethnic cleansing" of the Balkan wars and genocide in Africa, but also as a result of the growing recognition of the implications of migrant, refugee, and disapora cultures. In critical discourses, Benedict Anderson's influential notion of the "imagined community" defined the nation as a powerful yet fictional construct.[2] Within film studies, research on national cinemas shifted from the analysis of film industries to the textual representation of nationality. In fact, several recent studies have defined national cinemas in terms of their engagement with the concept of national identity.[3]

The historical emergence of Irish and African American cinemas at a time when events and critical discourses alike forced a reconsideration of totalizing national narratives partly explains the films' focus on deconstructing identity. A desire to address dominant misrepresentations of internal others—that is, the project of cultural decolonization—explains the intense focus on the dynamics of identification in these films.

Between 1980 and 2000, Irish and African American films embedded postmodern debates about identity within popular narrative cinema by focusing on modes of identification: acts through which characters temporarily relinquish the notion of a permanent, coherent self. These gestures reveal both a desire to move beyond the understanding of identity as a fixed essence *and* the difficulty of renouncing traditional, ontological notions of national, gender, and racial identity. Focusing on character identification speaks to the way identities are constructed through acts of exclusion and may be deconstructed through equally unsettling practices of appropriation, incorporation, and mimicry.

NONESSENTIALIST IDENTIFICATION: TWO EXAMPLES

Two examples help to illuminate my argument that identification expresses the tension between traditional and postmodern concepts of identity in recent Irish and African American films. In Alan Parker's *The Commitments* (1991), based on the exuberant novel by Roddy Doyle, Jimmy Rabbitte, a James Brown devotee and working-class hero, manages a band of disenfranchised Dubliners.[4] He convinces the band, called The Commitments, that the time is ripe for music that expresses "sex an' politics . . . [r]eal sex" (12). Adhering to the adage that one should write about what one knows, Jimmy tells the lads to look to their working-class background as a source of their own culturally distinctive sound:

> —Your music should be abou' where you're from an' the sort o' people yeh come from—Say it once, say it loud, I'm Black and I'm proud.
>
> They looked at him.
>
> —James Brown. Did yis know—never mind. He sang tha'.—An' he made a fuckin' bomb.
>
> They were stunned by what came next.
>
> —The Irish are the niggers of Europe, lads.
>
> They nearly gasped: it was so true.
>
> —An' Dubliners are the niggers of Ireland. The culchies have fuckin' everythin'. An' the northside Dubliners are the niggers o' Dublin.—Say it loud, I'm Black an' I'm proud. (13)

Jimmy expresses his working class culture—an identity he distinguishes from the culchies, the middle class city-dwellers who migrated to Dublin from the countryside—by identifying with African American music. This crosscultural identification astonishes the band members, yet rings "so true." Jimmy's vernacular reflects the author's interest in the oral and poetic capacities of language; this emphasis on oral performativity reappears in the form of numerous musical performances in the film.[5]

Jimmy's cohorts express their social alienation by performing music. They appropriate, but also translate, African American soul music, an emotionally expressive art form associated with resistance to racism.[6] They attempt to make the music their own by citing the linguistic effects of

English colonialism in Ireland and, specifically, the loss of the native tongue and the renaming of Irish cities and towns. During the band's first gig, singer Deco reroutes the "Night Train" by substituting stops on the Dublin DART train's northern line for U.S. cities, reclaiming Irish place-names while at the same time de-territorializing urban spaces.

The band's appropriation of soul music reveals a complicated, even paradoxical, view of race. Emphasizing the liberating effects of performing soul music, band philosopher Joey the Lips claims, "soul has no skin color" (44). Yet, in Joey's mind, other forms of music do. Charlie Parker "had no right to his Black skin," according to Joey, because he played jazz, an overly intellectual and individualistic form (108). Joey refers to his bandmates as "Brother" and "Sister," telling them: "Soul isn't words . . . Soul is feeling. Soul is getting out of yourself" (53). In his desire to get out of himself, Joey essentializes soul music as authentically black, despite his statement that it has no skin color. Joey might well be accused of being an agent of love and theft, the formula Eric Lott uses to characterize the racial dynamics of minstrelsy.[7]

The film's unconventional narrative structure underscores Joey's desire for transcendence through performance. The emotional intensity of the episodic musical performances subverts the narrative's forward movement. The emphasis on musical spectacle draws attention to precisely those moments when characters get outside themselves. Through soul music, members of The Commitments express the way their class position undermines their sense of national belonging yet also connects them with "the people" everywhere. The band advertises itself to a global audience, with a strong emphasis on its working-class appeal: "The Hardest Working Band in the World . . . Bringing the People's Music to the People" (73).

The hardworking members of the Commitments are actually out-of-work Irish youth who, like the poet Seamus Heaney's "Tollund Man," are "lost, unhappy and at home."[8] In Ireland, they go virtually unrecognized except in terms of stereotypes. Jimmy is approached by a local record producer, whose record label is called Eejit, a kitschy bastardization of the Irish pronunciation of "idiot." The producer is happy to learn that band members are on the dole because his company is subsidized by the Department of Labor, which approves of him signing the unemployed band members. The members of the Commitments attempt to both articulate and transcend their dire local situation by becoming a global band of "Celtic soul brothers."[9]

After the band breaks up, Jimmy encourages several former members to form a country-punk band. He plays them the music of The Byrds, once again encouraging the band to think of musical performance as a locus of cultural self-definition:

> —Joey said when he left tha' he didn't think soul was righ' for Ireland. This stuff is though. You've got to remember tha' half the country is fuckin' farmers. This is the type of stuff they all listen to. (139)

Jimmy's admonitions reinforce the idea that their music must somehow bear a specifically Irish resonance: it must combine the foreign and the familiar, in the terminology of James Joyce's Stephen Dedalus. Once again, the musicians move outside themselves in order to re-situate themselves at home. In the shift from urban soul to country rock, the rejuvenated band acknowledges the internal diversity of the Irish nation by considering the rural dimensions of Irish experience.[10] They continue to use music and performances to complicate what they understand to be an all-too simplistic notion of national identity.

Jimmy and Joey use the disembodying potential of music to recast the meaning of Irishness. They do so in response to contemporary social and economic dislocations that challenge their traditional notions of working-class Irishness. In the period under discussion, such disruptions include the erosion of the Catholic Church's cultural power; the continuing pattern of emigration for jobs abroad; the economic boom of the Celtic Tiger 1990s; the increasing rate of internal migration to Dublin; widening income disparities; and the numerous repercussions of Ireland's membership in the European Union. As part of an international renegotiation of Irish identities—of which the ubiquitous Irish pub and *Riverdance: The Show* are obvious examples—films like *The Commitments* explore Irishness through characters who identify with and perform otherness.

The central question of this book is to what extent, and in what ways, characters like Jimmy and Joey identify with others, get out of themselves, and, in so doing, explore the constructed nature of all identities. An example from recent African American cinema illustrates the way acts of character identification self-consciously acknowledge the way African American identities, like the Irish identities of the Commitments, are mediated through popular culture.

In Albert and Allen Hughes' *Menace II Society* (1993), practices of identification establish the young African American protagonist as a quintessential American antihero. In *Menace*, several characters look to, identify with, and emulate Hollywood figures. In doing so, they reveal the way popular culture representations help to construct African American identities, with important political implications.

The film's protagonist is Kaydee "Caine" Lawson (Tyrin Turner), whose nickname suggests his fractured identity. The name resonates with the biblical fratricide Cain, the white patriarch of American cinema, Charles Foster Kane, and Harlem Renaissance writer Jean Toomer's *Cane*.[11] Caine's story is familiar, particularly when read within the context of the "New Black City" film.[12] The South Central Los Angeles setting and first-person narration connect the film to both the "new ghetto aesthetic" and to classic gangster films of the 1930s.[13] Caine grows up in South Central, becomes involved in gang violence and crime, and becomes a successful cocaine dealer (yet another "caine"). Ultimately, Caine fulfills the "live by the sword/die by the sword" worldview the ghetto cycle inherits from its gangster film ancestors. He dies in a drive-by shooting instigated by a young man who seeks revenge.

At a critical turning point early in the film, Caine engages in an identification that crystallizes his persona as a gangster. Waiting in a hospital room after he has been treated for a gunshot wound, Caine watches *He Walked by Night* (Alfred Werker 1948). This act of televisual recognition reinforces the notion that Caine acquires his identity from film and television. Caine is fascinated by the white ethnic gangster made appealing by an earlier generation of Hollywood cinema. In the gangster films of the 1930s and their *film noir* descendents in the 1940s, the gangster is a social outcast who is nevertheless as quintessentially American as Horatio Alger.[14] The white gangster's ascent fulfills the American Dream and endorses the melting pot metaphor: he sheds his ethnicity in the process of rising to the top of the underworld.

Caine's identification with this figure, in contrast to his father Tat's (Samuel Jackson) association with another screen image—the renegade drug dealer Youngblood Priest (Ron O'Neal) of *Superfly* (Gordon Parks Jr. 1972)—suggests the son's desire for assimilation. Thus, these conflicting iconographies of masculinity reveal important historical contrasts. Their juxtaposition pits the Black action hero of the 1970s against the white-ethnic gangster. Tat's persona represents the culmination of decades of group protest and individual action aimed at dismantling the system whereas Caine's nostalgia for an earlier era privileges the gangster's ability to manipulate the system for his individual benefit rather than his interest in destroying it.

Caine's identification is set in relief by a subsequent scene in which character identifications reflect upon African American cultural identities. When Caine and his homey O-Dog (Larenz Tate) are forced to watch *It's A Wonderful Life* (Frank Capra 1946) on television with Caine's grandparents (Arnold Johnson and Marilyn Coleman), Caine's discomfort, boredom, and disbelief are made palpable through repeated close-ups. He cannot relate to the Capra film, whose pessimistic postwar vision of American capitalism is redeemed by melodramatic sentiment, and whose obsessive repetition at national holidays has reified its claims to exemplary Americanness.

Caine, Tat, and Grandpapa all identify with screen performances of American masculinity. Grandpapa admires Capra's hero George Bailey (Jimmy Stewart), a man whose arguable triumph is achieved when he recognizes his stake in the American dream of small-town family values.[15] In contrast to his grandfather, Caine prefers to emulate the classical gangster.[16] The gangster's antisocial violence reconciles his desire for capitalist-defined markers of success with his exclusion from legitimate means of achieving them. Thus he differs greatly from Capra's lily-white, suicidal George Bailey. Both are self-destructive figures, but the gangster takes aim at the society around him, not himself. Bailey's saga is reformist, targeting corrupt individuals, whereas Caine's gangster can be unintentionally revolutionary: he sheds light on the endemic problems of capitalism, exposing its ruthless underbelly.

Menace explores generational disparities through the three men's affinities for specific iconographies of celluloid masculinity. Whereas Caine identifies with the urban ethnic (but white) outlaw, Tat Lawson adopts the good badman persona of African American folktales and Blaxploitation fame, while Grandpapa admires the sentimental Capra hero. The screen identifications of Caine, his father, and his grandfather suggest that black masculinity is a historically variable construction, continually renegotiated through identification and performance.

In keeping with this emphasis on cinematic identification as a source of identity, the film makes explicit use of screen images to depict history. The film opens with simulated documentary footage of the Watts riots of 1965. Caine's voice-over situates those events as a historical parallel and backstory; his own story takes place several decades later, amidst urban deindustrialization, the dismantling of social support programs, challenges to affirmative action, police corruption, and the rise of movement conservatism during the Reagan administration and the first Bush administration.

Although they are located within very specific urban geographies (northside Dublin; South Central, Los Angeles), characters in these two films re-envision their local situation through music and film culture. Character identifications in *The Commitments* and *Menace* thus tap into a newly global context for performing identities. One way to conceptualize the spatial imperatives of these films—that is, their expression of local concerns in terms of global popular culture—is through Stuart Hall's familiar analysis of the nation-state's disintegration. Hall writes, "[W]hen the nation-state begins to weaken [. . .] the response seems to go in two ways simultaneously. It goes above the nation-state, and it goes below it. It goes global and local in the same moment" (1997a 178). These two films make explicit the role that popular culture identifications play in this doubled response, as gestures that reach above and below the nation as a paradigm for community and that also seek to move beyond an ontology of identity.

NONESSENTIALIST IDENTIFICATION

I characterize acts of character identification in recent Irish and African American cinema as nonessentialist identification because they express a character's desire to suspend the self and to explore otherness. A number of scholars have discussed the way postmodern culture has reconfigured identities. Richard Kearney employs the term "postnationalism" to characterize the inclusive political and aesthetic sensibilities of contemporary Ireland (1997). Although Kearney's term captures the sense of urgency with which the nation-state has been called into question, its suggestion of having moved beyond nationalism altogether seems premature. The events of the post-September 11 era seem to confirm the persistence of the nation as a military construct, to say the least.

Film scholar Mark Reid has described recent African American film and popular culture as exhibiting a "PostNegritude" aesthetic, which "creates, reveals, and exposes the nonessential nature of socially constructed ideas about race, gender, class, and nation" (1997 18). For Reid, PostNegritude involves "a creative dialogue of subcultures, of insiders and outsiders, of diverse factions" (1997 113). Expanding upon Reid's idea, I employ the term nonessentialist identification because the aesthetic Reid describes is evident in both African American and Irish filmmaking of the 1980s and 1990s. In Irish and African American films, character identification forms the locus of "creative dialogue" and plays a crucial role in the deconstruction of identity.

Most film scholarship on identification, including recent work on postcolonial identification, focuses on spectatorship. Postcolonial film theorists have studied the Eurocentrism of visual media, analyzed filmmaking practices that challenge and resist that regime, and elaborated instances in which colonial and ethnographic gazes construct primitive others.[17] These studies, like much of film theory, stress the psychosexual character of spectator identification and the viewer's mobility with respect to gender, race, class, and even species when introjecting on-screen figures. In *Threshold of the Visible World*, Kaja Silverman discusses a mode of spectator identification that relies upon both unconscious processes and secondary self-examination to foster a sense of estrangement from the self.[18]

Like Silverman, I am interested in pursuing the link between identification and self-estrangement, but from a different vantage point. I emphasize the social, political, and aesthetic dimensions of identification between and among characters, addressing the way character identification exhibits not only a potential for estrangement from the self, but also from dichotomous concepts of identity. Drawing upon Silverman's useful observations that identification always involves the body, I organize my analysis according to several key modes of embodiment (and disembodiment) that catalyze and enable character identification. I examine music and performance (chapter 2); pregnancy and maternity (chapter 3); violence (chapter 4); and genre (chapter 5), concluding with a discussion of contemporary Westerns that revisit the familiar American genre in order to challenge the racist underpinnings of traditional notions of the national body.

One paradox of cultural production in an era of globalization and standardization is that there are expanded opportunities for representing the complexity of identities and crosscultural affinities. Stuart Hall has written that marginality has never been such a productive space as it is now. Irish and African American films of the 1980s and 1990s exploit this moment and its opportunities for productive marginality. These films present identification as an aesthetic and political gesture that has the potential to redefine identity as an inclusive and ongoing process rather than a state of being.

CHAPTER SUMMARIES

In chapter 1, "Identifying Others," I review the recent history of Irish and African American cinema in the context of a longstanding connection between Irish and African American cultures. I consider Kaja Silverman's account of heteropathic identification and its dependence upon the body, extending her assertions to the analysis of character, rather than spectator, identification.

In chapter 2, "Sampling Blackness: Music and Identification in the Films of Neil Jordan and Spike Lee," I examine jazz and performance in Neil Jordan's *Angel* (1982) and *The Miracle* (1991), and in Spike Lee's *Mo' Better Blues* (1990), *Crooklyn* (1994), *Do the Right Thing* (1989), and *He Got Game* (1998). Jazz music offers Jordan and Lee's protagonists a way to get out of themselves, to identify with others, and to participate in a community of jazz musicians, past and present. More than merely embellishing the narrative with jazz music, both of these filmmakers convert jazz form into film style, replacing narrative continuity with circularity, riffing, and improvisation. Their cinematic adaptation of the jazz aesthetic reinforces the notion that identity, like music, is a process rather than a product.

Chapter 3, "'It's a Wise Child that Knows His Own Father': Pregnant Performances and Maternal Mythologies," explores films that foreground the improperly pregnant body as a process rather than a state of being. Although these films emerged amidst a heightened rhetoric surrounding teen pregnancy in Ireland and the United States, they also speak to longstanding colonialist representations of subaltern women's sexuality as well as the prescriptive patriarchal family values of Irish and black nationalisms. Within this framework, I discuss *The Color Purple* (Spielberg 1985), *Hush-a-Bye Baby* (Margo Harkin 1989), *Daughters of the Dust* (Julie Dash 1991), *The Playboys* (Gillies MacKinnon 1992), *Just Another Girl on the IRT* (Leslie Harris 1992), *The Snapper* (Stephen Frears 1993), *December Bride* (Thaddeus O'Sullivan 1990), *A Man of No Importance* (Suri Krishnamma 1994), *Beloved* (Jonathan Demme 1998), and *Blessed Fruit* (Orla Walsh 1999).

Chapter 4, "Culturing Violence: Masculine Identification in Irish and African American Gangster Films," considers recent revisions of the gangster genre. Contemporary versions of the gangster film situate their narratives within the context of the Troubles in Northern Ireland and urban gangs in the United States. They also make clear the importance of masculine identification to the gang community. The chapter includes readings of *Cal* (Pat O'Connor 1984), *Boyz N the Hood* (John Singleton 1991), *In the Name of the Father* (Jim Sheridan 1993), *Menace II Society* (Albert and Allan Hughes 1993), and *The Crying Game* (Neil Jordan 1992).

Chapter 5, "'Both Side of the Epic': Identification and the Nonessentialist Western," discusses the importance of identification within contemporary films that reference and revise the Western, and includes discussions of *Eat the Peach* (Peter Ormrod 1986), *Into the West* (Mike Newell 1992), *Posse* (Mario Van Peebles 1993), and *The Disappearance of Finbar* (Sue Clayton 1996). In these films, characters wrestle with the Western genre's radical individualism and colonialist ideology, seeking to undermine the stark contrast between colonizers and colonized. Pat Dowell describes the Western as "*the* cultural production that continuously refurbished a national foundation myth of agrarian equality" (6). Characters in these films confront and reconsider the basis for national foundation myths by relocating the frontier and/or by populating its hostile landscape with a cast of different others, including African Americans and Irish travelers. In so doing, they call into question the Western's, and the West's, colonialist paradigm of difference.

In these analyses, I am less interested in condemning or celebrating characters' identifications with powerful and/or disenfranchised others and more interested in analyzing the way identifications become a shorthand that signifies a desire for a changing politics and poetics of identity. I share the belief, voiced by Luke Gibbons, that "cultural representations do not simply come after the event, 'reflecting' experience or embellishing it with aesthetic form, but significantly alter and shape the ways we make sense of our lives" (1996a 8). These cultural representations reflect and have shaped contemporary thought, making contributions to our shifting understanding of self and other, and of our real and imagined communities.

CHAPTER ONE

Identifying Others

The central argument of this book is that recent Irish and African American films depict character identification as a process that violates the boundary between subject and object. Through acts of identification, characters inhabit and perform otherness. They circumvent essentialist models of identity that pit self against other, and us against them.

Irish and African American films of the 1980s and 1990s connect these processes of identification not only to the historical and interpersonal dynamics of colonialism but also to contemporary discourses about nation, race, and gender. In the period under consideration, critical discourses about Irish and African American identities, long shaped by practices and ideologies of race, colonialism, and nationalism, were confronted by and indeed helped to generate countervailing ideas and practices that forcefully asserted the constructedness of all identities.[1]

During the 1980s, models of national identity rooted in race and ethnicity were increasingly recognized as problematic and potentially ineffective. In the Republic of Ireland, according to Brian Graham, civic nationalism began to eclipse ethnic nationalism. Cultural geographer James Anderson argues that the Belfast/Good Friday Accords (1998), which address longstanding disputes over the status of the British province of Northern Ireland vis à vis the independent Republic of Ireland, reflect a belief that solutions to this entrenched conflict "require new policies and mobilization around non-national identities and issues" (216).

Discourses addressing African American and African Diaspora identities also shifted their focus in this period. Mark Reid distinguishes earlier black nationalist and Pan-Africanist movements from more recent postNegritude concepts and practices. PostNegritude cultural production encompasses analyses of class, gender, and sexual orientation as well as race; this aesthetic refuses to suppress the "polyvalence of diverse subjectivities" (Reid 1997 112–16).

The dilemma of how to negotiate the deconstructive effects of postmodernity and globalism found vibrant expression in Irish and African American film cultures, which depict the promises of anti-essentialism and the difficulties of relinquishing flawed (yet familiar) models of identity. These films address mass audiences, giving image and voice to widespread concerns about the perceived breakdown of ethnic, racial, and national identities. Through an emphasis on character identification, they interrogate the meaning and stability of Irish and African American identities.

Two films that I examine at length in chapter 5 use character identification to reconsider fixed and binary paradigms of identity in the context of the Western genre. In Mike Newell's *Into the West* (1992), a contemporary fable of marvelous realism, two Irish traveler boys adopt the personas of their favorite cowboy outlaws, Butch Cassidy and the Sundance Kid.[2] Although Butch and Sundance appeared on screen in 1969, long before the boys were born, Ossie (Ciarán Fitzgerald) and Tito Reilly (Rúaidhrí Conroy) are familiar with their exploits because of the ubiquity of the television set and the omnipresence of U.S. popular culture. They rent American Westerns on video and watch *Butch Cassidy* on their neighbors' television, literally becoming Butch's "Hole in the Wall gang," as they peer through the dilapidated wall into the neighboring apartment. And when the boys flee Dublin on horseback, headed for the West of Ireland, they envision themselves galloping into the Wild American West.

But Ossie needs his older brother's help in focusing his identificatory energies. Unsure of his entitlement to Western icons, he asks Tito, "[A]re we travelers Indians?" Although Tito replies that they are cowboys, the boys indiscriminately take on the attributes of both cowboys and Indians during their escape adventure, whooping it up around their campfire and warming tinned beans for dinner. The brothers enact "both sides of the epic," in the words of John Ford, the American film director who is consistently associated with both the Western genre and with Ireland (Peary 72).

In their polymorphous identifications, Ossie and Tito challenge several ideas related to national identities, and they expose the roots of those identities in concepts of racial difference. First, they debunk the notion that the differences between cowboys and Indians are so obvious that one instinctively would know the proper group with which to identify. Second, they deny any automatic identification with the victors of the cowboy-Indian conflict. Third, they force a reconsideration of the idea that Native Americans and travelers are "vanishing races" whose tales of cultural dispossession must be relegated to the space and time of the past. This point is reinforced by the temporal incongruity of the time travel film they watch as they hide out in a movie theater: *Back to the Future III* (Zemeckis 1990). Ossie and Tito are twentieth-century travelers, and, as such, they find it difficult to reconcile their existence with the notion of Indians (or travelers) as a vanquished and vanished people. Because Ossie and Tito fail to distinguish cowboy and Indian in their practices of identification, they call into question the narrative of conquest that constructs natives as savage others and subsequently uses that designation as a pretext to remove them from the landscape.

A 1993 Western challenges that system of difference as well. In Mario Van Peebles's *Posse* (1993), veteran actor Woody Strode narrates a tale that self-consciously situates African Americans within the plot conventions and visual iconography of the Western. Like Ossie and Tito, Strode's storyteller claims allegiance to both the cowboy ethos and to Indian culture. So does the legendary figure of Jesse Lee (Mario Van Peebles), whose diverse outlaw gang and black Indian mentor, Papa Joe (Melvin Van Peebles), support the film's project of recasting the colonial contest as a dispute over capital that is expressed through racial hatred.

Lee's gang grows out of a segregated military unit serving in the Spanish-American War that flees Cuba for the western frontier. Moving north and west, retracing the steps of African Americans who served in the Civil War then ventured west to become the Buffalo Soldiers who fought the Indian Wars, Lee's racially diverse posse heads for Freemansville, a town founded by Lee's father King David.[3] On the way to Freemansville, the posse's experiences catalog the deadly ambiguities of a national identity founded upon racial essentialism: African Americans fight on behalf of the United States in the Civil War, the Spanish-American war, and the Indian wars, yet face extinction "at home" by a Klan-like organization that terrorizes the frontier town. (The plot reiterates a number of elements contained in an earlier African American Western, *Buck and the Preacher* [Sidney Poitier 1972], a point I return to in chapter 5.)

FIGURE 1.1. Jesse Lee's multicultural posse in Mario Van Peebles's *Posse*. Courtesy of Photofest.

Rather than investing Western icons with Manichean attributes, with hero or victim status, *Posse* and *Into the West* indict capitalist individualism as the source of violence, exploitation, and community destabilization. In *Into the West*, corrupt Dublin police officers confiscate Ossie and Tito's horse—symbolically named *Tir na N'og* after the Celtic land of eternal youth—and sell the animal to a wealthy rural businessman. The new owner renames the animal "National Security," a telling moniker that displaces Irish mythology and replaces it with the economic, political, and strategic concerns of contemporary Celtic Tiger Ireland. "National" security—whether the term designates economic or strategic well-being—clearly accrues to the private coffers of businessmen.

In *Posse*, greed undermines community solidarity when a prominent citizen of Freemansville colludes with white racists. Carver (Blair Underwood) buys cheap land vacated by Freemansville residents who have been intimidated by the racist gang. Carver is a key player in the white gang's scheme to profit from the sale of land to the railroad. Through characters like Carver and the exploitive businessman, *Posse* and *Into the West* link capitalism's winner-take-all ethos to agencies or symbols of the nation-state, including the police force, the military, and the railroad.

The films' protagonists are distinguished from these unsavory characters by their identifications with multiple others and by their ability to imagine and act upon diverse, inclusive notions of self and community. In their multiple affinities, Ossie, Tito, and Jessie Lee's posse locate themselves outside the system of difference defined by the merger of American imperialism, free market capitalism, and Hollywood representation: they reject the oppositional logic of cowboy *or* Indian, black *or* white, victim *or* victor. These films do not simply reiterate familiar Western conventions but, instead, engage in a Bakhtinian "double voicing" as they adapt an older genre to new contexts.[4] By calling attention to characters' multiple identifications, these films question the dichotomous rhetoric of racial and national identities and they hint at the troubling implications of any political practice based on essentialism.

The discussion that follows lays the historical and theoretical groundwork for my contention that African American and Irish films of the 1980s and 1990s emphasize acts of identification and, in so doing, stage the conflict between essentialist notions of identity and the postmodern model of identity as performance. The next section examines the Afro-Celt connection, a political and aesthetic affinity between Irish and African American cultures that offers one historical context for examining these film cultures in tandem. The Harlem Renaissance and Irish Literary Revival of the early twentieth century were associated with modern nationalist movements. By contrast, the Irish and African American film "renaissances" that began in the 1980s articulate the challenges that fluid postmodern identities pose to black and Irish nationalisms. The final section of the chapter draws upon contemporary film theory to ground my analysis of character identification in these films.

First, a note on methodology. Setting Irish and African American film cultures side by side may seem to some readers to be misguided, or even irresponsible. Colonial settlement, forced evictions, land confiscation, transport, and enslavement have disrupted and defined Irish culture and diverse African cultures differently through centuries of modern history. Although they are diasporic cultures, the Irish Diaspora is primarily the result of emigration rather than a global dispersal emanating from the triangular trade in commodified bodies that produced the African Diaspora. In addition, the experience of racialization has differed greatly, particularly in the context of the United States, where Irish immigrants ultimately acquired whiteness, crossing a color line that African Americans could not. Finally, the Irish Free State (1922), which later became the Irish Republic (1949), is a formal state institution that represents the culmination of centuries of struggle among diverse Irish nationalists against British colonial rule. Of course, the geographical and symbolic borders of the Irish nation remain contested, not only because of the partition of Northern Ireland but also because a narrow vision of a traditional rural Irish Catholic culture dominated representations of Irishness within and outside of Ireland for much of the twentieth century.

The history of black nationalism reveals a wide variety of approaches to the national question in both symbolic and material terms. Many black nationalist leaders have looked to the continent of Africa as a source of national identity. In the eighteenth and nineteenth centuries, Paul Cuffee, Martin Delany, and Henry Turner sought to establish a black nation state by repatriation to Africa or relocation to Central America or Canada because they doubted that African American self-determination was possible in the United States. Oppsition to such schemes—particularly among abolitionists like Frederick Douglass and

Albion Tourgee—held that African Americans were appropriately considered "natives" of the United States (McCartney 19).

Three areas of divergence emerged in twentieth-century black nationalist movements, from the Pan-African Congress associated with W. E. B. DuBois to Marcus Garvey's African nationalism in the 1920s to the black nationalisms of the 1960s and 1970s. Philosophical and tactical disputes have involved, first, whether a separate nation is a prerequisite for African American self-determination; second, what is the proper geographical site or locus for a black nation; and third, whether a movement for black liberation ought to encompass U.S. racism, an interracial class analysis, and/or a global vantage point that expresses the reality of the African Diaspora as a "non-state nation" (Johnson 1998).

I acknowledge that profound differences in the historical experiences and the concepts of national identity have informed Irish and African American cultures. I nevertheless would make the case that reading Irish and African American film cultures in relation to one another helps to illuminate certain historical and representational questions that reading them as instances of a singular national or cultural tradition cannot. Certainly, I run the risk of perceptions that I am endorsing a notion of postcoloniality as "a universal constant," and reinforcing a metropolitan focus on culture as a "free floating ambience" (Radhakrishnan 1996, 155–57).

Yet I am struck by the way these two cinemas elaborate the process of identifying with others as a mode of self-recognition and redefinition that may produce personal transformation and political change. These films focus on the dynamics of diaspora in an era in which Irish-ness and black-ness were increasingly seen as flexible rather than fixed identities. On the one hand, these ethnonational identities have often seemed to signify entrenched and dichotomous categories of white-ness and black-ness; on the other hand, during the period under discussion, Irish and African American identities became readily procurable through commodities, including music and fashion, which promoted what might be called identity tourism. I would argue that the breakthrough moment for these film traditions occurred during this period not only because of a confluence of resources and talent, but also because these cinemas address contemporary conflicts over essentialism, authenticity, realness, commodification, appropriation, and the preservation of traditional cultures.

To examine these film cultures singly would fail to address the larger cinematic and social implications of practices of identification. Those implications extend to the way global popular culture creates the illusion of a public sphere, organized by communities of consumption, and, thus, reinforces the notion that identification is an efficacious political strategy. I address these issues throughout the book and return to them in the conclusion.

The outpouring of Irish and African American films after 1980 resonates with two earlier moments in history when Irish and black nationalist movements inspired, and were energized by, cultural production. Those moments were the Irish Literary Revival and the Harlem Renaissance at the turn of the twentieth century, and the civil rights protest era of the 1950s and 1960s. One major difference between these two earlier periods and the film boom after 1980 is that the emergence of these cinema cultures was not accompanied by revolutionary protest movements. One important question to consider, therefore, is the relationship between popular cinema and notions of the political: do these films endorse the idea that acts of identification stand in for (or are in themselves) acts of political solidarity? Do popular culture identifications, which may exploit the desire to consume images of otherness without any political investment or responsibility, become the preferred method for navigating the economic and political shifts of global capitalism?

Another important methodological issue raised by these film cutures concerns the concept of national cinema. To consider what it means to de-essentialize identity, it becomes necessary to break with certain traditions, such as a strict obeisance to the national cinema model. I depart from that tradition, which would consider Irish cinema in relation to British and European national cinemas and African American cinema in the context of U.S. cinema, because that framework circumscribes these cinema cultures within national borders. These films deconstruct that paradigm in both their production strategies and narrative concerns.

Ella Shohat and Robert Stam argue for the importance of "[speaking] of cultural/racial groups in relation, without ever suggesting their positionings are identical" (6). To speak these two film cultures in relation suggests that common, *not* identical, concerns permeate their contemporary expressions. Those concerns involve the desire to destabilize essentialist race, national, and gender identities and the often unexpected difficulties that process entails.

The proliferation of Irish and African American film production since 1980 bears examination in both historical and theoretical context. Although Shohat and Stam are interested in "dominant Europe's historically oppressive relation to its internal and external 'others'" (3), they refer to Ireland only to mention Jonathan Swift's satire. They discuss African American film only in the context of Hollywood images. I would argue that there is a critical need for a thorough account of the emergence of quasi-national film cultures that circumvent national and commercial cinema models.

Despite these limitations, Shohat and Stam's work provides important theoretical ballast to this study. Their injunction against recreating binary structures establishes a point of reference for the way this book pairs these two cinemas without pursuing equalization:

> Rather than recreating neat binarisms (Black/White, Native American/White) that ironically recenter Whiteness, while the "rest" who fit only awkwardly into such neat categories stand by as mere spectators, we try to address overlapping multiplicities of identity and affiliation. (6)

This book examines character identification in Irish and African American films because, I argue, it is through that device that African American and Irish filmmakers express their ideas about the "overlapping multiplicities of identity and affiliation" that undermine essentialist notions of identity.

AFRO-CELT CONNECTIONS: RACE AND NATION

A number of historical issues inform the dynamics of otherness and common gestures of identification that appear in the films under consideration. The interest in social and psychological alienation that pervades contemporary Irish and African American films derives from historical experiences of colonization, enslavement, and displacement.[5] Political historian Brian Dooley notes that slavery "was the defining historical experience for Black Americans, but it also played a fundamental part in the development of early Ireland" (7).

England's colonization of Ireland and Europe's colonization of Africa rested upon and crystallized the notion of racial difference and produced surprisingly similar renditions of natives as savages, "missing links," and human chimpanzees.[6] A particularly visual thrust dominates colonialist reportage, conveyed in letters, journals, engravings, paintings, and travel literature. By the late eighteenth century, Enlightenment thinkers employed numerous descriptions of Africans as ape-like and "introduced a commonplace of early travel literature into a 'scientific' context" (Gilman 176).

Jan Pieterse, among others, has speculated that colonial relations between England and Ireland "pioneered and prefigured" the power relations between European colonizers and their non-European territories (32). Michael Hechter argues that racism "came to full flower" in the British Isles as a system of differentiation of Anglo-Saxons and Celts (xvii). L. Perry Curtis demonstrates that Victorian-era political cartoons published in Britain's *Punch* magazine frequently visualized the Irish Celt in the primitive, simian mode used to depict Africans. In 1862, *Punch* suggested the Irish were the "missing link" between apes and Africans, a status previously attributed to the "Hottentot" (Khoi-Khoi) by Bory St. Vincent.[7] British Ethnologist John Beddoe's "Index of Nigrescence" grouped people who lived on the West Coast of Ireland and all Africans in the "Black" category.[8] Victorian novelist Charles Kingsley famously wrote to his wife about the "white chimpanzees" he saw in visits to Ireland.[9]

Racial classification, a system for differentiating groups of people in ontological terms, underpins the idea of nationality through these oppositions of civilized/savage, colonizer/native, and insider/outsider. According to Pieterse:

> These comparisons, in England between Irish people and Africans, and in the United States between the Irish and Blacks, were made under the heading of race, but this only serves as a reminder that, until fairly recently, the terms 'race' and 'nation' (or 'people') were synonymous. (214–15)

Liam O'Dowd has argued that the distinction between civic and ethnic nationalisms obscures the ethnic basis, and bias, of civic nationalism itself and "fails to register the process of ethnic domination and hierarchization central to constructing nation states" (177). Thus, even civic nationalism distinguishes citizens from foreigners and establishes categories of internal otherness based upon ethnic and racial identities.

Countermovements may challenge those hierarchies but adopt the same basic logic. Irish Catholics' demands for full citizenship in Northern Ireland, and African Americans' struggles for civil rights may reject racist hierarchies, but might not necessarily reject ethnic essentialism. Ethnic essentialism—"a belief in the real, true essence of things, the invariable and fixed properties which define the 'whatness' of a given entity" (Fuss xii–xii)—may be politically efficacious but may also simply reverse the terms of colonialist and nationalist hierarchies, leaving assumptions about the static character of identity and a binary construction of "us versus them" intact.

To counter racial hierarchies, and the economic oppression and social exclusion they foment, black and Irish nationalist movements have not only adopted similar strategies of ethnic nationalism but have also forged a historical affinity that George Bornstein has dubbed the Afro-Celt connection.[10] This connection dates back to the nineteenth-century abolitionist movement in the United States and the Catholic emancipation movement in Ireland.[11]

The "Great Liberator," Daniel O'Connell (1775–1847) fueled his movement for Catholic emancipation with oratorical attacks on slavery. In speeches delivered in Ireland and the United States, he frequently compared the plight of Irish Catholic peasants to that of African American slaves. O'Connell's rhetoric and civil disobedience campaigns resonated among American abolitionists intent upon liberating enslaved African Americans. Whereas O'Connell's program inspired American abolitionists, many in Ireland were moved by Frederick Douglass's experiences (Dooley 10). Douglass (1818–1895) traveled to Ireland in the early famine years of 1845–1846, appearing at meetings of the Repeal Association (which promoted the repeal of the 1800 Act of Union with Britain) and the Belfast Anti-Slavery Society.[12] After being presented with a Bible by the Belfast society, Douglass stated "whenever I feel myself to be a stranger, I will remember I have a home in Belfast" (10) and thanked his audience for its interest in "the cause of the wronged and oppressed slaves in America" (10). English and Irish friends raised money that Douglass used to purchase his freedom and to buy a printing press upon which he published the *North Star*, an abolitionist paper.

Connections between Irish and African American political leaders persisted well into the twentieth century. In the early part of the century, notions of a complete secession from dominant culture gained popular appeal among African Americans. Marcus Garvey, who agitated for the creation of an independent black state in Africa, and Eamon de Valera, an Irish Republican leader during Ireland's war for Independence (and later the President of the Republic), shared visions of and strategies for independence. U.S. military intelligence linked Garvey and the Irish-American Friends of Irish Freedom. In 1921, when Garvey was elected provisional president of an African empire at the Universal Negro

Improvement Association (UNIA) conference, he publicly recognized de Valera as the president of the newly formed Irish Free State at a time when Britain and the United States had not officially done so.[13]

Within the United States, however, relations between Irish immigrants and African Americans generally departed from this relationship of mutuality among political leaders. Labor historians such as Theodore Allen, David Roediger, and Noel Ignatiev have documented tensions between African American and Irish laborers in U.S. cities in the North, which, at the turn of the century, witnessed the conjunction of post-famine migrations from Ireland and the Great Migration of African Americans from the rural South. Noel Ignatiev emphasizes that experiences of racialization for the Irish and for African Americans were in many ways similar, but he points out that Irish immigrants, who were initially disenfranchised socially and economically on the basis of a non-white racial designation, "earned" whiteness by constructing themselves in opposition to African Americans, with whom they competed for jobs. Thus, despite the rhetoric of solidarity emanating from some political leaders, in the competitive economic circumstances of the labor market, and in a society circumscribed by the color line, potential affinities gave way to hostilities.

In the cultural arena, Irish and African American artists and activists at the turn of the last century sought to reclaim and valorize what had been designated "primitive" within colonialist representations. In many instances, literary production was marshaled in the service of political efforts to authenticate and validate racial otherness, whether Celtic or African. In late nineteenth-century Ireland, Irish nationalism underwrote the aesthetic rebirth of the Literary Revival. In the United States, the Harlem Renaissance coincided with and fueled political organizing and protest associated with the National Association for the Advancement of Colored People (NAACP), including protests of D. W. Griffith's *The Birth of a Nation* in 1914–1915, the Chicago race riots of 1919, and the development of Garvey's UNIA, which reflected the heightened political consciousness of many African Americans during and after World War I.

Mid-century civil rights movements brought the common struggles of African Americans and Irish Catholics in Northern Ireland into the public eye. Brian Dooley, among others, makes a convincing case that the nonviolent tactics and rhetoric of the black Civil Rights movement of the 1950s and 1960s inspired the Northern Ireland Civil Rights movement of the 1960s. These nonviolent protest movements sought to eliminate discrimination in education, voting, housing, and employment and to affirm the citizenship rights and humanity of African Americans and Irish Catholics.[14] Dooley writes that crosscultural influences between African Americans and Irish Catholics have largely been "underplayed" in historical accounts of the civil rights movements (3). Examples include the link between women's organizing in Birmingham, Alabama, which provided an impetus to widespread activism. The model of the Women's Political Council (which began in Birmingham in 1946) was repeated in Dungannon, Northern Ireland, where women formed the Homeless Citizens League in 1963.

Afro-Celt affinities have persisted in political organizing and in popular culture. During the 1970s, imprisoned IRA members' favored reading materials were books on Dr. Martin Luther King, Jr. A decade later, Irish rock band U2's songs "Pride (In the Name of Love)" (1984) and "Angel of Harlem" (1988) paid tribute to Dr. Martin Luther King, Jr. and Billie Holiday, respectively. Black activist and intellectual Angela Davis, whom Irish activist Bernadette Devlin McAliskey visited in prison in 1969, spoke out in 1997 on behalf of Devlin McAliskey's daughter's release from a London prison.

Literary scholars have documented the Afro-Celt connection in twentieth-century poetry and prose. Tim McLoughlin has explicated the connections between Irish and Zimbabwean settler fiction, whereas Joshua Esty has established the importance of the satirical scatology of Jonathan Swift, James Joyce, and Samuel Beckett to the post-independence novels of Wole Soyinka and Ayi Kwei Armah and their aesthetic of "excremental postcolonialism" (25). Laura Severin has argued that the work of late twentieth-century Scottish women poets such as Liz Lochhead, Valerie Gillies, Jackie Kay, and Carol Ann Duffy reflects the influence of the African American musical tradition, and, particularly, its critique of essentialist and masculinist notions of identity.

The dialogue between Irish and African American cultures was evident in 1990s popular culture in works such *Riverdance, the Show* (1994), where an encounter between Irish immigrants and African American tap dancers on the docks of New York culminates in a duel of footwork. The dancers mock one another's peculiarities of style and training, drawing attention to the contrast between the rigid and unmoving arms of the Irish and the loose limbs of the African American dancers, yet also challenging one another to deliver virtuoso performances. In the film *The*

Nephew (Eugene Brady 1998), a young African American man visits Ireland to meet the family of his dead Irish mother. The fifth installment of the Leprechaun horror franchise, entitled *Leprechaun V: In the Hood* (Rob Spera 2000), stages an encounter between an evil Leprechaun and hip-hop culture. Irish director Jim Sheridan's autobiographical film *In America* (2002) depicts an Irish immigrant family that develops a bond with a Nigerian artist in New York; his *Get Rich or Die Tryin'* (2005) is the story of an African American drug dealer who wants to become a rap artist (the lead role is played by rapper 50 Cent). The music of the Afro Celts, the band that scored Martin Scorsese's *Gangs of New York* (2002) and Terry George's *Hotel Rwanda* (2004), combines *uilleann* pipes and talking drums.

These popular culture collisions and collusions reconsider the supposed incommensurability of Irishness—a cultural identity that often morphs into an emblem of white-ness itself—and black-ness. In an essay on the representation of Irishness as innocence in American culture after September 11, Diana Negra discusses a comic scene in *Charlie's Angels: Full Throttle* (McG 2003) that juxtaposes Irish-ness and black-ness. Bernie Mac, using a fake driver's license that bears the name Paddy O'Malley, defends his identity as "Black Irish": the people who invented the McRib and Lucky Charms. Negra is correct in stating that the scene implies the "omnifarious nature of Irishness" (2004 54). Yet the joke also turns on two additional assumptions: that Irish-ness is as white as it gets and that black-ness is impervious to nationality or ethnicity. The unlikely combination of seemingly polar opposites underwrites the humor of Bernie Mac's attempts to "dilute" his black-ness with a presumed white Irish-ness.

Ranging from the profound to the prosaic, these moments of cultural juxtaposition represent attempts to breach the divide between white-ness and black-ness. Clearly, all identities are being renegotiated under the auspices of global capitalism and its commodification and branding of cultural identities as lifestyles. Ironically, it is often through projects aimed at cultural reclamation, such as *Riverdance* or *Stomp*, that Irish-ness and black-ness have been transformed into living brands to which anyone can gain access by patronizing the local Irish pub or busting the latest moves of a hip-hop star.

Whereas Irish and black cultural nationalist movements of the early twentieth century shared key features, as Tracy Mishkin's *The Harlem and Irish Renaissances* argues, and the civil rights era of the 1950s and 1960s renewed this connection, as Brian Dooley suggests, this book describes a third conjunction of cultures based on the creative response to a disintegration of national constructs. Mishkin argues that a major focus of the Irish and Harlem renaissances was an attempt to "mitigate the effects of what Paolo Freire calls 'cultural invasion' by investing their languages and/or dialects with dignity" (47) and to create "positive depictions in the arts" (37). The importance of folk culture and dialect is apparent in works by Charles Chesnutt, Paul Laurence Dunbar, Zora Neale Hurston, Langston Hughes, Yeats, John Millington Synge, and James Joyce, though not all of these artists saw their work as supporting a nationalist cause.

Early twentieth-century renaissances were concerned with the discovery and preservation of "authentic" Irish and black folk cultures. By contrast, late twentieth-century Irish and African American films stage an encounter between essentialist authenticity and the unfixing of identities. In the films under consideration, defying colonialist stereotypes by reclaiming and celebrating an authentic national identity gives way to expressions of hybridity and disarticulations of self.

WHY NOW? AFRICAN AMERICAN AND IRISH FILM

It's appropriate to ask why Irish and African American cinemas emerged as popular forms during the late 1980s, after almost a century of filmmaking. Economic factors as well as popular tastes explain this turning point. The timing of these film renaissances coincided not only with the rise of several individual directors, including Neil Jordan, Jim Sheridan, Spike Lee, and John Singleton but also with the development of audiences with a heightened interest in diverse representations of otherness. Against the backdrop of blockbuster franchises such as *Alien*, *Terminator*, *Rambo*, and *Die Hard*, low-budget independent films became profitable vehicles, and studios eagerly pursued profit-making opportunities in the wake of the success of films such as *sex, lies, and videotape* (Steven Soderbergh 1989), *The Wedding Banquet* (Ang Lee 1993), *Boyz N the Hood*, and *The Crying Game*.

Historically, two concerns have dominated Irish and African American filmmaking: a desire to resist dominant cinema's misrepresentations, and an interest in the development of a commercial industry to benefit, and employ, Irish and African American people. The prominence of both cultural and economic issues suggests that these cinemas might be best considered within the national cinema paradigm.

Certain historical aspects of Irish and African American film validate that perspective. An editorial published in *The Irish Times* as early as 1922 suggested that Irish cinema might develop along the lines of the "native dramatic movement," a cultural enterprise that contributed directly to the Irish nationalist movement (qtd. in Slide 22). The Republic of Ireland's attempts to develop a commercial film culture highlight the problems inherent in creating a cinema to function as both a mode of cultural expression and an economic growth industry.

Indigenous Irish cinema has been encouraged and hampered by the Irish Republic's adoption of a national cinema model and its emphasis on cinema as a commercial enterprise. The government-subsidized Ardmore Studios (established in 1958), the Irish Film Finance Corporation (IFFC), and the Irish Film Board have primarily served established directors from outside Ireland rather than supporting indigenous filmmaking. Brian McIlroy reports that most of the fifty-six films made between 1958 and 1976 at Ardmore were produced and directed by foreigners (20). Since the early 1980s, the Irish Film Board has provided funds to Irish filmmakers, but, as Terry Byrne writes, "it is still necessary for an Irish director to find a measure of success in the foreign market before being regarded as a good risk for funding by the home government" (191). In other words, international success is the most important criterion for national government support.

The fact that so many Irish films are cofinanced and coproduced within the European Union complicates the notion that Irish Cinema functions as a national cinema. Producing Irish films remains dependent upon externally acquired finance. Films such as *The Disappearance of Finbar* (discussed in chapter 5) and *December Bride* (chapter 3) were financed by consortia that included Irish, British, and Danish sources. So, to define a film as an Irish film in terms of production or narrative content becomes inordinately complex. In fact, some scholars emphasize the potential for formerly marginal filmmaking traditions to unsettle the nation-based model of the European art cinema. John Caughie has argued that 'other' Europeans (including the Scots and Irish, emergent states of Eastern Europe, and immigrants from former colonies), not American cinematic neocolonialism, pose the greatest threat to the notion of a European identity.[15]

African American filmmaking also has embodied the concerns commonly associated with a national cinema, including the desire to define an African American culture and worldview and to sustain a viable industry that trains and employs African Americans. From the earliest years of black American filmmaking, segregation and discrimination ensured that African American cinema would develop outside the Hollywood industry. In the 1920s, Oscar Michaux's *Within Our Gates* (1919) responded to D. W. Griffith's Klan epic *The Birth of a Nation* (1915), while Noble and George Johnson founded the Lincoln Motion Picture Company, whose goal was to depict "the negro as he is in his every day life" (Cripps 1993 50).

K. Maurice Jones has compiled a list that offers evidence of changes that occurred within African American film around 1980 (Jones 136). Jones writes that twenty-five major films were made by African American directors in the fifty-five years between 1925 and 1980, whereas thirty-eight were made in the fifteen years between 1980 and 1995. The discrepancy indicates the persistence of the black independent film tradition and points to its explosion after 1980, more than a decade after Hollywood began to deal with race through the social problem films of the 1960s.

Black American cinema's link to domestic protest politics became apparent during the 1970s Blaxploitation cycle in films by Ossie Davis (*Cotton Comes to Harlem* 1970), Melvin van Peebles (*Sweet Sweetback's Baadasssss Song* 1971), and by white directors like Larry Cohen (*Black Caesar* 1975). These wildly popular films express a politicized violence practiced by outlaw heroes. Politically incendiary and commercially successful, their formula was taken up and repeated by the industry. It's no coincidence that contemporary black films such as *Posse* and *Menace II Society* hearken back to those vivid and provocative representations that brought African American antiheroes the screen.

However, as Clyde Taylor points out, African American films produced after 1980 must be situated within a different political climate: one that witnessed a "backlash against black empowerment" (187). The ability to forward black nationalist claims was compromised, partly, Adolph Reed contends, because the electoral politics that replaced movement politics was not based on racial exclusivity.

> Because black power activism's sole category was race, radicals were generally unprepared to respond when the new, mainstream, black political elite gained momentum in the late 1960s . . . (204)

The idea that racial identity defined a political identity was called into question, and this factor contributed to the development of Jesse Jackson's Rainbow Coalition in the 1980s.

African American popular culture also began to challenge the idea of an immutable, authentic black identity as well. Tricia Rose describes hip-hop culture, perhaps the most important black aesthetic expression to emerge in recent years, as the mesh of "Afro-Caribbean and Afro-American musical, oral, visual, and dance forms" and situates its development in the environment of post-industrial urban America (23). The broad and inclusive vision of films like *Daughters of the Dust, Posse,* and the equal opportunity comedy *Undercover Brother* (Malcolm Lee and Gregory Dark 2002) emphasize the importance of reclaiming African American histories while also looking at the complexity and constructedness of racial designations in both historical and contemporary terms.

Although they carry the vestiges of the traditional national cinema paradigm, I would argue that Irish and African American cinemas are best discussed in light of views forwarded by Robert Burgoyne and Susan Hayward that link the concept of a national cinema to the interrogation of national identity. Burgoyne defines Hollywood as a national cinema because it "unambiguously articulates an imaginary field in which the figures of national identification are deployed and projected" (6). In other words, Hollywood activates cinema's powerful capacity for promoting identification in the service of nationalist ideology.

Hayward argues that the national cinema model is a problematic framework because the fiction of the nation no longer holds. One important reason to reconsider the concept of national cinema, she argues, is that the "internal" diversity of nations has come to be increasingly recognized. Citing radical changes instigated by the social movements of the 1960s, Hayward argues that recent popular culture texts "undermine the strict borders that nationalisms police" (95). As a result, "identity co-existing with difference(s) has become a reality—the very thing that nationalisms seek to deny" (95).

In their emphasis on character identification, recent Irish and African American films deconstruct those borders that nationalisms police. They address the "internal" diversity of both individuals and national formations, making reference to the perpetual dislocations of colonialism and racism. They speak to the affinities among people within the "third space" of Homi Bhabha's postcolonial diasporas and the traveling cultures theorized by James Clifford who experience "intercultural positionality" (Gilroy 1993 6). In recent Irish and African American films, intercultural positions are explored through acts of character identification enabled by a model of identity as performance.

IDENTITY AS PERFORMANCE

Recent Irish and African American films re-evaluate race, gender, and nation in light of the fluid notions of self that emerged during the last two decades. That debate has been carried out in critical theory and cultural studies as well as in visual culture. In *Gender Trouble*, Judith Butler argues that the gender system is not merely a social construct to be obeyed but a series of repeated gestures or performances that can be both enacted and resisted. Richard Dyer's work on whiteness, as well as that of Diane Negra and Gwendolyn Audrey Foster, reveals the way that ethnicities are performed and reproduced through films texts, star personas, and promotional materials.

The idea that identities are performances challenges notions of individual and cultural authenticity that defined an earlier era. Irish cultural critic Fintan O'Toole sees the now-canonized literature of the Irish Literary Revival as permeated by a defensive posture that fostered a "countermyth of national purity" and produced the "true Irish Gaelic peasant." (1997 28). He further argues that the Irish often make strategic choices around their ambiguous racial identity—"black or white or anything in between" (1997 25)—through playful identifications with Indians and African Americans. Richard Kearney suggests that these multiple identifications are "far more inclusive than the ethnic nation-state in that [they embrace] the exiled along with the indigenous [. . .] not only different Irish peoples but [. . .] different racial confections as well" (1988 5).

In a critique that resonates with that of O'Toole, Phillip Brian Harper considers appeals to black authenticity problematic. Harper sees unavoidable contradictions in African American investments in African identities:

> However much U.S. blacks might want to underscore our identification with "Africa" (a concept whose highly problematic character I leave almost entirely aside in this analysis), it seems likely that the widespread adoption of *African American* bespeaks much more loudly our peculiarly—and *narrowly*—"American" disposition. (73)

Harper goes on to question the masculinist character of black authenticity and the "conformist demands the concept implies"(ix). Manthia Diawara also offers a vigorous critique of the way Africa becomes conflated with authenticity. Diawara disparages contemporary Afrocentrism as "Afro-kitsch," an "imitation of the discourse of liberation" that fixes the meaning of blackness rather than deploying blackness as performance (1999 181). Diawara calls for a "modernist meta-discourse" that would

> [focus] on such zones of ambivalence as identity formation, sexual politics [. . .] and attempt to prevent [blackness] from falling into the same essentialist trap as whiteness. (1999 181)

Contemporary Irish and African American cinemas focus precisely on Diawara's zones of ambivalence. They do so, I would argue, as a reflection of the postmodern belief in both the possibility and desirability of subjects divesting themselves of limiting identity positions. In getting out of themselves, in revealing their multiple identifications, characters attempt to resist the limitations of identity politics. Their successes and failures, in psychological and political terms, mark the possibilities and limitations of the paradigm of identity as performance.

THE THEATER OF POPULAR DESIRES

> It is a theater of popular desires, a theater of popular fantasies. It is where we discover and play with the identifications of ourselves, where we are imagined, where we are represented, not only to the audiences out there who do not get the message, but to ourselves for the first time.
>
> —Stuart Hall, *"What is this 'Black' in Black Popular Culture?"*

> [Irish culture] is demolishing the colonial opposition of Self and Other and re-inventing the ideal of the Self as Other . . . the foreign native, the white black, the civilized barbarian. It is enjoying the benefits of a long history of being on the borders of two worlds and turning its dread status of being neither one thing nor the other into the playful pleasures of being both and neither.
>
> —Fintan O'Toole, "Going Native"

Stuart Hall and Fintan O'Toole view acts of identification as gestures of playful transcendence and of deadly seriousness. But are they also political? Diana Fuss claims that the very notion of identification has a specific, colonial history. Freud's psychoanalytic concept of identification was developed "within the larger cultural context of colonial expansion and imperial crisis" (1999 295). Moreover, she argues, Frantz Fanon's founding premise is that politics are embedded within psychic structures. "What Fanon gives us, in the end," she concludes, "is a politics that does not oppose the psychical, but fundamentally presupposes it" (1999 322). Thus, the idea that one can transgress the boundaries of individuation, to inhabit, occupy, empathize with, perform, or introject another carries with it the traces of the colonialist imagination.

Performance theorist Elin Diamond also views identification as political, arguing, "because it bridges the psychic and the social, identification has political effects" (391). Diamond goes on to claim, "the wholeness and consistency of identity, is transgressed by every act of identification" (396). If, as Fuss and Diamond argue, political circumstances shape and are shaped by identification practices, then transgressing the boundaries of the self is not necessarily liberatory. To analyze the political character of identification, Diamond's acts of destabilization and transgression must be situated historically.[16]

One way to historicize spectator identification would be to document actual audience practices. Recent cultural studies work that challenges psychoanalytic concepts of identification examines the ways that spectators insert or project themselves into films, or resist such temptations. Stuart Hall's taxonomy of official, negotiated, and oppositional reading strategies and the work of Dick Hebdige, Angela McRobbie, and Jacqueline Bobo all highlight the ability of spectators to engage with and disengage from characters and texts.[17] This body of work debunks the notion—deriving from the Frankfurt School and film apparatus theory—of mass culture as a purveyor of false consciousness and film identification as evidence of the medium's internal colonization of the spectator.

Another way to historicize processes of identification is to analyze the way they function within film texts. In this method, identification, as part of the film's story and discourse, becomes one aspect of the "cultural gaze." Kaja Silverman defines the cultural gaze as "the cultural constructedness of the images through which the subject assumes a visual identity" (19). In their explicit focus on character identification, recent Irish and African American films suggest that one important aspect of the contemporary cultural gaze is the belief in one's ability to relinquish the self and perform other identities. They also emphasize the way image consumption assists in the self-conscious practice of donning and doffing identities.

In exploring identification, many film theorists focus on the relationship between the spectator and the camera, which Jean-Louis Baudry and Christian Metz termed *primary identification.* Apparartus theories divorce spectators from the complications of narrative and character, however, in their emphasis on the viewer's identification with the camera and their neglect of *secondary identification* (between viewer and character) and, especially, *tertiary identification* (among characters on screen). I would argue that tertiary identification—the relationships expressed between and among on-screen characters—represents an important site for examining notions of postmodern subjectivity. Characters' acts of identification reflect contemporary beliefs about the politics and poetics of identity.

Unlike psychoanalytic critics such as Metz and Silverman, I do not focus on the the spectator's unconscious as the privileged site for acts of identification.[18] Instead, I examine narrative structures as well as visual and aural strategies that enable the expression of character intersubjectivity. Certainly, films with an emphasis on character identification may affect spectators at the unconscious level. It's also likely that the point-of-view structures that convey character identification draw upon the spectator's primary and secondary identification with the camera and characters. But my interest lies in the textual representation of characters who get outside themselves in order to engage with others and with otherness, and the implications of those acts. Do characters who apprehend their own experience through/as others become politically empowered and/or psychically entangled by their identifications?

Silverman insists that cinema's "identificatory lure [. . .] represents the potential vehicle for a spectator self-estrangement" (65), which may lead to a process of self-redefinition. Identification forces the viewer into a previously unimaginable subject position, which Silverman terms "heteropathic identification." Such identification

> is the privileged mechanism whereby the spectator can be not only integrated into a new social collectivity, but also induced to occupy a subject-position which is antithetical to his or her psychic formation (i.e., to his or her self). (91)

Heteropathic identification has the potential to counter essentialism by recognizing the possibility of occupying different subject positions. In my focus on character identification, I displace the locus of this transaction from the psyche of the spectator to the screen. Rather than focusing on the spectator's unconscious processes, I suggest the way characters identify within the context of the narrative might present to audiences on a conscious level the idea that such heteropathic identifications are desirable, valuable, or, perhaps, unavoidable.

Despite my focus on character identification, I find Kaja Silverman's argument that the body plays a central role in maintaining a culture's existing categories of identity compelling (92). She repeatedly emphasizes the relation between the body and identification, variously referred to as "alter[ing] the terms of bodily reference"(89); a "deliteralization of the spectator's body" (89); "the cinema's propensity for carrying away the spectator" (89); and "spectatorial abduction" (89). I use these ideas to explore acts of character identification.

In the chapters that follow, I analyze the way that Irish and African American films alter certain terms of bodily reference as their characters suspend themselves, identify with others, and perform other identities. Chapter 2 examines the way jazz and other musical performances enable heteropathic identification in the films of Neil Jordan and Spike Lee, two prominent *auteurs* of Irish and African American cinema. Chapter 3 focuses on the fascination with the pregnant female body in numerous Irish and African American "women's films." These films foreground pregnancy not only to critique gender essentialism but also to expose its connections to racial and national identity. Chapter 4 addresses the role that masculine identification plays in the reproduction of violence in contemporary Irish and African American gangster films. Chapter 5 considers the way contemporary Irish and African American films revise archetypes of individual and national identities produced by the quintessential colonialist narrative: the Western.

Character identification in these films is not necessarily politically progressive, enabling acts of solidarity or intervention, nor is it consistently regressive, prompting withdrawal from politics or the embrace of traditional structures of identity.[19] Nor are acts of identification free of eroticizing, appropriating, and fetishizing others and otherness. These films enact the pleasures and confusions associated with the fading efficacy of old paradigms for individual and communal identities and the dearth of new models of affinity.

CHAPTER TWO

Sampling Blackness: Music and Identification in the Films of Neil Jordan and Spike Lee

Music is our witness and our ally.
—James Baldwin, "Of the Sorrow Songs"

Neil Jordan and Spike Lee are two of the most prominent directors working in Irish and African American cinema. Their careers took off during the 1980s as their success with small independent films led to larger-budget projects and broader audiences. The two directors also happen to share a key aesthetic interest: music. In several of their films, jazz music serves as a focal point for narratives about the struggles of artists and musicians. In other films, characters' personas are defined by and expressed through the music they listen to.

Music also functions as a formal element that contributes to the unconventional structure of many of Jordan's and Lee's films. In Jordan's *Angel/Danny Boy* (1982) and *The Miracle* (1991) and in Lee's *Crooklyn* (1990), *Mo' Better Blues* (1994), *Do the Right Thing* (1989), and *He Got Game* (1998), music is performed, repeated, riffed upon, and sampled. In its common usage, "sampling" refers to rap music. I use the term here as ethnomusicologist Tricia Rose has defined it: for her, sampling establishes a reference point for recontextualization. Sampling suggests the existence of a tradition against which, and into which, a musician performs. In Lee's and Jordan's films, when characters sample music, they identify with (primarily) African American composers and musicians from the past and present. By sampling music as performers as well as fans, they use music's disembodying potential to get outside themselves, engaging in heteropathic identification. They occupy previously unimagined subject positions. In this way, the films show that musical performance can challenge essentialist notions of race and national identity.

On a narrative level, Lee and Jordan select specific songs that refer to social alienation, such as "Strange Fruit," and "Fight the Power." In so doing, they situate their characters' experiences within a tradition of creative African American responses to violation and disenfranchisement. They also elicit viewers' "affiliating identifications": knowledge about ideas and events that exist independently of the film, which viewers use to enhance the significance of the music (Kassabian 3). Whether as musicians or loyal fans, Lee and Jordan's characters inhabit the lyrics and musical notes of others. They take "someone else's" music and make it their own, adding their interpretation and social context to the ongoing life of the composition.

But on a formal level, the structure of repetition and revision that dominates the music that these directors employ—primarily jazz and rap—presents identity as a continual process. Music does not clearly distinguish subject and object, nor does it obey the laws of linear time. As Claudia Gorbman writes, "musical time is abstract time; once begun, a piece's musical logic demands to work itself through to the finish" (24). The nonlinear dynamics of repetition and revision undermine conventional narrative form in the films of these directors. By using musical identifications to get out of themselves, characters in Lee and Jordan's films challenge the chronological relation between past and present as well as the architectural division between self and other.

Cultural critics from Theodor Adorno to Fredric Jameson have disparaged musical repetition as a formal device that colludes with capitalist processes of mass-market commodification. Yet Tricia Rose writes that repetition "sometimes work against market forces" (72). Rose argues persuasively that "repetition is an important and telling element in culture, a means by which a sense of continuity, security, and identification are maintained" (68). For Rose and James Snead, repetition in black music establishes an economy of circulation and equilibrium that counters the capitalist model of accumulation and growth. In Jordan and Lee's films, musical identifications work against the forces that support essentialist ideas about identity as a state of being rather than a contextual and relational process.

As they explicitly challenge traditional ideas about racial and national identity, Jordan's and Lee's characters implicitly question traditional notions of masculinity. Musicians explore the fluidity of identity through performance, participating in creative, masculine exchange. This emotionally satisfying and aesthetically productive activity may threaten standard assumptions regarding masculinity, including the presumption of heterosexuality. The explicit sexualization of black musicians has the potential to invoke stereotypes, "idealizing a black other as spontaneous, transgressive, and ecstatically free of bourgeois restraint" (Gabbard 2). However, performances in these films also make a variety of African American masculinities visible, from the "explicitly virile" performances of Louis Armstrong and Dizzy Gillespie to what Krin Gabbard has called the "post-phallic" style of Wynton Marsalis and Terence Blanchard.[1] By activating characters' identifications through music and performance, Lee and Jordan call attention to, and often destabilize, parameters of masculinity.

JORDAN AND JAZZ: CELTIC SIGNIFYING

Music frequently functions as a narrative and structural element in Neil Jordan's films. Jordan has said that he often associates a film with a particular song that captures the story's emotional texture. Within Jordan's oeuvre, *Danny Boy* (1982), *Mona Lisa* (1986) *The Crying Game* (1992), *The Butcher Boy* (1997), *In Dreams* (1999), and *Breakfast on Pluto* (2005) all derive their titles from popular songs.

In *Danny Boy* (first released as *Angel* in the U.K.) and *The Miracle* (whose working title was *Stardust*), jazz music serves as a narrative element and structural motif. Jordan's Irish male protagonists idealize jazz music; through performing, they forge identifications with African American others.

Jordan's Irish characters are drawn to African American culture, suggesting their desire to affirm their own experience of W. E. B Du Bois's second sight: the peculiar burden of racialized subjects who must always see themselves through the eyes of others.[2] They express their alienation by embodying the figure of the African American jazz musician. Although

Jordan's protagonists ultimately come to terms with the notion that identities are constructed, they do not necessarily celebrate postmodern performativity. Danny and Jimmy learn that identities may be consciously constructed, yet they are ultimately forced to acknowledge circumstances over which they have no control.

Formally, these two films exhibit a fundamental restructuring of narrative form as a result of characters' musical identifications. Film theories dealing with narrative disruption tend to focus on visual spectacle.[3] But in *Danny Boy* and *The Miracle*, auditory "spectacle" interrupts the linear unfolding of the narrative. Jordan samples the jazz tradition so that it functions as a reference point for his recontextualization. He allows the music to inform the film's visual style and the story's structure. In other words, he translates jazz into film style.

Jordan explicitly locates himself within the jazz tradition, paying homage to African American jazz musicians and suggesting a resemblance between Irish and African American experiences of political and psychological repression. Henry Louis Gates has argued that jazz music provides one salient example of signifying, a term that describes the double-voiced quality of a text that speaks to other texts.

> Black jazz musicians [. . .] perform each other's standards on a joint album, not to critique these but to engage in refiguration as an act of homage [. . .] this form of the double-voiced implies unity and resemblance rather than critique and difference. (xxvii)

Jordan draws upon a perceived resemblance between Northern Ireland and the United States in an interview in which he discusses his choice of the Billie Holiday/Lewis Allan song "Strange Fruit" as the musical centerpiece for *Danny Boy.*

> You could almost transpose the whole lyrics over to Ireland . . . there you're speaking about a situation where human beings killed people they didn't know for reasons which had nothing to do with any kind of human emotion whatever. It was just to do with racial differences; and it's a similar kind of situation that I was talking about in the film. (qtd. in Kearney 1982 302)

While it may be difficult to fully endorse this connection between Irish Catholics and black Americans, the differences ascribed to Irish

Catholics in Northern Ireland are based on racial classifications developed in British colonial discourses. These racial distinctions go back as far as the sixteenth-century writings of Edmund Spenser, who differentiated the Celts and the Anglo-Saxons in classical colonial terminology of savagery versus civilization.

In Jordan's films, Irish characters speak as African Americans through music. This aural impersonation complicates the paradigm Toni Morrison has described with respect to the American literary tradition, wherein the Africanist presence must be silenced and erased.

> [T]o notice [race] is to recognize an already discredited difference. To enforce its invisibility through silence is to allow the black body a shadowless participation in the dominant cultural body. (9–10)

In these two films, Jordan enforces a different version of "shadowless participation": no African American characters appear on screen. In this instance the jazz tradition stands in for the black body, a palimpsest of composers and performers that emerges aurally, not visually.

In Jordan's films, African American music is both audible and expressive, and it is linked to sexuality and aggression. In the course of paying homage to figures such as Charlie Parker and Louis Armstrong, Jordan recirculates assumptions that jazz is a spontaneous voicing of the soul. In both *Danny Boy* and *The Miracle*, jazz is a means by which characters explore their sexuality and enact violence. Jordan's characters and viewers may, therefore, "consume fantasies of black male sexuality mediated through white performers" (Gabbard 45).

But Jordan's use of jazz is more than simply appropriation, in terms of both content and form. Using jazz to structure male coming of age narratives in *Danny Boy* and *The Miracle*, Jordan references an indigenous Irish rebellion against decades of Irish Catholic political and sexual orthodoxy. The Catholic Church waged a long campaign against dance halls and jazz music, which are two omnipresent tropes in Jordan's work. Father Peter Conefrey's opposition to jazz culminated in a public demonstration in 1934. In the *Catholic Pictorial* in 1926, Conefrey associated socialist rebellion and sexual permissiveness with jazz.

> Jazz is an African word meaning the activity in public of something of which St. Paul said "Let it not be so much as named among you." The dance and music with its abominable rhythm was borrowed

> from Central Africa by a gang of wealthy Bolshevists in the USA to strike at Church civilization throughout the world. (qtd. in Gibbons 1996a 101)

Thirty years after the priest's denunciation, during Jordan's adolescence, similar ideas about jazz circulated in America, but with a different valence. In 1957, writer Norman Mailer described a cross-race identification of the white hipster with black men: "The hipster has absorbed the existential synapses of the Negro, and for practical purposes could be considered a white Negro (4)." For Mailer, "jazz is orgasm, it is the music of orgasm, good orgasm and bad, and so it spoke across a nation" (4). Despite their vastly different cultural locations, and their differing opinions about the value of jazz, Conefrey and Mailer both credit the music with the potential to break down social and psychological boundaries. The music's physicality and formal aesthetic of suspension may permit individuals to overcome the social stratification of racial difference and, perhaps, even the structure of identity itself.

ANGEL OF DEATH

In *Danny Boy*, Jordan's first feature film, a musical triumvirate shapes a narrative of sudden death and an excruciatingly violent retribution. That trinity includes Verdi's "Requiem," "Strange Fruit," and the Irish standard, "Danny Boy." Danny (Stephen Rea), a young saxophonist, befriends a mute girl named Annie (Veronica Quilligan) prior to a performance at the Dreamland Ballroom, a rural dance hall near Derry in Northern Ireland. The name of the dance hall situates this rural enclave squarely within the Irish tradition of the *aisling* or dream poem. Annie waits for him outside after the performance and they make love in a concrete construction pipe near the entrance to the ballroom. From their vantage point inside the pipe—a circular image that foreshadows Danny's eventual entrapment—Danny and Annie witness the killing of his band's manager by masked gunmen. Danny watches the assassins shoot and kill Annie as the dance hall explodes in flames.

The film documents Danny's quest for revenge. By avenging Annie's death, he becomes enmeshed in the Troubles that permeate Northern Ireland and loses control over his actions. As he tracks down the killers one by one, he loses himself first in his music and then in a series of identifications with his victims. Danny relinquishes his musical identifications for a role in the drama of dehumanizing violence.

During the final scene, in the ruins of the Dreamland Ballroom, Danny realizes that the two police officers on the case have manipulated him, inciting his murderous revenge spree to suit their own needs. Danny learns that the British state is implicated in the "indigenous" violence between Irish Protestants and Catholics. Those who perpetuate the violence transform individual loss into a renewed commitment to a corrupt national identity.

Richard Kearney's excellent analysis of the film focuses on Danny's gradual substitution of violence for art, signified in a scene where he takes his saxophone from its case and puts a machine gun in its place.[4] Kearney argues that the film's strength lies in the way it addresses the psychological motivations for violence:

> Jordan investigates that fundamental nexus between aesthetic creativity and violence which has become one of the most frequent stamping grounds of contemporary art. (1988 177)

Kearney emphasizes the psychological undercurrents of the film, specifically noting that "the deep-structure unfolds 'synchronically' by repeating key visual and sound motifs, [while] the surface structure progresses 'diachronically' according to the standard conventions of a sequential plot" (179). He also identifies several critical motifs that operate at a "counter-narrative" level, including dancing, music, and the laying on of hands. Fascinating as his analysis is, Kearney does not address the critical importance of jazz, except to mention the overtly political implications of the lyrics of "Strange Fruit," which is performed by Danny's band immediately after his first revenge killing.

I would extend and reframe Kearney's analysis by suggesting that a jazz aesthetic dominates *Danny Boy* and provides the framework for the film's exploration of creativity, violence, sexuality, and dehumanization. The repetition and revision of the jazz aesthetic expresses Danny's multiple identifications as victim and violator, as Irish citizen and British subject.

Initially, the film connects Danny's musical performances to his sexual desire *for* another person, not his desire to *be* another. During the opening credits, Danny plays a diegetic saxophone riff outside the Dreamland Ballroom. When Annie touches the instrument, he tells her "it's a saxophone." The saxophone is repeatedly associated with Danny ("the Stan Getz of South Armagh") as we see him fondle, fiddle with, and clean the instrument.[5]

Danny's musicianship is associated with sexual conquest. Prior to the gig, Danny propositions Deirdre (Honor Hefernan), the band's singer; during the show he engages in flirty banter with a new bride; and afterward he makes love with Annie. Given this phallic association, it is not surprising that, after the bombing of the ballroom, Danny has lost his saxophone and fears that he also has lost his ability to play. When he tells his Aunt Mae (Marie Kean) he has lost his sax, her reply emphasizes the metaphorical significance of the instrument: "We've all lost something," she responds. Without the sax, Danny also has lost his ability to express his anger, rage, and sorrow. Danny has lost his voice. Like Annie, one of the film's first victims, he is mute.

When Danny eventually expresses his feelings, he does so in a sequence that underscores the jazz aesthetic of repetition and revision through Jordan's precise manipulations of sound and image. After leaving the hospital, Danny stays at Aunt Mae's house. He discovers his uncle's soprano saxophone stored under a bed (a further suggestion of the instrument's sexual connotations). As Danny plays a mournful cascade of notes, he looks out the window, sees a British soldier, and imaginatively revisits the scene of the killings. A montage sequence alternates between images of plenitude (Annie covering Danny's eyes from behind outside the dance hall) and violence (the murder of his manager; the burning dance hall). This imagistic and musical riff begins with the following shot sequence: Annie's hands, Annie being shot, and a tiny bell tinkling. As the sax's cascade of notes speeds up, growing more insistent and shrill, the saxophone repeats a single phrase that is synchronized with the images. The sequence peaks with the shot of Annie's hands repeated three times and closes with the shot of the bell. Danny uses the music to transport himself backward in time to the moments of erotic fulfillment before Annie's death. Yet that process is suspended—the repetition of image and sound is akin to a skipping record, a flawed CD. Try as he might, Danny has difficulty moving beyond that moment of destruction to perform creatively.

Danny's inability to recover from his loss transforms him. After Danny leaves the hospital and rejoins the band, he and Deidre finally consummate their flirtation. Their relationship is threatened by Danny's increasing alienation and withdrawal, however. When she asks him about his changing emotional state, he tells her his problem is "like a nothing

FIGURE 2.1. Danny plays "Danny Boy" in Neil Jordan's film of the same name: the music expresses his identity crisis. Courtesy of Photofest.

you can feel, and it gets worse." Later, Deidre will tell Danny that he is dead, and that he looks just like the police: "them, like you, only in uniform." John Hill works with this metaphor, noting that Danny "only appears to have escaped death at the film's beginning" and may symbolically be dead already (1988 179).

Danny struggles with his increasing depersonalization, denying the impersonality of violence by studying his victims and forging an identification with each one. When Danny finds a gun hidden in his first victim's apartment, he fits together the pieces of the automatic weapon, which visually rhymes with his previous manipulations of his saxophone. The stranger's weapon replaces the saxophone: the former an instrument of his masculinity and creativity, the latter of destruction. He scours the beach house of another victim, looking at personal pictures and having a conversation with the victim before shooting him.

Danny's multiple identifications with Annie, with his victims, and with the two paternalistic police officers who ostensibly work the case contribute to his sense of losing himself. When Deirdre tells Danny they'll be playing "his tune"—"Danny Boy"—he replies, "that's not my tune, that's everyone's." Danny's music becomes inextricably connected to his obsession with revenge. He tracks down one potential suspect during a performance: believing the new bride's husband to be one of the gunmen, he renews his flirtation with the bride in order to learn more.

In identifying with the husband, Danny goes further in relinquishing his individuality than he has with previous victims. During his performance, the bride asks Danny if she has seen him play before, to which he replies, "We all look the same." Danny initiates a sexual liaison with her in order to locate the estranged husband. Together in bed, they compare Danny to her husband, collapsing sexuality (the reason he gives for asking questions) and violence (the actual reason he asks them):

> BRIDE: I think you're jealous!
>
> DANNY: I want to know everything he ever did with you. Am I like him? [They kiss.]
>
> BRIDE: You're like him now.

When he finds the husband the next day, Danny draws his gun. The interchange between the men suggests their growing similarity as well as their mutual recognition of the depersonalized face of violence:

DANNY: How'd you do it?

MAN: It's not that hard when you put your mind to it. You may know yourself.

DANNY: How did you shoot her?

MAN: It's easy, just pull the trigger.

Danny does pull the trigger, making the man his third victim.

The soundtrack underscores Danny's loss of identity. Musician and murderer collapse as the nondiegetic jazz music eclipses the band's performances. On several occasions jazz riffs alert viewers to Danny's acts of identification and their profound effect on his identity. Those moments include the scene in which the police approach Danny and take him to the morgue (where he furthers his identification with the victims), when the bride tells of her husband's absence on their wedding night, and just before Danny witnesses the band's new manager making protection payments to paramilitaries.

It is fitting then, that a jazz riff sets the stage for the final confrontation between Danny and Bonner, the police officer who, Danny finally learns, has been involved in the paramilitary violence, and Bloom, the officer who has set Danny up in order to find the perpetrators. The film returns full circle to the Ballroom. "Here we are again," Bonner remarks as he drags Danny into the ruins of the dance hall. Bonner completes the analogy between creative musical performance and destructive violence: "It's a lot easier to play than the saxophone," he says of his gun, "You only have the one tune." Poised to kill Danny, Bonner is killed by Bloom, his superior officer. Danny returns to the position of witness. Verdi's "Requiem," the music that accompanied the film's first scene of violent killing, plays over the sound of Bloom's helicopter in the film's closing moments.

The film closes with a nearly overwhelming sense of despair, in large part due to its narrative circularity, embodied in the vicious-cycle imagery of the spinning helicopter blades. John Hill criticizes the film for this dead-end sensibility and its structural circularity, because, through this abstraction, political questions "are rendered irrelevant by virtue of the film's emphasis on the metaphysical origins of violence" (1988 179). Brian McIlroy similarly indicts the film for its political ambivalence and its allegiance to magical and mythic elements (2001 70–74).

Danny's acts of mourning and revenge undermine his sense of self and uncover anxieties related to national identity. Danny becomes like his victims because he is convinced that racial hatred explains the intractable sectarian violence. But he learns that the British state, no impartial arbitrator, is the locus of violence and profits from the clash of bodies and identities in Northern Ireland. The presence of British troops in the province, the film reveals, does not result in the enforcement of the law but, instead, has introduced new forms of state-sanctioned violence that exploit fervently held ideas of racial difference. Danny's ability to relinquish his sense of self through musical performance makes him the ideal candidate to perform the script presented by the agents of the British state.

Jazz music is critical to the film's narrative and to Jordan's visual style. Danny's music allows him to get out of himself when he performs; but when he trades his saxophone for a weapon, he is unable to transcend the social context of sectarian struggle. His stubborn refusal to take sides—his motive is to avenge Annie's death—is irrelevant. Racial oppositions that feed the national conflict have continued to construct him, unwittingly, all along.

In *The Miracle*, Jordan again employs jazz to structure a male-coming-of-age narrative. This story is less obviously concerned with the Irish national conflict, yet its focus on a family of performers illuminates the constructed nature of gender roles, and family relationships with a nod toward Irish-American hybridity.

"NIGHT IN TUNISIA": THE ALTO BREAK AND OEDIPAL RIFFS

The source for *The Miracle* was Jordan's own 1976 short story "Night in Tunisia," which deals with an adolescent boy nurturing his artistic talents and discovering his emerging sexuality. In both the story and the film, the boy performs jazz as a means of escaping his adolescence, of moving from child to man. He also seeks to transcend an Irishness associated with the previous generation's failures, embodied by his father. The film foregrounds the fact that the boy's transition is based upon masculine identification; his performances mimic those of his own father and of jazz forefathers. As in *Danny Boy, The Miracle* conveys the boy's journey through both a jazz score and discrete musical performances.

Several passages from the short story highlight moments of heteropathic identification that occur when the boy hears the Dizzy Gillespie composition that lends the story its title. They also suggest the degree to which Jordan's writing style borrows from jazz. The protagonist's father is a brass man whose career is in decline, and the boy has rejected the saxophone in favor of the guitar. But then father and son listen to Charlie Parker's famous 1947 recording of "Night in Tunisia." Here Jordan's writing approximates Parker's cascading style.

> He heard the radio crackle over the sound of falling water and heard a rapid-fire succession of notes that seemed to spring from the falling water, that amazed him, so much faster than his father ever played, but slow behind it all, melancholy, like a river. He came out of the toilet and stood listening with his father. Who is that, he asked his father. Then he heard the continuity announcer say the name Charlie Parker [. . .] (Jordan 42–43)

This scene crystallizes connections Jordan makes among music, orality, sexuality, and transcendence. In an earlier scene of sexual initiation, the protagonist witnesses another boy play with a condom. "[He] put his mouth to the mouth of the French letter and blew. It expanded, huge and bulbous, with a tiny bubble at the tip" (38). The protagonist's preference for the saxophone's disembodied, aural eroticism is made clear in a scene where the same boy puts on a condom and masturbates. In contrast to the sensual fluidity of Parker's playing, the protagonist focuses on the dead-end quality of the act. "He saw how the liquid was caught by the antiseptic web, how the sand clung to it when the thin boy threw it, like it does to spittle" (43).

In contrast to the act of masturbation, jazz is orgasmically transcendent. The Parker solo freezes space and time by occupying both simultaneously, an example of aural spectacle.[6] After dissatisfying encounters with the other boys on the beach, the main character returns home to the piano, "trying to imitate that sound like a river he has just heard" (46).

> The notes soared and fell, dispelling the world around him, tracing a series of arcs that seemed to point out a place, or if not a place, a state of mind. . . . He decided it was a place you were always in, yet always trying to reach, you walked towards all the time and yet never got there, as it was always beside you. (46)

After playing a recording of Charlie Parker's "Night in Tunisia," he finally picks up the alto saxophone and allows his father to help him find the notes.

> When his father came back at two in the morning, he was still playing . . . He forgot the raft and the games of pontoon and the thin boy's jargon. He stayed inside for days and laboriously transferred every combination of notes he had known on the piano onto the metal keys. [. . .] He fashioned his mouth round the reed till the sounds he made became like a power of speech, a speech that his mouth was the vehicle for but that sprang from the knot of his stomach, the crook of his legs. (47)

The boy masters a new language; one whose power comes from his sexually marked and yet disarticulated body.

The boy in the story adopts what Krin Gabbard calls the "appealingly unconventional paradigms of masculinity" that jazz presents (1996 97). He becomes assertive, yet does not challenge his father in a typical Oedipal struggle. No maternal figure appears in the story to complicate the relationship between the men and their music. Or, perhaps, the missing mother might be seen as the musical instrument. Father assists son, rather than competing with him, in a quest for physical and aesthetic transcendence.

In the story, Jordan indulges fantasies of masculine bonding through identifications forged in the context of the musical group. Charlie Parker's playing speed and improvisations from the top of the anchoring chord are only two reasons he was recognized as the most important jazz soloist since Louis Armstrong; his location within the jazz combo is equally important to this story.[7] Parker, along with Dizzy Gillespie, is credited with the innovations of 1940s and 1950s bop, a combo-centered style that depended upon group cohesion as well as instrumental virtuosity and improvisation, displayed in landmark (and fetishized) solos like the famous alto break in Parker's 1947 recording of "Night in Tunisia."[8] In the story, the father-son combo functions in such utopian terms. The combo eclipses the family as a community in which individuality and artistry are prized. Men come together through musical performance.

The story displaces generational, political, and sexual conflicts into the ideal and uncomplicated realm of jazz performance. Although a reviewer for *Irish Stage and Screen* noted that the "only bond between the father and his son is their common love for Charlie Parker music and playing the saxophone" (7), they also share a desire for an innovative, performative alternative to conventional masculinity. Their shared experience of transcendence through jazz generates new possibilities for masculine bonding, and father-son relations in particular. Those bonds are forged outside the framework of sexual difference or heterosexual relationships.

When Jordan reintroduces the mother into this scenario in *The Miracle*, however, these masculine identifications shift. Musical performance become a means by which the boy identifies with his mother and father but also wages an Oedipal struggle. His coming-of-age saga becomes a performance that renegotiates sexuality and nationality. In translating the story to film, Jordan presents the maternal figure in somewhat conventional terms—as a return of the repressed—and reframes the story as one in which all identities are constructed and performed.

THE MIRACLE: JAZZ SPECTACLE

In *The Miracle*, Jordan focuses on a different strain of jazz than in "Night in Tunisia," taking as his touchstone the Hoagy Carmichael classic "Stardust." The song was made famous by swing soloist Louis Armstrong, whose musical persona emphasized an exuberant phallicism. The analogy between musical instruments and the phallus in American film has been well documented by Krin Gabbard. In *Jammin' At the Margins: Jazz and the American Cinema*, he writes that:

> Although many Americans now recall Louis Armstrong as a smiling clown, he regularly used his trumpet to express phallic masculinity along with a great deal of sexual innnuendo that was already an essential element of jazz performance. (139)

and reports further that

> members of Armstrong's band are said to have referred to their accompanying figures on Armstrong's 1931 recording of "Star Dust" as "the fucking rhythm." (143)

In *The Miracle* that rhythm provides the backdrop for a story of repressed sexuality and family secrets. A young musician named Jimmy (Niall Byrne) asserts his sexuality and musicianship, rejects his father and seeks transcendence through transgression.

Renee Baker, Jimmy's absent mother, returns to the seaside town of Bray, because she is performing in nearby Dublin. Her reappearance disrupts the intact and continuous life story her husband Sam (Donal McCann) has crafted. Renee is unaware that Sam has told Jimmy that she is dead. The ineffable Renee (Beverly D'Angelo) is an American stage actress/singer whereas Jimmy's overly present, overly embodied father, Sam, is an Irish jazz musician who drinks too much. Jimmy's destiny, it seems, is to experience his own identity through theatrical performances of one kind or another.

The film is framed by an attention to the way narratives are constructed and identities performed. Jimmy walks the boardwalk by day with a girl named Rose (Lorraine Pilkington) whose histrionic claim that she and Jimmy are "too friendly to be lovers, too close to be friends" belies her obvious feelings for Jimmy. Her phrase also reflects the highly improbable romances she and Jimmy concoct as they prowl the boardwalk. They often indulge in flights of verbal acrobatics, describing the skin of the Nuns who visit the ocean as "pellucid." Each one concocts narratives, often revising and elaborating upon the scenarios the other one has introduced. That these narratives are conveyed orally is significant: they are performed texts, they exist only in the moment of the telling.

Another important motif is a shifting romantic triangle, which underlines the importance of the film's unconventional Oedipal triangle. The first triangle emerges during Renee's first visit to Bray. When Renee appears on the boardwalk, arriving by train from Dublin, she is fodder for Rose and Jimmy's amusement. Rose speculates that the glamorous Renee must have gotten off at the wrong stop; Jimmy is wordlessly entranced. They follow her to the beach stairs where Renee is framed between them; a visual metaphor foreshadowing the effect she will have on Jimmy and Rose's relationship as well as Jimmy and Sam's. Jimmy, who doesn't know Renee is his mother, falls in love with her. He comes to resent his father for keeping them apart. Rose, jealous of Jimmy's obsession with Renee, takes up with a circus performer.

Jimmy's relationship with Renee is couched not only in terms of these triangulations, but also in terms of his identification with her. Jimmy pesters Renee at the beach, rides the same train into Dublin, and follows her to the Olympia Theater where she is performing a stage version of *Destry Rides Again*, the 1939 musical-comedy-western featuring Jimmy Stewart and Marlene Dietrich.[9] Jimmy steals a poster bearing Renee's image and puts it up in his room.

Although Jimmy's parents collude in keeping Renee's identity a secret, Jimmy eventually discovers the truth. Even the truth is delivered through an image. Jimmy's access to the primal scene is photographic but not cinematic; he finds a photograph of Renee and Sam together in Renee's purse.[10] For a director as indebted to Hitchcock as Jordan is, Jimmy's violation of Renee's purse may be seen as a foreshadowing of their scandalous sexual liaison later in the film.[11]

In formal terms, Jimmy's identification with Renee is governed by a jazz aesthetic of repetition and revision. Attending her performance over and over again, Jimmy watches Renee playing the phallic Frenchy to her counterpart's nonviolent Destry; she shoots, sings, smokes, and, ultimately, dies taking a bullet intended for Destry. The nightly repetitions of her death scene, complete with a bloodstained costume, evoke Renee's symbolic death in the film, just as Jimmy's endless train rides signal the fetishistic quality of his desire for her.

Moreover, the film's narrative pattern is shaped by full-length jazz performances. These performances are too integral to the story to be seen merely as interruptions of the narrative. Krin Gabbard warns that, "since narrative is indisputably what most audiences crave, then a film about jazz or a film with jazz cannot dwell on the music for too long (6)." But this film coalesces around jazz performances, flouting the convention of narrative priority. This formal choice is consonant with the film's self-conscious approach to stories, which are constructed and reconstructed as the storyteller goes along. Jimmy's life story unfolds as a process of repetition and revision.

As in "Night in Tunisia," jazz is liberating when it recognizes the individual artistry and the sexual expressiveness of the performer. Jimmy rejects his paternal identification, quitting his father's dance hall band and its passé uniform of matched Hawaiian shirts. He resents playing when no one appears to be listening. Instead, he performs with Renee and accompanies a circus contortionist, identifying with and desiring both women. Jimmy clearly enjoys the challenge of matching his playing to the acrobat's body's movements in rehearsal, and a moment of heteropathic identification occurs when the camera circles Jimmy, his eyes trained on the woman. The performance emphasizes the sexual charge of Jimmy's performance as well as his moment of identification. Later, the camera frames him between the contortionist's legs during the performance. He becomes her phallus, mingling identification with sexual assertion.

Another, more spontaneous, performance reveals the way that music allows Jimmy to mingle identification and sexual desire. During an after-party for *Destry Rides Again*, he accompanies Renee on the piano as she sings "Star Dust," a song about memories. Significantly the camera circles Jimmy and Renee at the piano as it does in the scene where he plays for the contortionist, suggesting the blend of identification and sexual tension. In both scenes, Jimmy establishes himself as a solo musician (in contrast to being one of many in his father's band), yet he always performs in relation to another, inhabiting a shared rhythm.

The scenes in which Jimmy plays the saxophone for the acrobat and the piano for his mother have all the hallmarks of a Mulveyan spectacle. They do not further the narrative but, instead, reiterate the fact that the identities of Jimmy, Renee, and Sam are based on performance. Emotions are conveyed within the confines of theatricality, as Jimmy rejects his father in the midst of a performance and connects with his mother through performance.

The jazz aesthetic emerges not only from these performances but also in the temporal suspension and repetition of scenes where Jimmy travels in a seemingly endless loop on the train between Bray and Dublin. Unbeknownst to him at that point in the film, he keeps returning to a presumed point of origin (his mother) only to relive the shock of her absence by witnessing her death on stage every night. Like the boy discovering the solos of Charlie Parker, Jimmy's journey becomes detached from real time. The various performances in the film—Renee's, Sam's, Jimmy's, the circus performances—assume a heightened prominence as a result.

Luke Gibbons considers repetition to be a device that acknowledges the past as relevant to the present, a view similar to Tricia Rose's notion of sampling as recontextualization. Gibbons suggests the difficulty of obeying a strict separation between past and present.

> The impossibility of gaining direct access to the past is not because it is sealed off, as in a time capsule, but because it is part of an unresolved historical process which engulfs the present. (1996a 157)

Musical repetition in performances allows Jimmy to sample identities as he resituates himself in relation to his father and mother. He rewrites his own story as he performs. In performance, past and present collapse.

The film's sense of timelessness informs its mise-en-scène. Critics have remarked that the look of the film is nostalgic, evoking a sense of the 1950s, or seems to exist outside time. A number of reviewers called *The Miracle* Jordan's home movie, as if its small budget and Irish location secured a return to Jordan's proper origins. Yet this is a film in which origins are muddled, if not hopelessly untraceable.

In moving beyond himself, Jimmy challenges gender and sexual boundaries. Jimmy's identification with his parents as performers deconstructs gender differences to the extent that he identifies with both his mother and father, as well as with the woman contortionist. Although tinged with sexual desire, Jimmy's heteropathic identifications permit him to combine the stereotypically masculine and feminine practices of voyeurism and exhibitionism.

In the process of performing otherness, Jimmy crosses another boundary, violating a sexual taboo. His increasingly complex identifications make it difficult to recognize any stable identity, and this process culminates in an extremely shocking moment: Jimmy and Renee have sex on the boardwalk after the secret of their relationship has been revealed to him.[12] In its radical insistence on performed identities, the film refuses to endorse genealogy—a classification system that regulates social interaction based upon biological concepts of identity—as an unassailable framework.

In its treatment of identification and performance, the film points to the difficulty of obtaining access to any original, essential, definitive identity, whether it is biological, ethnic, or cultural. The film's structural circularity and focus on the family crisis underscore an anxiety regarding origins. In its use of jazz to privilege moments of suspension, the film rejects chronological history, which would make it possible to trace a lineage, secure an identity based on the past. Instead, *The Miracle* offers layered performances: for example, when Renee performs the stage version of a classic American film, *Destry Rides Again*, she is reversing the usual progression from stage to screen.

At the film's conclusion, Rose frees the circus animals (in a doff of the hat to W. B. Yeats's "The Circus Animals' Desertion"), and the specter of elephants trudging past churches lends an absurdist quality that alleviates some of the shock of Jimmy and Renee's sexual encounter. The carnival, which overturns hierarchies and defies boundaries, has invaded the real world. Although normalcy is restored when Renee leaves and Jimmy and Rose become friends again, Jordan reminds viewers that stories and, by implication, identities are constructions. Jimmy and Rose walk along the beach as Jimmy revises his own recent history, turning it into a fiction. The conclusion suggests that only stable ground for identity is the process of creation and revision—moments when the self as such is both suspended and created through visual, verbal, or musical performance. Jimmy emerges as the narrator of his story, his identity a process that has been influenced in important ways by Renee and Sam to shape his narration.

In both *Danny Boy* and *The Miracle*, jazz music functions as a metaphor for filmmaking. In Jordan's hands, jazz and cinema are intellectual and sensuous traditions that continually reconsider the relation of past to present. His stories focus on jazz musicians and are structured around music and performance. Jordan's characters sample jazz in ways that extend, destroy, and experiment with identity, including sexual identity.

Jordan does more than merely appropriate jazz. Jordan samples jazz, finding within its form a reference point for the recontextualization of essentialist identities. He participates in the ongoing project of de-essentializing identities through characters who continually redefine themselves through musical performances.

In a similar vein, Spike Lee uses music to examine and question racial and national identities in the United States. Lee's take on DuBois's double consciousness emerges as an analysis of synechdoche: the linguistic and literary trope that universalizes by allowing a part to stand in for a whole. Because Americanness is based on exclusivity and whiteness, the relationship of African Americans to national identity is a continual struggle to be considered a part that can also stand for the whole.

SPIKE LEE: SAMPLING DOUBLE CONSCIOUSNESS

It is widely held that Spike Lee's first feature, *She's Gotta Have It* (1986) set the stage for "New Black Hollywood," a that term suggests greater participation by African Americans at all levels in the U.S. film industry than was achieved even thirty years after Lee's debut film.[13] In an interview, Lee discussed the fact that his work addresses "this whole American myth that it doesn't matter what color you are, creed, or nationality, as long as you're American, you'll be treated the same and viewed the same" (qtd. in Rhines 111). That myth elides the reality of racial difference that W. E. B. DuBois wrote about a century ago when he argued that black Americans are always conscious of a doubleness: "An American, A Negro . . ." (45). The incommensurability of the two names forms a linguistic representation of DuBois's notion of double consciousness: the double vision of always seeing and being seen. If race defines Americanness, the possibility of identifying as an American is compromised by identifying as a Negro, black person, or African American.

Lee addresses this problematic of double identification by invoking sports and music, two realms of celebrity, performance, and entertainment that challenge the divisive construct DuBois defined. Both activities offer avenues for self-expression and bodily transcendence for those who participate and for those who observe. The rhetoric that national identity is based upon a harmonious blend of diverse cultures might actually become reality through such encounters. When characters get out of themselves through the physicality of music and sports, they move beyond an "either/or" and "us/them" structuring of identity.

Music serves as a source of heteropathic identification in Lee's films. Like Neil Jordan, Lee features music as a central formal and thematic device in many films. *She's Gotta Have It* contains a four-minute color dance sequence that pays homage to Vincente Minnelli; *School Daze* (1988) includes full-fledged song and dance numbers. *Do the Right Thing* was recognized for its timely and audacious rap soundtrack, while *Summer of Sam* (1999) used a wide-ranging soundtrack of 1970s rock and disco music to convey its characters' barely-suppressed rage. In *Mo' Better Blues* and *Crooklyn*, musician characters function as avatars of black creativity, and they are identified with musical forefathers.[14] Lee's commitment to affirming a black musical tradition is evident in disc jockey Mr. Señor Love Daddy's roll call in *Do the Right Thing* (his radio program also is heard in *Mo' Better Blues*); in repeated references to John Coltrane in *Mo' Better Blues*; and in Lee's interest in the musical tastes of the five children in *Crooklyn*.

Yet Lee's jazz films go further than historical recovery. They also challenge the idea of essential, authentic black identities. Lee reveals the diversity of black musical styles and their relationship to other musical forms, and in so doing, rejects racial essentialism. In *Mo' Better Blues*, Bleek Gilliam (Denzel Washington) laments the fact that black people don't patronize their "own" music, but the way Lee employs music in that film signifies the impossibility of any individual or group owning a musical style. Furthermore, characters' identifications range across a broad array of black music, defining and giving expression to the beliefs and values of numerous diverse figures, from the urban Carmichaels to their rural Virginia relatives.

In *Mo' Better Blues*, *Crooklyn*, *Do the Right Thing*, and *He Got Game*, musical identifications define moments when characters venture beyond themselves and question the synechdochic relationship between race and nation. Music is an appropriate medium for working through this question of synecdoche—that is, for asking what are the conditions under which a part may stand for the whole of America—because musical forms associated with African American musicians, such as jazz and rap, "rise" to the level of American music only after they are seen to have matured beyond their ethnic origins.[15] As Jon Pareles writes, "[Jazz] was born on the margins of society and nurtured in bordellos and saloons, and despite the fact that it has transformed the world's music, it is still treated as tainted by cultural arbiters who should know better" (22). Beyond this historical fact, on a formal level, music defies the distinction between part and whole because, to be successful, a musical composition must add up to more than the sum of its parts. The relation between instruments, tempo, vocalization, solos, and combinations, makes or breaks the performance. Finally, while using music to intervene in the problem of synecdoche on a thematic level, Lee takes advantage of the music's formal properties to counter traditional narrative form and to experiment with film language.

Lee's musical identifications emphasize the relation between part and whole in the context of the family, the musical group, the neighborhood, and the nation. Lee's two jazz films, as well as *Do the Right Thing* and *He Got Game*, take music beyond mere accompaniment to raise the question of which parts—or which cultures—are recognized as American.

MO' BETTER BLUES: (P)ART AND WHOLE

Spike Lee pursued the jazz film project that culminated in *Mo' Better Blues* because he was frustrated by what he saw in Bertrand Tavernier's *'Round Midnight* (1986) and Clint Eastwood's *Bird* (1988). They were films that, from Lee's perspective, erased black jazz musicians or treated them with contempt. By contrast, Lee presents his contemporary jazz musicians as ordinary working stiffs. In *Mo' Better Blues*, Bleek's quintet works regularly. Even though they are underpaid, they support themselves and their families, and they avoid drugs.

In *Mo' Better Blues*, Lee adopts a metacritical approach to synecdoche, treating it as a social and psychological issue. In the film's opening moments, Lee uses comedy to establish that the relation of part to whole is a central question of the film. Over the familiar logo of Universal Studios, audiences hear rapper Flavor Flav of Public Enemy read out the letters. On its own, the visual image is pure American fantasy, a nostalgic version of a studio logo that calls up associations of leisure time and amusement parks, whereas the rapper's distinctive hip-hop style and direct address issue a challenge to the historical suppression of black literacy. It also questions that logo's claim to universality. Is Flavor Flav's voice the sound one would expect to accompany this overdetermined image of universality? The fact that music will mediate the relation of part to whole in the film is underlined by cinematographer Ernest Dickerson's initial cut to extreme close-ups of a trumpet, lips, and body parts.

The film documents Bleek Gilliam's struggle to become part of something larger than himself. Rather than bringing him closer to others, his musical talent sets him apart. He finds it difficult to join a larger community and he seems to resent black people for their lack of interest in his music. Bleek also refuses to submit to normative masculine identifications, deferring his entry into adult masculinity (associated with monogamous heterosexuality and reproduction) by refusing to commit to one woman.

The film's opening montage contains numerous jazz references and underscores the fact that Bleek defines himself through musical performances. The sequence juxtaposes a scene from Bleek's childhood with one from the present day. Bleek practices scales on his trumpet (a detail that links him to mid-career Coltrane) because his mother refuses to let him play with his friends. Those friends subsequently call him a mama's boy. A cut to the present establishes Bleek in the midst of a performance at the Beneath the Underdog club (a reference to the title of jazz pianist Charles Mingus's autobiography). Bleek's quintet consists of his trumpet, Shadow Henderson (Wesley Snipes) on saxophone, a bass player (Bill Nunn), a pianist (Giancarlo Esposito), and drummer Rhythm Jones (Jeff Watts). Bleek's childhood friend Giant (Spike Lee) is the group's inept manager. He is also an obsessive gambler with a knack for picking losing baseball teams.

Bleek never manages to connect with the members of the quintet except on stage. When performing, Bleek is in charge, and he invests his persona with humor and reaches out to the audience. Potential fraternal associations among the quintet are thwarted by his single-minded pursuit of his own musical "voice," however, and dissention is fueled by Giant's accusations that Shadow hogs the spotlight with his flashy solos. Bleek tolerates longtime buddy Giant, but, in his self-absorption, neglects to register Giant's financial incompetence and instability—two factors that intensify the disgruntlement among the quintet members. Ironically, this male community offers Bleek no means of getting outside himself. The whole is destined to remain less than the sum of it parts.

Moreover, Bleek rejects identifications with earlier musicians, including members of the jazz pantheon. Despite obvious visual and musical references to John Coltrane, Bleek does not listen to or identify with Coltrane. He remains impervious to others in his professional and social life. He appears uncommitted to anything or anyone but practice and performance: his girlfriend Indigo (Joie Lee) accuses him of being a dog. He confirms her accusation when he later makes love with Clarke (Cynda Williams) an aspiring jazz singer (whose name recalls jazz bassist Stanley Clarke). He distances himself from both women by taking refuge in masculine prerogative: his inability to relate to them emotionally is "a dick thing." He uses synecdoche to represent his connection to them (or lack thereof), reducing his investment in these relationships to a single body part.

Lee takes pains to establish the importance of parts and whole by suggesting that Bleek's only source of identity derives from music. The film's cinematography bears out Bleek's over-investment in music as a process of self-involvement. As Bleek practices, visualizing and enacting his performance, a camera revolves around him. This moment of intense solipsism and transcendence also carries erotic weight, suggested when the same circular camera captures Bleek and Clarke having sex.

The notion that sex is a substitute for jazz is conveyed in a scene of foreplay that depicts Clarke caressing Bleek's horn. Yet the superiority of jazz's solitary pleasures relative to the intimacy of heterosexual intercourse is evident in Bleek's injunction to Clarke, after she playfully bites him. He tells her "Don't play with my lips." This interchange foreshadows the violent attack on Bleek later in the film, when thugs beat him with his trumpet. In these scenes, the instrument—which functions as a part of Bleek that he mistakes for his whole identity—mediates moments where the self might be lost: in the midst of sexual desire and during brutal violence.

Bill Lee's "Mo' Better Blues," W. C. Handy's "Harlem Blues," and John Coltrane's "Love Supreme" are the three signature musical pieces in the film that introduce a temporal pattern of repetition and revision. Lee's memorable blues piece, with its melancholy trumpet line and symmetrical chord progressions, refers to the love (or sex) that one settles for in the absence of real love. The song expresses Bleek's unloving relationships with women, where body parts rather than whole persons dictate human relating.

The difference between the two blues songs—"Mo' Better Blues" and "Harlem Blues"—reflects the fundamental opposition between Bleek and Shadow. Bleek seeks musical transcendence without "opening up" to the voices of others, and without regard to the identifications possible within the quintet or the jazz tradition. He has minimal respect for his audience. By contrast, Shadow's joy in performing music lies precisely in his ability to forge identifications with other jazz musicians and his understanding of what audiences want to hear. Wesley Snipes' performance, which makes Shadow appealing *because* of, not despite, his commercial enthusiasm, helps the character rise above the stereotype of the audience-pleasing poseur.

The conflict between Shadow and Bleek links racial identity with aesthetic production. Bleek adopts a cultural nationalist perspective. He states, "jazz is our music, black music" and laments the fact that black people are not aware of or as supportive of jazz musicians as they should be. "It incenses me that our own people don't realize our own culture," he complains to Shadow, "if we had to depend upon black people to eat, we would starve." Shadow replies: "If you play the shit that they like, then they come." Shadow's pragmatic stance embodies the higher value he places on identifying with and performing for others.

By comparison with Bleek, Shadow seems to possess a less aesthetically rigorous commitment to jazz. Yet Shadow listens to and prizes the work of earlier jazz artists like John Coltrane. In one scene, Bleek nonchalantly returns a borrowed Coltrane album to Shadow by using Giant as an intermediary. Shadow handles the album with delicacy and care, commenting on its rare and exalted status. In another scene, he attempts to bask in the shadow of the master to impress Clarke: he visits the store where she works and tries to buy a stack of Coltrane tapes. He may overvalue these musical figures through commodities, using objects as a way of asserting who he is in a culture that defines individuals through their consumption habits. But his ability to forge connections and identifications with previous masters and with struggling newcomers like Clarke allows him to embrace audiences composed of any and all interested listeners.

By contrast, Bleek is only interested in creating himself in the music. He literally "tunes out" all others and rejects the possibility of breaking down rigid boundaries of identity that the music offers to its artists and fans. In the film's final performance scene, Clarke sings "Harlem Blues" with Shadow's band. Shadow makes manifest his ability to balance solos with the integrated sound of the group when he steps in to assist Bleek, who struggles with his solo. He also tempers the all-male combo by introducing heterosexual romance, as he is now Clarke's sexual and musical partner.

Bleek comes to Shadow's performance a broken man. A year earlier, Bleek was drawn into a conflict between Giant and enforcers coming to collect unpaid gambling debts and was beaten with his own trumpet. Without his music, he almost ceases to exist. In the early moments of the scene where he is attacked, Bleek is on stage, and rapid crosscutting uses his frenzied trumpet solo to accompany images of Giant's imminent beating. The music is reminiscent of Coltrane's "sheets of sound" technique, where rapidly playing scales complicates harmonic texture. This overt reference to Coltrane's experimentation becomes important to the film's conclusion.

His lip damaged, Bleek's rehabilitation involves staying home alone, listening to his own music on tapes. The trauma has resulted in his complete withdrawal from the world. He simulates his performances and mutters to himself. One of the few barely intelligible phrases is "John Coltrane-tenor sax—got to improvise." This moment of identification with Coltrane's improvisation does not necessarily signal Bleek's abandonment of an individualistic ethos: instead, it sets up the contrast between Bleek and his son. "Coltrane's playing was controversial," writes David Rosenthal, "on 'All Blues,' for example, his solo makes concessions neither to the audience nor to the rhythm section" (147). At this point in the film, Bleek's ability to improvise—to recontextualize his aesthetic and personal situation through his own music and that of others in a manner that is meaningful to anyone but himself—remains highly questionable.

At Bleek's final performance, Shadow's success ratifies the latter's view of jazz as a shared musical form, not an arena for selfish pleasures. After Bleek's humiliating experience on stage, he rushes to Indigo, demanding that they get married and have a son. Bleek abandons music to literally become his own father and raise himself differently.

The circularity of the narrative is highlighted by the visual rhyme of the closing and opening scenes in the same Brooklyn brownstone. When Indigo "saves" Bleek's life by marrying him and giving birth to their son, she assumes the role of Bleek's mother. In the film's final scene, she demands that their son Miles practice his trumpet, but Bleek indulgently permits him to go out and play. Bleek embraces the conventions of family life; as a patriarch with ultimate authority, he overrules his wife and, the film suggests, ensures his son a normal upbringing that involves playing well with others.

Two aspects of the film's final moments signify Bleek's struggle to use music to define himself as an individual whose identity is a process of relating to others. The first is the symbolism of his son's name. To shift from John Coltrane to Miles Davis as a figure of identification speaks volumes. Miles Davis is accorded a status in the jazz pantheon at least as exalted as that of John Coltrane, but for a very different reason. Davis was best known for bringing his musical brilliance to bear in the context of community; that is, his own playing was often viewed as secondary to the combination of talent he drew to himself over his long career. Davis is recognized for his ability to maintain artistic integrity, not by narrowing his focus but by allowing the ideas and talent of other musicians to permeate his own sensibility. (In fact, the malleability of his aesthetic led a number of critics to dismiss Davis and argue that his experiments with electric jazz fusion were a bastardization of jazz.) Whereas Davis asserted his position as both the maestro and a part of a whole; Coltrane is best remembered for *becoming* whole all on his own through his increasingly spiritual and introspective approach to jazz.

The second signifier of Bleek's transformation is the montage sequence that traces his entry into family and domestic life. The sequence fastens the spirituality associated with Coltrane's "A Love Supreme" to home movie images that are reminiscent of the opening of Scorsese's *Mean Streets* (1973). If Lee's "Mo Better Blues" is about sex and unrequited love (the problematic coupling of two separate parts), and if Handy's "Harlem Blues" is about black social experiences (where the part is refused incorporation into a whole), "A Love Supreme" is about spiritual apotheosis (where the part transcendently becomes the whole).

Lee pairs Coltrane's music with images of birth: dawn bursting through a bedroom window, against which Indigo's swollen belly is silhouetted. The symbolism of new beginnings is carried through shots of Bleek and Indigo's wedding and scenes of childbirth. The supreme spiritual love to which Coltrane's piece alludes is visually rendered as the loving bonds of family. The images suggest the possibility of creative transcendence through the sacrament of marriage and the birth of a child. Yet the sequence can be read ironically as well; Bleek has relinquished the very music that held out the promise of the sublime.

In this montage, music elevates the actions depicted to the level of a love supreme; the music stitches together the parts into a seamless whole and endows them with meaning. To fully appreciate the technique in this sequence, it's important to look at an earlier montage that works to a vastly different effect. A scene depicting Bleek and his father throwing a baseball calls attention to the fact that it is composed of separate parts. An upbeat jazz score with bright trumpet notes accompanies the ball throwing. The fact that Bleek's relationship with his father is distant is suggested when the brief outing segues into a montage that juxtaposes the interests of father and son—baseball and jazz—rather than merging them. Here, the camera captures figures of identification (Coltrane, baseball players) and draws parallels between father and son in terms of their abiding interests. But those parallels—the baseball team and jazz combo, sites of individual and group accomplishment—also suggest the differences between the two men. Bleek's father urges him to pursue a conventional family, not to lose himself in his work. At this earlier point in the narrative, the music and editing refuse to stitch together images to form a whole, as they do in the Coltrane-inspired sequence.

Finally, Lee's use of music also draws upon complex references to black aesthetic history. David Breskin argues that the film's mise-en-scène feels dated; he reads a 1940s sensibility in Lee's costuming and character names (191). Yet if references to Coltrane and Davis are any indication, Bleek's crisis is more appropriately situated in the 1960s, a period that not only witnessed the decline of bebop and the proliferation of new, conflicting styles but also gave birth to coalition politics. In *Riffs & Choruses: A New Jazz Anthology*, Burton Peretti argues, "Just as the civil rights movement broke into various conflicting groups, so did jazz—fragmented into modal, "free" and "outside" styles—face a crisis of identity and lose its revolutionary fervor" (189). The experimental jazz scene of the late 1960s and early 1970s became diverse and contentious in ways it had not been during the rigor of the bop era. Furthermore, audiences no longer supported bebop—a fact that resonates with Bleek's despair over his audience. If the film's high priest of jazz, John Coltrane, "was the sound of hard bop revitalizing itself [. . .] seeking out new modes of expression while retaining the school's mixture of high-modernist self-awareness and hipness" (Rosenthal 150), then the film's new avatar, Bleek's son Miles, represents a jazz that reaches out to embrace, incorporate, and adapt other musical styles. This historical moment is the point where Lee situates his second jazz film, *Crooklyn.*

CROOKLYN: GENDERED FAMILY TIES

Set in a fictionalized Brooklyn, Lee's *Crooklyn* places the cool jazz of *Mo' Better Blues* in opposition to the exuberance of 1970s popular culture. The film covers a traumatic and transitional period in the life of the fractious Carmichael family as seen through the eyes of the family's only daughter, ten-year-old Troy (Zelda Harris). Troy's coming of age takes place during the illness and after the death of her mother Carolyn (Alfre Woodard).

The family patriarch, Woody Carmichael (Delroy Lindo) is a jazz musician whose commitment to the now-unpopular jazz of the previous generation prevents him from supporting his family. As Marc Anthony Neal writes, "Woody Carmichael is in many ways a living embodiment of the marginalization of high African American art in the black community as well as a useful example of the lack of public spaces provided specifically for jazz music and jazz musicians" (152). The fact that the jazz on which he's staked his identity has been eclipsed by popular music is evident in the soundtrack of top 40 hits that functions as a musical score. In contrast to the performance aesthetic of *Mo' Better Blues*, Lee structures this film along the lines of New American Cinema directors like Francis Ford Coppola and Martin Scorsese, who use songs or fragments of popular songs to comment on the film's events and characters. That transformation from free-form jazz to the rhythms of commercial popular culture acts as a metaphor for the expanding locus of cultural identification for Woody's children.

Woody is a jazz pianist and composer whose professional identity is based upon an identification with bebop pioneer Thelonious Monk. A photograph of Monk graces the top of Woody's piano. Moreover, Woody wears Monk's signature sartorial accouterment—a hat—when he composes. Woody has married Carolyn, a teacher, and their union has produced five children. Unlike Bleek, Woody persists in a jazz career and faces a conflict between his work and his paternal role. As Krin Gabbard has noted about jazz films in general, the music is associated with emasculation, which here takes the form of financial dependence. After a contentious discussion about family finances, Carolyn orders Woody out of "her" house. When he arranges a solo concert that he thinks will turn his career around, the scanty audience consists of friends and family.

Woody's fervent identification with those who compose and perform "pure" music relegates him to the status of misunderstood artist, resented husband, and distant parent. The family lacks cohesion: Woody's pursuit of his dream breaks the family into parts. Woody and Carolyn's five children, along with other denizens of the neighborhood, are defined through identifications with a variety of popular musical styles. For example, next-door neighbor Tony plays Welsh sex-symbol Tom Jones's smash hit "It's Not Unusual" on his synthesizer. His off-key performance invades the Carmichaels' aural space, disrupting their dinner (the children retaliate by throwing garbage in Tony's yard). Another space in the film is defined by music: in the food shop down the block, owned by a Puerto Rican man, Latin rhythms dominate in songs like "El Pito" (Never Go Back to Georgia) and "Puerto Rico."

Despite bell hook's contention that the Carmichaels "represent an alternative to the bourgeois norm" (11), the Carmichael children clearly are products of the contemporary popular culture of sports, radio, television, and music. Their figures of identification include African American athletes and musicians as well as white musicians and celebrities. Clinton's room is plastered with images of Muhammed Ali and Walt Frazier, traditional celebrity role models. As they watch television, the boys dance to "Soul Train." The two youngest children, Troy and Joseph, express their heteropathic identification by singing along to "I Woke Up in Love This Morning," as performed by the Partridge family, a lily-white television family whose structure reverses that of the Carmichaels. On television, the white mother and children enjoy careers as pop musicians and the father is absent.

Scenes such as these are why Neal calls *Crooklyn* "postindustrial nostalgia, loosely described as a nostalgia that has its basis in the postindustrial transformations of black urban life during the 1970s" (151–52). The film's retrospective appeal is conveyed through costumes, hairstyles, and, most importantly, the soundtrack. No fewer than twenty-five hit songs are listed in the credits, including tracks from The Jackson Five, Curtis Mayfield, and Sly and the Family Stone, the Delfonics, Jean Knight, and the Stylistics.

When Troy is sent to stay with relatives in the South, the vast difference between her progressive, Afrocentric urban lifestyle and the Southern lifestyle of Aunt Song, Uncle Clem, and Cousin Viola is typified not only by Viola's predominantly white Barbie doll collection, but also through music: an instructional 45 rpm record and the television music that inspires Viola and Aunt Song to sing along. Whereas scenes of Troy and Viola playing are accompanied by the Jackson Five's "1-2-3," Viola and her mother sing along with white evangelists, whose lyrics include: "1,2,3; the Devil's after me; 4,5,6; he's always throwing sticks." Although Troy clearly is dubious about her relatives' religious fervor, later she sings Viola and Song's version of "1,2,3." After she visits her ailing mother in the hospital, Troy turns on the television and seems to find comfort as she sings along with the Afro-Sheen jingle. Her attempts at heteropathic identifications are literally pathetic: the pathos arises from her misplaced identifications with advertising that establishes black urban identities through hair products and with a dimly understood religion associated with the uptight Southerners.

Unlike *Mo' Better Blues*, the film's structure is based on the pop song aesthetic. Troy's coming-of-age story unfolds as a series of vignettes; the pace conforms to the three-minute pop song. Whereas mainstream radio stations broke away from the three-minute format during the 1960s, the advent of MTV music videos in the 1980s re-imposed a standardized treatment of visual and sound combinations that Lee draws upon. In the film, popular 1970s songs are not played in their entirety; instead they are utilized diegetically and nondiegetically to build the emotional texture of a particular scene, and then fade out as another vignette develops. This pattern may be intended to suggest the perspective of a ten-year-old child or the episodic daily-ness of the characters' lives, but it nevertheless draws upon the rhythms of popular music culture rather than experimental jazz. One example of the pairing of sound and vignette in cinematic shorthand is the use of Curtis Mayfield's "Pusherman" to introduce the neighborhood's sad-sack drug users, two glue sniffers who terrorize the children for their lunch money.

An example of the layering of music and vignette to produce a more complex resonance occurs when Lee weaves several bars of Jimi Hendrix's "Hey Joe" into a scene of Troy walking home at night to discover that the police have come to the Carmichaels' brownstone. The police arrest Vic, the Carmichaels' tenant and a Vietnam vet who slapped Tony during an ongoing dispute. The use of Hendrix—whose music is often associated with Vietnam in films like *Apocalypse Now* (Francis Ford Coppola 1979)—signifies Vic's connection to the war. (This offers yet another version where a part stands for a whole: the soldier's body stands for the nation). The lyrics emphasize Troy's position as a witness to violence. Its tempo and instrumentation suggest both sympathy for the perpetrator of violence and weariness with the cultural context that promotes reaction rather than prevention or mediation.

In *Crooklyn*, jazz is displaced to the periphery of African American urban life. As in *Mo' Better Blues*, Lee emphasizes the conflict between artistry and the practical necessities of family life. In both films, the family reigns supreme; this is signified by the use of Coltrane's paean to elevate the rituals of marriage and childrearing and by Troy's final transformation to female adulthood. She agrees to attend her mother's funeral, accompanied by the Ohio Players "Ooh Ooh Child."

The onus of maturity falls upon Troy in this film rather than on the patriarch Woody. Troy becomes the family's conscience and spiritual foundation. The film's final scenes reveal her complete identification with her mother. In a sequence that crosscuts Troy's memories of Carolyn combing Troy's hair with a scene of Troy combing Joseph's hair, Troy assumes the maternal position physically and psychologically, repeating the phrases Carolyn used and adopting her stern demeanor. More than any of the male Carmichaels, the film seems to say, Troy's life is irrevocably changed by her mother's death. As bell hooks writes, "becoming a mini-matriarch because her mother is sick and dying requires of Troy that she relinquish all concern with pleasure and play; that she repress desire" (13). Troy is unaware of the possibilities offered by "selfish" creativity, and her range of identifications is circumscribed.

Lee's musical identifications, which signify characters' relationships to something larger, be that family or community, expose the existence of a gendered status quo. Troy sees herself as part of the family, not part of a musical group or sports team. Assuming her mother's role provides an opportunity to become an important part. In this context, it is important to note that, of the more than two dozen pieces of music Lee uses to organize the episodic narrative, only two songs are sung by women: "Mr. Big Stuff" by Jean Knight and "Rock Steady" by Aretha Franklin. If music carries the potential for individual transformation, and offers a means of joining a community, then the dearth of women musicians underscores the fact that women cannot be figures of identification and suggests the inevitability of the domestic world that entraps Troy. That world is "an insidious anti-woman, anti-feminist vision of black family life" (hooks 14).

In *Mo'Better Blues* and *Crooklyn*, Lee uses musicians and musical forms to explore the troubled relation of part to whole, of individual to group identity. In both films, an obsession with creating the music, rather than an ability to identify with other players, composers, and audience members, sets the stage for tragedy. That obsession prevents artists from experiencing the bonds of family and the solidarity of community. In both films, the solution to the synecdochic problem of reconciling blackness and American-ness, is to create a whole in the form of the nuclear family, organized by traditional gender roles. In the following two readings, I examine the way Lee's interest in synechdoche moves beyond family and jazz combo to encompass the neighborhood and the nation.

CODA: IRRECONCILABLE IDENTIFICATIONS IN *DO THE RIGHT THING* AND *HE GOT GAME*

Spike Lee juxtaposes sound and image in *Do the Right Thing* and *He Got Game* to signal the way racial divisions work within individuals and across American culture. Music that functions as a source of identification also offers a possibility for destabilizing apparently irreconcilable differences. Like Jordan, Lee uses music to structure his narratives and to inform his visual style. In *Do the Right Thing* and *He Got Game*, Lee's juxtapositions of music and image highlight the way that music might create a sense of wholeness but fails to do so in the racially polarized United States.

In *Do the Right Thing* when Sal's Famous Pizzeria burns, Smiley (Roger Guenveur Smith) attaches a decorated photograph of Martin Luther King, Jr. and Malcolm X to the wall. Throughout the film, Smiley has been hawking these doctored photographs of black political consensus. The gesture of placing the picture on the wall is highly ironic. The riot's two primary antagonists, the boom box-toting Radio Raheem (Bill Nunn) and the volatile neo-nationalist Buggin' Out (Giancarlo Esposito), have instigated a boycott of Sal's for the precise reason that no African Americans graced Sal's photographic Wall of Fame, reserved, according to the proprietary Sal (Danny Aiello), for "American Italians," with emphasis on the former.

The irony, of course, is in the fact that the African American icons are afforded pride of place only when the business is engulfed in flames. They offer identificatory possibilities on the wall only in the context of annihilation, an instant before the structure succumbs. At the same time, Sal's prized photos of assimilated celebrity and success—including Al Pacino, Marlon Brando, and Frank Sinatra—are also immolated. Tragically, the only shared space is figured as a space of destruction. Visual images that elicit identification are consumed by a kind of violence based upon individuals' unwillingness to expand their range of potential identifications.

At the heart of the conflict between Sal, Radio Raheem, and Buggin' Out lies the question of identification. More specifically, the characters question the modes of identification available within the diverse Brooklyn neighborhood. Outsiders like Sal and the Korean grocer own the businesses. The one African American figure who engages in public, civic discourse is disc jockey Señor Love Daddy (Samuel Jackson). His voice and music engulf the neighborhood, assisted by fluid camerawork that catches the drift of his music and talk as it flows over the inhabitants.

He is an unambiguously unifying force, admonishing his listeners to lighten up and feel the love rather than give in to animosity.

The predominant means of signifying one's identity, and one's group affiliation, is music. The Public Enemy song that is Radio Raheem's anthem—"Fight the Power"—accompanies him in life and lingers after his death. Señor Love Daddy's roll call of famous and forgotten black musicians is accorded a privileged position in the film as well as on the community's streets, where the names at first clash with, and then blend into, the rap music of Public Enemy.

Sal's inability or refusal to identify with the community in which he claims membership—at one point he proclaims his satisfaction at having fed the block's inhabitants for twenty five years—incites the violence that destroys his pizzeria. Just prior to the attack on Sal's, members of the community call on him to join in their resistance. At the moment of truth, Coconut appeals to Sal, making reference to the brutality of the white police officers: "They didn't have to kill the boy." Sal replies, "You gotta do what you gotta do," thus condoning the killing of Radio Raheem. Sal's refusal to stand with the neighborhood against the white police officers motivates Mookie to throw a garbage can through the pizzeria's plate glass window.

The Korean man who operates a grocery store across the street from Sal's avoids a similar fate for his business by asserting his identification with the angry black residents in search of justice—"I'm black," he shouts, as he fends off the angry crowd with a broom. His timely and self-interested gesture of solidarity is not rebuffed. Despite the growing hostility of the residents, his overt gesture of heteropathic identification suffices.

The fact that music and sports have the potential to encourage such heteropathic identifications and thus to breach racial difference is made clear earlier when Mookie discusses popular culture with Sal's son Pino (John Turturro). Pino is hostile toward African Americans, yet he does admit that he admires Michael Jackson and Prince, two important "crossover" stars of the 1980s. Pino's ability to identify with and appreciate prominent African Americans does not temper his hostility on a day-to-day basis. So, although Mookie's attempt to talk to Pino raises the possibility that popular culture identifications can break down ignorance and racism, it also shows that identifications are not sufficient to the task of changing racist practices. Pino considers the black sports and music celebrities who are objects of his identification "white." This circular logic casts Pino's racism as a kind of white autism: he is unable to identify across the color line, thus he must make his heroes white, or at least not black. Pino's racial conundrum might be traced to his Italian American heritage and his need to perform that identity in a manner that supports his own claim to whiteness.

Unlike Mookie and Radio Raheem, Sal prefers his ethnic identifications to be visual and silent. His wall of fame is repeatedly depicted as a lifeless gallery of photographs, devoid of movement or sound. No one plays or listens to music in Sal's pizzeria—music's potential for blurring cultural boundaries may be as threatening to him as adding images of African Americans to the wall. Sal's space functions as an enclave in both symbolic and experiential terms; the images on the wall enshrine the past successes of individual Italian Americans. Sal's refusal to have his space infused with music—and especially Radio Raheem's rap—indicates his disinterest in truly sharing his cultural history or values and learning about those of others. The absence of music suggests the sterility of his environment and the lack of interchange, especially when the pizzeria is compared to the sound-filled spaces of the rest of the neighborhood.

In *Do the Right Thing,* Lee specifically asks how a collection of parts—photographs of Pacino, Brando, King, and Malcolm X and the music of black, Latino, and white artists—fails to produce a coherent whole that is greater than its sum. (It's notable that those parts—images and sound—are also the parts that create the whole of the film medium.) Lee is unable to solve this problem, but comes close to a diagnosis by disarticulating images and sounds, revealing the way various kinds of identification both shore up and tear down notions of individuality, race, and national identity.

HE GOT GAME

In *He Got Game,* Spike Lee brings to the fullest expression his twin passions for music and sports. Formally, this is Lee's opportunity to fully develop the montage technique he experiments with in the Coltrane–baseball and "Love Supreme" sequences in *Mo' Better Blues. He Got Game* weaves together a cautionary tale of sports success with a story of familial breakdown. In a sense, basketball replaces jazz as the masculine domain that threatens to destabilize traditional forms of family and community. It also functions as the link between protagonists Jake (Denzel Washington) and Jesus Shuttlesworth (Ray Allen), an estranged father

FIGURE 2.2. Playing basketball becomes a means of asserting an American identity in Spike Lee's *He Got Game.* Courtesy of Photofest.

and son. One reviewer calls the film "*Do The Right Thing* meets *Crooklyn* on a basketball court" (Carr, D1).

The plot concerns Jesus's struggle to make a decision about his future. A high school senior and basketball hotshot, he must choose between attending college or entering the NBA. As he weighs his options, Jesus's entire world shifts around him as his family and friends jockey for position. Jesus comes face to face with the way the system of professional sports threatens to exploit his talent and rewrite his identity in order that some entities (universities, NBA teams, merchandisers) might extract the maximum commercial benefit from his status as a figure of identification for fans.

In the film, music expresses Jesus's talent, his love for the fame, and his vulnerability to exploitation. Lee employs two forms of music—the popular classical music of Aaron Copland and the more contemporary music of Public Enemy—to express the seemingly intractable problem of synecdoche that prevents African American subjects and African American culture from being acknowledged as sites of identification for all Americans.

Most reviewers have commented on the seemingly irreconcilable musical styles Lee uses to orchestrate the saga of the sacrificial sports figure: the rap of Public Enemy and the orchestral folk of Aaron Copland. Mike Clark writes "though the score sounds schizophrenic on paper, Aaron Copland and Public Enemy are a surprisingly harmonious fast-break combination" (*USA Today*, 11E). Janet Maslin writes that the film reaches for a "wider scope" than Lee's other films and she singles out the soundtrack as a prominent element of that expansive reach (1998 16).

Maslin and a number of other reviewers imply that the film's emphasis on Copland signals Lee's interest in moving beyond "narrow" issues pertaining only to African Americans. In other words, the music of Copland, but not that of Public Enemy, is appropriate for underscoring the peculiarly American narrative of the rise from obscurity to sports celebrity. Jay Carr argues that Lee's use of rap music is to be expected since he wants to "project a heightened street flavor," but that employing Aaron Copland's "portentous sonorities" is a dramatic musical departure aimed at a "specifically American myth." (D1). In *Sight and Sound*, Rob Falson similarly invokes myth in his comments on the film's opening sequence, which pairs Copland's "John Henry" and images of bodies in motion: "Such an arresting opening declares both Lee's passionate love of basketball [. . .] and his continuing commitment to producing mythic cinema from a Black-American perspective" (45).

These reviewers suggest that Lee's use of Copland "elevates" the sport of basketball to the level of ballet while it also attaches his narrative to a mythic universality. But that endorsement of Copland's music's universality obscures a subtle and underlying rejection of rap music and narratives about African American experiences as "American" forms. In this view, to achieve mythic status, Lee must draw upon white Americana. The jazz, blues, and rap Lee uses in most of his films are indigenous American forms. Jazz, drawn from folk sources and "elevated" to a serious art form, certainly shares a great deal with Copland's aesthetic. Yet, it would seem from the critical commentary, only Copland's folk classicism is capable of nationalizing images of black bodies.

While *He Got Game* certainly aims directly at the heart of American mythologies—including the Coney Island hucksterism Maslin alludes to and the Horatio Alger story—Lee's juxtaposition of Copland and Public Enemy carries with it more than a little irony. That confrontation—not unlike the conflict between Bleek and Shadow, or between Sal and Radio Raheem—creates the conditions for a dialogue about the apparent incommensurability of black and American identities.

In a film about the appropriation of black bodies, arguably a modern parable of enslavement, the choice to use the music of Public Enemy and Aaron Copland raises more than one question about Americanness. But for my purposes, the way music undermines identity, and therefore highlights the problem of national identity remains the paramount issue. In *He Got Game*, Lee poses the following question: what are the conditions under which all artifacts of American folk culture—the music of Copland and African American rappers, Sal's wall of fame, and the game of basketball—might be raised to a "higher" or more universal level? Juxtaposing rap and Copland forces one to consider the reasons for designating one style high culture and the other popular culture. If Copland's work signifies Americanness, Lee suggests, then under what conditions will important and popular black musical forms like jazz and rap ascend to that pinnacle of universality? In the terms of this book, if heteropathic identifications forged through the out-of-body experiences that music and sports can offer do not lead to a system of functioning synecdoches, then what experiences might produce that outcome?

CONCLUSION: FRAMEWORKS OF MUSIC AND IDENTITY

Neil Jordan and Spike Lee use music to suggest the slipperiness of identity, its performative and contextual, rather than essential, nature. Jordan's characters are transformed as they come to recognize the constructed character of identity. They do not find in those moments of transcendence a solution to the predicaments of history and location, however. They realize their self-constructions are partially produced by, and therefore also limited by, the historical dynamics of family and nation.

Jordan's interest in character identification across race and nationality through music offers a new possibility for theorizing identification through the voice. Because Jordan's saxophone-playing protagonists adopt the persona of the jazz musician by playing the instrument, they recontextualize themselves as African American performers. This re-positioning sheds light on Danny and Jimmy's uneasy relation to national identity but also may perpetuate certain stereotypes of black emotion and spontaneity. The characters' bodies mediate between composer and instrument, suggesting a conflation of desire and identification, of passivity and activity. In a similar aesthetic of suspension, jazz performances, with their circular structure, thwart the progress of narrative itself.

Whereas Jordan employs music to transport his characters "out of Ireland," Spike Lee relies on musical identification to de-essentialize blackness, to reveal the diversity of black musical forms, and to question the doubleness or disparity that marks the difference between black and American identities. He appeals to the tradition of black musical creativity not merely to correct the historical record but also to suggest the diversity that belies any notion of "a" black community.

Lee's formal juxtapositions of image and music suggest music's capacity for unifying disparate elements. Lee uses music as a model for undermining essentialist identities, but cautions that even music's invitation to engage in heteropathic identification seems unlikely to permeate the rigidly nonsynecdochic structure of part to whole that shapes American national identities.

CHAPTER THREE

"It's a Wise Child that Knows His Own Father": Pregnant Performances and Maternal Mythologies

A number of Irish and African American films made during the 1980s and 1990s focus on pregnant women and mothers. Unlike the classical maternal melodrama, however, these problem pregnancy films do not situate the discourse on women's sexuality within the realm of character psychology. Instead, they cast a wider net and implicate social practices and ideologies of gender in the construction of women's bodies, sexualities, and maternal activities. Not only do these films question gender essentialism, they also consider the way such gender ideologies contribute to the construction and maintenance of national identity.

This chapter explores a number of films that reject the political and religious discourses that define woman as mother, yoking female sexuality to biological and social reproduction. The films articulate links between mother figures and national identity and make clear the public stakes of supposedly private matters of gender and sexuality. This diverse group of problem pregnancy films includes Steven Spielberg's *The Color Purple* (1985), Margo Harkin's *Hush-a-Bye Baby* (1989), Julie Dash's

Daughters of the Dust (1990), Thaddeus O'Sullivan's *December Bride* (1990), Gillies MacKinnon's *The Playboys* (1992), Leslie Harris's *Just Another Girl on the IRT* (1992), Stephen Frears's *The Snapper* (1993), Suri Krishnamma's *A Man of No Importance* (1994), Jonathan Demme's *Beloved* (1998), and Orla Walsh's *Blessed Fruit* (1999).

By expressing an interest in the social implications of unauthorized reproduction, these films explicitly reject the generic codes of the maternal melodrama, a genre that experienced a mini-revival during the 1980s and 1990s with films such as *Fatal Attraction* (Adrian Lyne 1987); *Baby Boom* (Charles Shyer 1987); *Mermaids* (Richard Benjamin 1990); *The Hand That Rocks the Cradle* (Curtis Hansen 1992); *Little Women* (Gillian Armstrong 1994); and *The River Wild* (Curtis Hansen 1994).[1] Whereas the maternal melodrama foregrounds maternal sacrifice, these problem pregnancy films locate scandalous pregnancies and mothering in a community context rather than attributing the problems they create to the inately excessive quality of the maternal psyche.

According to Lucy Fischer, cinematic maternity invariably generates a crisis (22). Certainly, the physical state of pregnancy has served as a congenial subject for informational documentaries, avant garde meditations, and gory horror films—Stan Brakhage's birth films, Roman Polanski's *Rosemary's Baby* (1968), and the *Alien* series are paradigmatic texts in this regard. Pregnancy frequently functions as comic relief in narrative feature films. Here, however, I examine narrative films in which the state of pregnancy signifies the social crisis of the maternal.

Irish and African American problem pregnancy films are popular narrative films that draw attention to the corporeality of the maternal body to forward a critique of essentialist ideas about gender. They question ideologies of mother and country. In the process, they show pregnancy and mothering to be social acts that redefine subjectivity, not states of nature. In fact, these films often couch pregnancy and mothering as performances.

In these ways, the films reflect upon the way the "visibly pregnant woman makes the possibility of a continuous subject/ivity real" (Phelan 170). Whereas music presents opportunities for getting outside oneself in the jazz films of Jordan and Lee, female characters in problem pregnancy films grapple with the ways that pregnancy and motherhood confound the distinction between self and other. Pregnant women embody heteropathic identification because the subject positions they occupy are previously unimaginable, and they remain intangible to many in their communities. Pregnant women in these films explore the social meaning of their bodies, attending to both the traditional and radical forms of identification they make possible, and often liberating themselves from restrictive gender roles in the process.

As these characters explore this unique perspective on identity as process and reject the one-to-one correspondence posited between woman and mother, they destabilize the binary and essentialist system of difference that defines gender and national identities. In addressing these questions, the films draw upon contemporary and historical discourses that link women's sexuality to national identity.

THE POLITICS OF MATERNITY

Irish and African American problem pregnancy films emerged during hotly contested public discussions of pregnancy in both Ireland and the United States. These discussions focused on socially unauthorized sexual behavior, such as nonmarital or teen pregnancy, and homosexuality. In Ireland, referenda were held on the constitutionality of abortion (1983 and 1992) and divorce (1986 and 1995). In the United States, demonization of the pregnant African American teenager during the Reagan era formed the social and political backdrop to these films. *Just Another Girl on the IRT* and *Hush-A-Bye-Baby* depict these fraught debates directly, but the vast majority of problem pregnancy films do not. I am not suggesting that any of the films simply reflect or respond to contemporary political discussions. What I am proposing is that these films situate pregnant women at the center of public debates in ways that emphasize the connections among maternity, colonial history, and national identity.

During the 1980s and early 1990s, the notion of scandalous pregnancies occupied center stage in the public arena in Ireland and in the United States. In Ireland, the struggle over the religious and political significance of the maternal body intensified in the wake of several highly publicized cases involving unmarried pregnant women: Joanne Hayes and the Kerry babies in 1983, Ann Lovett in 1984, the X case of 1992. The moral and legal dilemmas raised by these emotionally charged situations catapulted personal tragedies onto an international stage.[2]

In the United States, Reagan-era indictments of black teen pregnancy and "welfare queens" coincided with the rise of the religious right and underwrote the dismantling of public support programs. Adolph

Reed, Jr. points out that, in official rhetoric, households headed by poor women of color were vilified as "baby factories" and became synonymous with social pathology. Reed's research speaks to the ideological character of the campaign to use black women's sexual and reproductive choices to drive national policy: the hysteria about the epidemic of black teen childbearing contradicted statistics indicating black teen fertility rates had declined since 1970 (191–92).

As traditional sexual ideologies garnered renewed interest in both Ireland and the United States, profound questions were raised about public policy and its relation to Catholic orthodoxy in Ireland and to racist schemata in the United States. The fact that women's sexuality has played, and continues to play, a central role in national narratives is made evident by both the proliferation of problem pregnancy films during the 1980s and 1990s and by their specific narrative concerns.

In addition, many of the stories themselves are set during historical periods when concepts of national identity were being vigorously renegotiated. *December Bride*, *Daughters of the Dust*, *Beloved*, and *The Color Purple* deal with the upheavals in the late nineteenth and early twentieth centuries, a period of social and economic change that redefined Irish and American national identities. Efforts to secure Home Rule in Ireland were in full force, exacerbating sectarian divisions, particularly in Ulster, where *December Bride* is set. In the United States, between 1890 and 1910, a quarter of a million southern blacks, like the characters in *Daughter of the Dust*, left the Jim Crow south for the urbanized north in search of jobs and better lives. *The Color Purple* and *Beloved* deal with the legacy of slavery as it has continued to inform pregnancy and reproduction for black women after the U.S. Civil War and well into the twentieth century.

A second set of films is set after World War II, right around 1960. This era was a period of revolutionary transformation in Ireland: rapid economic shifts reversed the Republic's social and economic insularity and wartime neutrality, particularly through the communications technologies of television.[3] *The Playboys* and *A Man of No Importance*, set in this era, examine maternity as performance, rewriting one nationalist tradition associated with the Irish theatre.

The last group of films is set in the 1980s and 1990s, and includes *Just Another Girl on the IRT*, *Hush-A-Bye Baby*, *The Snapper*, and *Blessed Fruit*. These films speak directly to the contemporary politics of sexuality and reproduction in the United States and in Ireland in the 1980s and 1990s. So, for example, the Reagan administration's gag rule prohibits a counselor from informing Chantel (Ariyan Johnson) about her options in *Just Another Girl*, while the Catholic Church and British army circumscribe Irish women's choices regarding pregnancy in *Hush a Bye Baby* and *Blessed Fruit*. Caught up in the politics of the period, these pregnant women resist their identification as mothers by disavowing their physical states, by refusing to divulge "the name of the father," and by adopting an ironic stance toward social pieties. They suggest that, to address the cultural shifts of postmodernity that have reconfigured national identity, the literal and symbolic dimensions of maternity must also be addressed.

While these films speak directly to contemporary concerns, they also reference histories of colonial subjugation and highlight the role maternity plays in collective memories. Luke Gibbons cites Toni Morrison's *Beloved* (1988) to make the point that social traumas of the past are embedded in the present:

> But while the past may be a distant country, it is not so different for those cultures engaged in a centuries-old struggle against western colonization [. . .] [w]ould anyone seriously suggest [. . .] that novels such as Toni Morrison's *Beloved* are valuable merely for their recreation of the ordeal of slavery as it was endured 150 years ago but have little to do with the lived experience of the African American population in the contemporary United States? (1996f 172)

The dynamics of colonialism that these films grapple with through the maternal figure involve "a relation of structural domination and a suppression—often violent—of the heterogeneity of the subject(s) in question" (Mohanty 256). As colonial practices have suppressed the heterogeneity of female (and male) subjects, images of powerful mothers have proliferated in both the colonialist and anti-colonial/nationalist discourses. The films in this chapter take aim at these cultural and religious mythologies of matriarchal power. In order to appreciate the critiques that these films level, I offer the following condensed cultural history of women's sexuality and reproduction in Irish and African American contexts.

COLONIALISM, NATIONALISM, AND MATERNITY

Narratives growing out of colonial experiences often represent women as a troubling border between colonizers and colonized, as a foreign yet familiar body. The Chicana figure of "La Malinche" refers to Malintzín Tenépal, the woman who acted as a translator for Hernán Cortés. A number of Mexican writers attribute the mixed heritage of their culture to her and describe the *mestizo* (mixed) people she mothered as *los hijos de la chingada* ("children of the fucked one"). Rosa Linda Fregoso writes about the pivotal role of La Malinche as both sexual victim and scapegoat:

> Mexican writers [such] as Octavio Paz and Carlos Fuentes have traced the pathology of Mexicans (*mestizos*) to La Malinche's rape by the conqueror. In their view, La Malinche facilitated the ultimate downfall, giving birth to the *mestizo* people. (16)

Here, the violated woman produces living embodiments of a people's cultural domination, the mixed people. Her fertility is responsible for cultural disintegration.

In Irish history, the image of the wronged woman has been used to represent Ireland as a violated nation. Richard Kearney notes that the bardic poetry prior to the seventeenth century used terminology of the "fatherland" to characterize Ireland. After the flight of the Earls of Tyrone and Tyrconnell in 1607 that marked the end of the Gaelic order as a political system, the poets transpose women "into desexualized, quasi-divine mothers" in "idioms connoting a motherland" (119). Eventually a composite Mother Ireland figure—the *Shan Van Vocht*, or poor old woman—appeared in the nationalist ballads of the 1798 rebellion. She is an old woman who urges her sons to sacrifice themselves for Ireland.

Although Irish nationalist movements have encompassed Catholics and Protestants across several centuries, for the last century, Irish nationalism has been inextricably intertwined with Catholicism. In the latter half of the nineteenth century, post-famine Ireland was characterized by a growing tenant-farmer class whose survival depended upon "familism." Familism describes a shared set of attitudes, sanctioned by a Catholic Church experiencing what Emmett Larkin has called a "devotional revolution." The church enforced strict codes regulating sexuality and marriage.[4] These practices were not solely aspects of religious devotion, but influenced Irish culture broadly. David Cairns and Shaun Richards conclude, "among the tenant farmers, sex was a subsidiary to a more important, material, transaction—the passage of farms and dowries from generation to generation" (61). After independence was achieved in the

1920s, views and practices that equated women, mothers, and the nation were ensconced in the ideology of the Irish Free State and, eventually, written into the Irish Constitution.

Nineteenth-century Catholic political leaders such as Charles Stewart Parnell defined Irishness in terms of Catholic culture, whereas the Anglo-Irish literary revival celebrated pre-Christian Ireland as a means of asserting the Irishness of both Catholics *and* Protestants. Revival poet William Butler Yeats glorified the Celt, offering "the myth of Mother Ireland as symbolic compensation for the colonial calamities of history" and idealizing a "Celtic paganism *pre-existing* the colonial rupture of Ireland into sectarian denominations" (Kearney, 1988 113; emphasis in original). By the end of the nineteenth century, "two female images had become potent social, political, and moral forces in Catholic Ireland—the images of Mother Ireland or Erin, and the Mother of God, often linked through iconography to Mother Church" (Innes 41). The ideology of national identity at the time of the 1916 Easter Rising was fully bound up in the imagery of a Virgin-Mother Ireland:

> Since the women of colonized Ireland had become, in James Connolly's words the "slaves of slaves," they were, in a socio-political sense at least, the perfect candidates for compensatory elevation in the order of mystique. The cult of virginity undoubtedly corroborated this process of sublimation. Woman became as sexually intangible as the ideal of national sovereignty became politically tangible. (Kearney 1988 119)

Although Connolly and others recognized the specific oppression of women, in post-independence Ireland the Church's influence overrode the radical democratic notions of leaders such as Connolly. Historian Margaret Callaghan argues that, shortly after Independence, nationalist energies originally aimed at the British enemy were redirected toward an internal foe: immorality (Hug 77).

After the establishment of the Irish Free State in 1922, Catholic orthodoxy was formalized in law for a population more than 90 percent Catholic. The Censorship of Publications Act of 1929 prohibited books advocating contraception, the 1935 Criminal Law Amendment prohibited the sale and importation of contraceptives, and the 1937 constitution officially endorsed the Irish woman's domestic role as a national goal. Article 41.3 banned divorce, and 41.2 stated that

> 1. by her life within the home, woman gives to the state a support without which the common good cannot be achieved.
> 2. The State, shall, therefore, endeavor to ensure that mothers shall not be obliged by economic necessity to engage in labor to the neglect of their duties in the home. (qtd. in Beale 7)

Historian Jenny Beale emphasizes the linguistic slippage between points one and two; "woman" and "mother" are viewed as synonymous by the Constitution (7). Legislation prohibited married women from civil service jobs, banned divorce, and prohibited contraception and abortion. Most of these laws were in effect until the 1970s, when a series of reforms removed the special status of the Catholic Church in relation to the state.

The desire for access to employment and for reproductive self-determination led Irish feminists and other activists of the 1970s (and since) to bring sexuality and reproduction into the public sphere. These actions are in direct conflict with the culture's lingering Mariolatry, wherein sanctioned public representations of sexuality are asexually maternal (Mother Ireland) and virginally maternal (the Virgin Mary). Cheryl Herr writes that the illusory power of the matriarch may be one reason why the "turmoil of Irish history is illogically laid, by both genders, at the feet of women" (1995 293). She continues,

> although Ireland itself is generally thought of as a woman who demands and gets considerable sacrifice, the actual power exercised by Irish women is severely constrained to a certain familial and ideological zone that does not disarm the more powerful patriarchal syntax of the culture. (1995 293–94)

Given Herr's observations, it might seem ironic that contemporary political discussions and cinematic representations related to Irish women have organized themselves around the Virgin Mary, mothers, and reproduction. Yet the image of the mother provides a recognizable position from which the public voices of women can be heard. According to Luke Gibbons, the collection of "harrowing narratives" that focus specifically on unwed maternity in an Ireland still governed by Catholic dogma offers a potent alternative to patriarchal politics:

> The silencing of women's stories and of marginalized voices during the referendum campaigns of the '80s allowed Irish people to delude themselves that they were dealing with cut-and-dried issues. [. . .] It

> is tempting to see such stories simply as individual case histories that put a human face on the impersonal abstractions of politics. But these charged "family romances" themselves operate politically, as alternative national narratives to the official discourses of faith and fatherland. (1992 13)

Irish problem pregnancy films disrupt the automatic identification of woman with Mother Ireland, whether figured as the *Shan Van Vocht* or the Catholic Virgin Mary. They resist the relegation of the woman as mother to silent intangibility and the erasure of women's sexual desire by the sacrificial Madonna. They present alternative narratives that view identity as a work in process and national identity as open to renegotiation.

Matriarchal mythologies associated with African American women in the United States center on the cultural trauma and disruption accomplished by chattel slavery. Echoing the rhetoric associated with La Malinche and with representations of Ireland as a wronged woman, African American discourses have cast African American women as "conduits" for hybridity, as symbols of the inability to resist physical and psychic colonization by dominant European culture. Hortense Spillers argues that North American racist ideology casts African American women not merely as the source of cultural hybridity but as the point of intersection of species. "Slavery did not transform the Black female into an embodiment of carnality at all," she writes. "She became instead the principal point of passage between the human and non-human world" (1992 76). Echoing the arguments of anti-lynching activist Ida B. Wells, Spillers writes that black women labored under an altogether different sex and gender system than that of bourgeois white women. This critical difference—the absence of a domestic model to characterize black femininity—meant that the enslaved woman's sexuality was necessarily public; no private realm existed where matters of sex and reproduction were concerned. Her sexuality was not only public, but also the property of her owner. And so was her maternal capability:

> even though the enslaved female reproduced other enslaved persons, we do not read "birth" in this instance as a reproduction of mothering precisely because the female, like the male, has been robbed of the parental right, the parental function. (Spillers 78)

These dynamics—ensconced within the legal system—define African American motherhood itself as illegitimate. Under statutes, the enslaved mother's function was to pass on the condition of being a slave to her children. Two laws passed in Virginia in the late seventeenth century ensured, first, that indentured servants and slaves who bore children by their masters would be punished with two additional years of service and, second, that "Negro women's children to serve according to the condition of the mother" (Hening). The full text of Article XII, enacted in December 1662, reads:

> Whereas some doubts have arisen whether children got by any Englishman upon a negro woman should be slave or free, Be it therefore enacted and declared by this present grand assembly, that all children borne in this country shall be held bond or free only according to the condition of the mother, And that if any Christian shall commit fornication with a negro man or woman, he or she so offending shall pay double the fines imposed by the former act. (Hening)

The "Black Code" of Louisiana, enacted in 1724, contained two articles on the status of African and African American women and their children:

> Article IX enacts that children born from the marriages of slaves shall belong to the master of the mother.
>
> Article X enacts that if the husband be a slave and the wife a free woman, the children shall be free like their mother. If the husband be free and the wife a slave, the children shall be slaves. ("Black Code")

Through these laws, African American motherhood could only proliferate its own illegitimacy, enacting a transfer of negative cultural capital in the form of an inability to possess oneself in a culture where property possession defined citizenship.

Eliminating the institution of slavery itself and the laws regulating it has not eradicated the problem of black maternal illegitimacy. These laws, Spillers contends, influenced the 1965 Moynihan Report, a narrative rendering a perceived social system of African American matriarchy pathological because it prevents black men from exercising their proper masculinity. Spillers argues:

> the dominant culture [. . .] actually *misnames* the power of the female regarding the enslaved community. Such naming is false because the female could not, in fact, claim her child, and false, once again, because "motherhood" is not perceived in the prevailing social climate as a legitimate procedure of cultural inheritance. (79–80, emphasis in original)

The misrecognition of the power of the maternal, manifested in numerous sociological as well as literary and cinematic texts, is the result of material practices as well as the erasure of black women's labor. Black women historically have mothered white children while an approving white culture framed domestic work within the confines of private and family matters. Black women mothering their children and participating in the reproduction of African American *culture*, as Spillers points out, remain points of contention within a white-dominant culture.

During the 1980s, well-intentioned attempts to analyze black women's "real lives" merely echoed the conventional wisdom of important books on social policy, including George Gilder's *Wealth and Poverty* (1981), Lawrence Mead's *Beyond Entitlement* (1986), and Charles Murray's *Losing Ground: American Social Policy 1950–1980* (1984). These books and television programs—including PBS's "The Vanishing Family: Crisis in Black America"—cast black women as figures of blame, primarily because of their sexual choices. K. Sue Jewell finds a common theme among them: black women's sexual irresponsibility is the cause of their children's low social and economic status (150–51).

The image of the African American mother found its way into politics—including presidential campaigns—as a national symbol of degenerate sexuality, profligacy, and greed. Myths of black matriarchy also justified a laissez faire approach to economic trends and a rollback of government programs aimed at alleviating economic distress. In the 1980s and 1990s, against a backdrop of urban deindustrialization and the declining provision of prenatal services and abortions for low-income communities, black motherhood increasingly became a subject for public condemnation, which was one impetus for Leslie Harris's *Just Another Girl on the IRT.*

The "problem" of black maternity is not merely a feature of dominant white discourses, however. Jacquie Jones argues that the 1990s ghetto films construct the black mother as blameworthy. She is marginal to the narrative, but highly visible on a rhetorical level. "After all, according to the news of the early eighties it was those teenage, female-headed households that produced these boys" (96). In an essay on Spike Lee's *Crooklyn* (1994), bell hooks indicts Lee for ultimately endorsing a "repressive patriarchal valorization of Black family life [. . .] in no way opposed to the beliefs of white mainstream culture" (14). Many critics have argued that the rise of hip-hop culture and rap music has for the most part reinforced the notion of sexually deviant and promiscuous African American women.

Between 1980 and 2000, Irish and African American problem pregnancy films addressed the profound and lingering influence of maternal myths within Irish and African American cultures. The films reframe the maternal role as a personal and social process. They also suggest that maternal identifications and pregnant performances offer a better account of women's subjectivities than previous models that sanctify (and vilify) an essentialist definition that equates women with their maternal capacities.

PREGNANT HISTORIES: *BELOVED* AND *THE COLOR PURPLE*

The Color Purple and *Beloved* are films based on immensely popular Pulitzer prize-winning novels by African American authors Alice Walker and Toni Morrison. The films reveal the links between the American institution of slavery and black women's sexuality and reproduction. They speak on two levels, emphasizing maternal mythologies in dominant culture as well as within black communities, offering an important corrective to representations of black mothering as wholly illegitimate or as based on a natural instinct. Reproduction and mothering become acts that women undertake and experience, rather than ontological necessities they endure. The films document the fact that identifying with maternal figures can be both damaging and liberating.

In Walker's *The Color Purple*, Celie (Whoopi Goldberg), an illiterate black woman, rises above the oppressive circumstances of poverty and abuse in the early years of the twentieth century in the U.S. South. The novel, which assumes the form of Celie's letters, documents her liberation as she gradually takes control of her education, her sexuality, her creativity, and her economic security. She becomes the author of her life. Morrison's *Beloved*, a poetic novel set in the 1870s, deals with the aftermath of slavery as experienced by Sethe (Oprah Winfrey) a woman haunted for nearly two decades by the ghost of her eldest daughter, Beloved.

Both films explicitly situate pregnancy in the context of the colonization of African American women's bodies and psyches by white and black men. *The Color Purple* opens with a series of visual reversals that suggest the impropriety of Celie's imminent maternity. Celie and her sister Nettie (Akosua Busia) romp in a field of tall flowers; camera angles hides Celie's distended belly until the end of the credits sequence. The juxtaposition of innocent child's play amidst the lyricism of the natural world with Celie's swollen belly produces a sense of grotesque distortion, of nature defiled. Celie looks far too young to be a mother. As Celie runs out of the high grass to a clearing, her body is silhouetted as the music slows and darkens in tone.

In the next scene, a stormy night shot in gothic style with extreme camera angles, Celie gives birth to a daughter she names Olivia. The circumstances of the birth convey the complexity of what Lucy Fischer calls the maternal crisis. Conveying the epistolary form of the novel, Celie's voice-over provides context: Pa has raped her and this is her second child. Incest adds to the crisis represented by Celie's pregnancy: she is young, she had been violated, and she will be violated again. Celie's father takes baby Olivia and admonishes Celie to remain silent so that she will not break her mother's heart. Through his acts of incest and theft, Pa conflates Celie and her mother, reducing their subjectivities to their sexual and reproductive roles. Furthermore, although he forces her to identify with her mother's grief, he denies Celie the chance to act as a mother to her own children. Pa then forces her to go live with Mr. (Danny Glover) to raise his children.

Celie's lack of control over her own body and her peripheral status in her own story is visually suggested in scenes where actions affecting her take place without her in the frame. When Mr.'s son Harpo throws a rock at her, she is off screen when it hits her. She is also off screen or near the edge of the frame when Mr. slaps her and when she contemplates cutting Mr.'s throat. The camera implies that Celie has internalized her oppression. She identifies with Mr.'s view of her as a marginal subject, as evidenced in her advice to Harpo after he has married. Celie tells him to beat his wife Sophia to make her comply with his wishes.

Two modes of identification permit Celie to center herself in the frame of her life and to distance herself from Mr. and his children. When a rebellious nightclub singer, a woman named Shug Avery, enters Celie's life, Shug (Margaret Avery) enables Celie's heteropathic identification. Celie notices that Mr. treats Shug well even though Shug rejects him. The magnetic Shug enflames Celie's desire on several levels. Celie wants to be like Shug as much as she wants Shug's approval. She dresses up like Shug. She kisses Shug. Celie's identification with a sexual woman, and her identification of herself as a sexual woman, allow her to eventually challenge Mr.'s abuse.

Celie also engages in another form of heteropathic identification: she escapes from her reality by reading Charles Dickens's *Oliver Twist.* The story tells of an orphan's trials and tribulations and culminates in an unexpected reunion with the family he never knew he had. The Dickens reference not only adds significance to the stormy night of Olivia's birth (which recalls Dickens's *David Copperfield*), but also reveals that Celie identifies with others across race, gender, and national identity.

In the film's conclusion, the importance of this literary identification becomes clear. In a Dickensian *deus ex machina,* Celie learns that Pa was not her biological father and that her father left the farm where she and Nettie grew up to the two sisters in his will. The closing scenes depict a rapprochement between Celie and Mr., now called Albert. His renaming not only humanizes him, but also suggests that both Celie and Albert recognize that they are subjectivities in process.

Celie learns to value her multiple and evolving personas. Reading and writing open up possibilities of connecting with others, and her identification with and admiration for the glamorous Shug unleashes her sexual potential. In the film's conclusion, Celie has assumed a position of authority as landowner and entrepreneur. It is important to note that her identity and authority are not based upon her maternal role (the only sanctioned position permitted by her stepfather and Mr.). Celie does not reject her status as a mother: she vigorously embraces the opportunity to know her children, but that role does not define her identity.

In Toni Morrison's *Beloved,* directed by Jonathan Demme, maternity is both an embodied process and the site of cultural crisis. Sethe, a pregnant mother of three, escapes from the Sweet Home plantation, gives birth to her fourth child on the banks of the Ohio River, and joins her mother-in-law Baby Suggs near Cincinnati. When the plantation's Schoolteacher comes to return her to slavery, Sethe kills her unnamed toddler daughter, Beloved, rather than allow her to be taken into slavery. For the next eighteen years, Beloved's ghost haunts Sethe's home. The haunting is one manifestation of the way maternity might be viewed as a process. Sethe cannot remain the same person she was at Sweet Home, a fact that becomes apparent when the ghost child grows up and returns in mortal form. Shortly after Paul D (another survivor from Sweet Home) arrives, Beloved (Thandie Newton) appears as an eighteen-year-old woman, ready to reclaim her mother.

The physical process of pregnancy embodies the many horrors at the heart of this story. Scenes of Sethe's flight from Sweet Home suggest the ways that African American maternity has been stripped of legitimacy and black women stripped of self-determination. Sethe's body defines her in the eyes of Schoolteacher and his minions, who steal Sethe's breast milk in a scene shot with extreme angles and dramatic camera movement. Sethe's body is divided further, rent by Schoolteacher's whip. Cinematography distinguishes scenes of the plantation and Sethe's flight from her life in Cincinnati in a tangible way, using color. The flashbacks are yellow and overexposed, contrasting the palpable heat of Southern plantation life with the blue-gray underworld existence that Sethe sleepwalks through in Ohio.

Sethe's flight north might be defined as a move from object to subject, yet the film prevents such easy distinctions. Sethe is both object and subject, whether at Sweet Home or in Cincinnati. On her journey, her continuously shifting subjectivity is represented by the active processes of pregnancy and childbirth. Sethe ought to be moving from the slave state of Kentucky to the free state of Ohio; she ought to be giving birth to herself and to her second daughter, Denver, at the same time. But the events and metaphors are not so straightforward. Over the course of the film, Sethe proceeds through stages of self-determination, her identity a process of detaching herself from an overidentification with her maternal role and the blame associated with it.

During the flight to freedom, a virtually immobile Sethe lies in the Kentucky woods, dragged along the ground by a minimally helpful young white girl named Amy Denver. Enlarged and unwieldy, her bare feet shredded, Sethe embodies liminality: she is neither one nor two, neither a slave nor a free woman. Stepping into the boat for the trip across the Ohio River, Sethe's water breaks. Assisted by Amy, Sethe gives birth to her child in a boat rapidly filling with river water. Like Sethe's body, the river breaks down the distinction between slavery and freedom by mingling the supposed freedom of the North (Ohio) with slavery (Kentucky). Despite traversing the watery boundary and giving birth to Denver in ostensible freedom, Sethe cannot escape Sweet Home. Under Fugitive Slave Laws, her humanity and her maternity are attributes associated with property ownership. Sethe does not cross the Ohio River to freedom but rather becomes a fugitive harboring stolen property: herself and her children.

The film's grotesque visual treatment of Sethe's pregnant body and Beloved's ghost reiterates the way that slavery rendered black maternity a site of negative existence. Beloved's fierce, childlike desire to re-inhabit and possess Sethe leads her to bewitch Paul D, who eventually moves into the barn. When Beloved appears to him as a child seductress, their coupling is visually associated with her disembodiment as pulsating red lights punctuate the scene. When Beloved—dead child, nubile ghost—becomes pregnant, she embodies the scandal of maternity as both an emptiness and excess. Paul D leaves the women to themselves.

The household of women is transformed into a womb-like space dominated by the bond between Sethe and Beloved. Sethe spends her meager savings baking sweet things and buying dolls for the insatiable ghost. Visually, these scenes imply a suffocating intimacy. Rapidly moving cameras swirl around the interior of the home; canted angles, dollies, and streaming decorations contribute to the sense of the house as a womb-like environment. The insularity of the home represents Sethe's complete identification with herself as a mother; given a second chance, she embraces the self-sacrificing maternal role to the exclusion of all else. Beloved exacts a financial, physical, and emotional toll: she is as demanding as a child but the intensity of her needs is consistent with her physical manifestation as a young adult woman.

In contrast, Denver reaches out to women in the community. When they come to Sethe's house to exorcise the ghost, Sethe clambers out onto the front porch with a naked, hugely pregnant, wild-haired Beloved. She is a "child having a child" in the parlance of the 1980s, but she seems like a bloated void, more likely to swallow up anyone and anything she comes into contact with than to give birth, which requires an act of creation. She is an image of all-consuming, selfish, monstrously illegitimate maternity.

The shocked women continue to sing and pray. But Sethe only lets go of Beloved's hand to launch an attack on a man whose hat reminds her of Schoolteacher's distinctive silhouette. Reenacting Beloved's death, Sethe moves outside herself and repossesses herself, turning her aggression toward the man who tried to rob her of her self and her children. At that moment, released from her mother's grip, Beloved dissolves into a screaming mouth and disappears completely.

The film concludes with Sethe reassessing her overidentification with maternity. As she convalesces, Paul D tries to convince her that she can remake herself, that her identity is a process. She, not her daughter, is "her own best thing." As a ghost story, the film renders pregnancy and maternity violent and horrific. But those troubling aspects of maternity are shown to be the social and psychological repercussions of a social context in which racism and economic exploitation construct African American women as illegitimate mothers. Sethe's struggle illuminates the need to develop a view of mothering as a legitimate social practice, not as an instinctual and uncontrollable state of nature or a monstrous act that, by definition, can only reproduce abjected subjects.

DAUGHTERS OF THE DUST AND *DECEMBER BRIDE*: MATERNITY, CULTURE, AND COMMUNITY

Two problem pregnancy films set at the turn of the twentieth century examine the way gender ideologies underwrite a community's identity. The pregnant women characters in *Daughters of the Dust* and *December Bride* withhold the name of the father, asserting their right as mothers to establish cultural continuity. In these films, mothers are the catalyst for rethinking individual and community identities, in part because the action is set at pivotal historical moments when the relation of minority groups to national identities underwent important changes.

Daughters of the Dust, set in 1903 on the coastal Sea Islands of South Carolina and Georgia, considers the plight of the Peazant family, which is poised to move north on the eve of the Great Migration of the twentieth century. This diverse, extended family wrestles with desires and fears associated with leaving the islands, which have allowed them to maintain some connections with their African ancestors, and assimilating into the national community on the mainland. For Nana Peazant (Cora Lee Day), the family elder, the gathering of the clan is a time to honor the past and carry the beliefs of the ancestors into the future.

Pregnancy functions as a focal point for the entire family's struggle to resolve the past and begin anew. Eula Peazant (Alva Rogers), married to Nana's grandson Eli (Adisa Anderson), is a pregnant woman whose physical state symbolizes the sexual economy of chattel slavery. A white man has raped her and her husband now questions the child's paternity. Eli seeks revenge, but any retaliation raises the specter of lynching. Moreover, as Nana Peazant points out, Eli's anger stems from his view of Eula as property. Nana must remind Eli that he does not own his wife.

Dash's film builds upon the crisis of Eula's pregnancy and the family's crossing to the mainland to suggest the liminal processes of identity.

All of the characters reflect on their lives, identify their affinities with figures from the past, and project themselves into the future. Cousin Viola (Cheryl Lynn Bruce) sums up the film's reflective process in her citation of Shakespeare's *The Tempest*: "What's past is prologue."

The Peazant family's geographical location underlines this liminal quality: they are situated between mainland modernity and Ibo tradition. The fluid quality of the Peazants' identities is marked by the camera's panoramic shots of the islands. Overhead shots from an airplane depict unspoiled beaches and, like the story told in several scenes in the film, invoke the arrival of the "salt water Africans" on those shores. The merging of land and water, of memories of Africa and the tangible, grounded connection to North America, suggests that a history prior to enslavement as well as slavery inform present-day events. The characters identify with their Ibo ancestors, even though the "facts" of the Ibo story are in dispute. One version, which Eula narrates, tells of the Ibo loosening their chains and flying back to Africa; another, told by Bilal (Umar Abdurrahamn), who is said to have witnessed the events, is that they sank in the water.

Dash links these important ancestral identifications to the problem pregnancy by presenting Eula's unborn daughter (Kai-Lynn Warren) as the film's narrator. The child acts as a condensation of the characters' histories. She identifies with the old souls and wears a blue ribbon in her hair, visually connecting her to the indigo plantations they worked. She also represents the next generation, the first to be born on the mainland, and, therefore, serves as a repository of future hopes and fears. The unborn child signifies that the future grows out of the past and that any present moment is an unfolding. Embodying Eula's child in this tangible manner emphasizes the fact that subjectivity is an individual and a social process that relates past events, present circumstances, and future aspirations.

The motherless Eula forges identifications with Nana and Yellow Mary (Barbara O. Jones). Like Eula, Mary has been violated. Hired by a wealthy family to be a wet nurse after her own child died, Mary is sexually abused by her employer. Though she hired herself out to the family, her experience as a purchased maternal body is more akin to enslavement than wage labor: "When they went to Cuba, I went with them. I nursed their baby, and took care of the other children. That's how I got 'ruint' . . . I wanted to go home and they keep me" (Dash 126). The reference to Cuba reinforces the parallel between Mary's narrative and the African slave trade. Mary returns to the Peazant family marked by her difference: she has become a prostitute and may be a lesbian, suggested by her choice of companion, a woman named Trula (Trula Hoosier).

The tensions associated with Eula's pregnancy and Mary's return to Ibo Landing reach a climax at the family picnic. Eula rebels against the family and announces her identification with Yellow Mary, the family's despised other. Confronting their silent disapproval after the picnic, Eula exhorts the family to cease scapegoating the two women. Her impassioned speech exposes the manner in which African American women's bodies materialize the trauma of slavery and are, therefore, re-victimized within their families and communities.

In the climactic scene, Eula confronts the family members assembled on the beach: "If you're so ashamed of Yellow Mary 'cause she got ruined. . . . Well, what do you say about me? [gesturing to her pregnant stomach] Am I ruined too?" (Dash 155). Eula focuses on the link between mothers and daughters, foregrounding the way the negative cultural capital of sexual victimization is transferred through generations:

> Deep inside, we believed that they ruined our mothers, and their mothers before them. If you love yourselves, then love Yellow Mary, because she's a part of you. Just like we're a part of our mothers. . . . We carry too many scars from the past. Our past owns us. . . . Let's live our lives without living in the fold of old wounds. (156–57)

Eula and Yellow Mary symbolize the unspoken fears regarding the cultural and physical vulnerability of African Americans in the United States, but the film highlights women's resistance. Eula resists the pathological dynamic of blame through her identification with her mother (who comes to her in a dream), with Yellow Mary, with Nana, and through her grasp of the continuity of past and future.

For Nana and Eula, maternity is not a static identity defined by white culture or by black men but part of a constant process of personal, community, and cultural renewal. Dash expands this metaphor of continuity by making reference to the film medium itself. Viola's companion, Mr. Snead (Tommy Redmond Hicks), is a still photographer hired to record the historic moment of the crossing. He is associated with visions of the continuity of time. Snead sees the unborn child through his camera lens and gives stereoscopic toys to the Peazant family children that suggest the modern era's definitive art form: the moving picture, whose technology animates static images in order to create the illusion of continuous movement.

Like Eula Peazant, Sarah Gomartin (Saskia Reeves) of *December Bride* flouts social conventions and asserts her right to participate in the process of cultural inheritance. Sarah makes her life with two brothers, Hamilton (Donal McCann) and Frank Echlin (Ciaran Hinds). The threesome scandalizes their strict Ulster Presbyterian community in the north of Ireland as they expand their land holdings and raise two children. All the while, Sarah refuses to marry, giving her own surname to her children. Sarah defies social and religious norms at a time when Ulster Protestants, a minority, feared the prospect of Irish Home Rule and began to assert their cultural identity as British subjects. Thus Sarah's rebellion is not merely a proto-feminist assertion of women's rights but also a challenge to the ossification of essentialist national identities during a period in Irish history when Irish identities were fiercely contested.

Sarah redefines her maternal role through acts of identification with father figures. The child of a sharecropper, she asserts her right to own land. Her obsession with owning and working the land is reflected in the film most important visual motif. The film opens with, and constantly returns to, an image of Sarah silhouetted against the sea and sky on the literal edge of Ireland. As that silhouette, she merges with the Irish land—a familiar trope of femininity deriving from bardic poetry and from images of Mother Ireland.

Martin McLoone has written that O'Sullivan's treatment of the Irish landscape challenges traditional imagery of Ireland. For example, several scenes ironically undercut conventional romanticized portrayals of the Irish landscape through the use of the Lambeg drum (an emblem of Protestant militancy), which serves as a "reminder that the industrial workers of Belfast are only part of the Protestant story and that the romantic nationalism of the Catholic Ireland is only part of the story of Irish landscape" (McLoone 2000 209). One extended sequence recalls John Ford's *The Quiet Man* (1952), although it replaces Ford's farcical horse race with "the earnest marching and the banners of the Orange parade" (209). Thus, McLoone concludes, this film engages in a debate about the cinema's traditional representations of Irishness (211). Because

FIGURE 3.1. In Thaddeus O'Sullivan's *December Bride*, Sarah defines her status as an equal among the men of the Echlin family: the two sons and the patriarch. Courtesy of Photofest.

the film consistently links Sarah to the landscape, this discourse on cinematic romanticism encompasses gender as well as national identities.

In an interview with director Thaddeus O'Sullivan, Luke Gibbons notes Sarah's gender rebellion: she is typically aligned with paternal figures, and specifically, with Hamilton and Frank's absent father, who dies early in the film (1990 11). At the film's opening, Sarah must go to work for the Echlin family as a domestic servant because her father has died. Sarah grows close to the Echlin family patriarch, Andrew, who takes to calling her "daughter." Sarah, Andrew, Hamilton, and Frank set out in a small boat to borrow a ram for mating season (another suggestion of absent paternal figures). A storm threatens their journey home. When the boat capsizes, tossing the four of them into the ocean, Andrew lets go of the keel, exclaiming, "there's too many."

After Andrew's death, Sarah, Hamilton, and Frank become increasingly isolated from their Presbyterian community as they reconfigure the family unit. Sarah rejects the church because the minister turns Andrew's conscious act of sacrifice into the will of God. Andrew was "[p]lucked from the deep by the Almighty's hand," Mr. Sorleyson proclaims. Sarah retorts, "No one was taken, no one was spared. That man let go to let us live." O'Sullivan elaborates on Sarah, Hamilton, and Frank's iconoclasm and their resistance to social and religious orthodoxy:

> The mainland community are synonymous with religion. They think they are free but they confine themselves in walls of their own making, either physically or metaphorically. On the other hand you have Sarah, Hamilton and Frank. They have to find other systems which will work for them—a community of three—and of course they have their cynical reasons. She is interested in land and security of a sort, but she knows she can't get accepted by the community because she is a sort of outcast—not just because she's a servant girl, but because of the person she is. (Gibbons 1990 11)

When her mother (who has entered domestic service with her) decides to leave the Echlins, Sarah asks Ham and Frank for a job. She becomes sexually involved with Frank, then with Hamilton. Scenes of Sarah pairing off with one of the brothers are followed by scenes in which the three characters sit at the kitchen table, discussing the economics of farming and developing plans to acquire more land.

Sarah, who refuses to marry either brother, confirms the scandal of their living arrangement by giving birth to two children. Moreover, she usurps the position of patriarch when she gives her children her surname. She names them Andrew, after Hamilton and Frank's father, and Martha, after her mother. At the record office with infant Andrew, Sarah defies the state's interest in paternity and inheritance, telling the clerk that she has no husband. When asked for the father's name, she replies "not certain." Given Ulster traditions, Sarah's rejection of the church and refusal to marry could only result in absolute censure after the birth of the children. Analyzing data collected by the Irish Folklore commission, Fionnuala Nic Suibhne writes:

> Because the event of childbirth was so private and mysterious the woman who had given birth was regarded as being outside society and outside the church. It was only through churching that she could be accepted back as a member of the community and the church [. . .] it is clear that women would have had themselves churched to put an end to the event of childbirth so that they could be accepted back into the community. (21–22)

But Sarah performs no social rituals to mark her sexual or economic ties to the Echlin brothers or to re-assimilate into the community after having children. Sarah has no need for the Ulster community; she defines her identity apart from theirs and remains detached from local and national identity politics, which are obliquely suggested through the sounds of the drums and the Orange parades that Frank attends.

Like the Peazants' Sea Islands, the geography of the Echlin farm enforces its inhabitants' seclusion: it is separated from the mainland by a narrow land bridge. The deterioration of the bridge marks Sarah, Hamilton, and Frank's growing isolation. After Mr. Sorleyson's final visit to the farm, when he urges Sarah to marry one of the brothers, he must wade through knee-deep water to return to town.

When Andrew and Martha are young adults, Sarah's commitment to her ideas about family becomes a source of strife. Martha confronts Sarah because her own potential marriage is jeopardized by her mother's unmarried status. "Down below" in the mainland community, Martha is referred to as the "daughter of Jezebel." She tells Sarah that she wants to marry but cannot: "What have I for a name? A bride enters the church on the arm of her father. I don't know which of them two. . . ." The film's depiction of the community's multigenerational memory regarding unauthorized reproduction is also in keeping with Ulster tradition.

> The accident of the child's birth was with it for a life-time, insofar as the community never forgot it and one of society's greatest censures was often used against the child in later life, that is, prevention of marriage. At a time when the "right" match was of considerable importance, parents would not want their child matched with a so-called "illegitimate." (Nic Suibhne 14)

Martha succeeds by appealing to Sarah's paternal identification, reminding Sarah of Andrew's sacrifice for the next generation. Martha implies that Sarah must make a similar sacrifice so that the young may live. Sarah finally acquiesces, becoming a "December Bride" by marrying Hamilton. She stands between Ham and Frank during the ceremony. She forms a legal relationship with the Echlins so that her daughter may participate in the life of the community. She accepts maternity as an ongoing process and responds to her adult daughter's demands by changing her marital status.

Significantly, Sarah is silhouetted with Martha at dusk in the film's closing shot. The visual rhyme of the opening and closing shots suggests that, although Sarah's idiosyncratic individualism has been relinquished for the proper transmission of names and property rights, her daughter may more strongly identify with Sarah than with the paternal figures in her life. Sarah has not entirely rewritten maternity, but she has demonstrated its social and material dimensions.

In *Daughters of the Dust* and *December Bride*, Eula Peazant and Sarah Gomartin reject the paternal prerogative by refusing to name their children's fathers and by resisting cultural disapproval of their improper pregnancies. Eula makes public the presumed illegitimacy of African American maternity within both dominant culture and her African American family and exhorts the Peazant women to reject the shame of double victimization. Sarah refuses marriage and appropriates the paternal power to name her children. When the stigma of her impropriety is visited upon her children, however, Sarah marries.

In both films, motherhood is revealed to be anything but a fixed state of being that defines women's subjectivities. Instead, mothering is shown to encompass historically situated acts and choices that play a critical role in cultural survival. Given the importance of the sea to both of these films, it's appropriate to couch their depiction of mothering in those terms. In *Daughter of the Dust* and *December Bride*, mothering may anchor the family and community, but anchors are subject to the drift caused by the ocean's deep currents.

THE PLAYBOYS AND *A MAN OF NO IMPORTANCE*: THEATRICAL PREGNANCY

Two Irish films of the 1990s, *The Playboys* and *A Man of No Importance*, depict the plight of young Irish Catholic women who become pregnant outside of marriage. These problem pregnancies symbolize the tension between traditional and postmodern notions of Irishnesss and make apparent the critical importance of maternity to Irish national identity. Significantly, both films are set around 1960, the beginning of a decade of transition that ultimately produced a more urban and international Ireland. Tara McGuire (Robin Wright Penn) in *The Playboys* and Adele Rice (Tara Fitzgerald) in *A Man of No Importance* call Irishness itself into question as their pregnancies point out the fragility of the public/private divide as it relates to gender and sexuality. These challenges are crystallized in a theatrical metaphor that dominates both films. By linking pregnancy to Irish theater, the films not only suggest that femininity, pregnancy, and maternity may be roles and performances (not ontological states), they also imply that this view is indisputably part of an Irish national tradition.

In *The Playboys* a traveling theatrical troupe in 1950s County Cavan wreaks havoc on a traditional village. But a carnivalesque performance arises from within the town as well, as unmarried villager Tara McGuire refuses to name the father of her baby boy. From the opening scene, Tara's predicament is depicted in terms of public performance. Her water breaks in the midst of a church service, so the birth effectively upstages the solemn performance of a Catholic Mass.

Tara continues to scandalize the villagers when she refuses to name her baby's father. Even worse, she becomes romantically involved with Tom Casey (Aidan Quinn), one of the players. Drawing on Catholic tradition, Tara ironically identifies with the Virgin Mary, an unwed mother, and she forms a union with a man who is clearly not her child's father. The blessed and the blasphemous aspects of this updated holy family are reflected in a scene depicting the village hay pitching: Tom, Tara, and her son ride in on a donkey and Tara wears a blue shawl. One villager exclaims "Jesus, Mary, and Joseph!"

Tara's name evokes two geographical sites of national trauma: it refers to the Hill of Tara, the seat of the high kings of Ireland and thus an emblem of precolonial Irish glory, and to the displacement of that glory onto the U.S. South. The Ireland–United States connection reaches fruition late in the film.

Framing the scene in which Tara's baby's paternity is revealed, the players stage a production of *Gone With the Wind*, the 1939 film that has just reached this provincial town's movie theater.[5] The history of this film's Irish reception is an important element of *The Playboys*' challenge to Irish ideologies of gender. *Gone With The Wind* was not screened in the Republic of Ireland when it was released because the official film censor, Mr. James Montgomery, required so many cuts that the distributor withdrew it. Ironically, Mr. Montgomery vigorously objected to the childbirth scene.[6] Thus, while the state of maternity was formally recognized within the Irish constitution, the embodied process of becoming a mother—involving sex and childbirth—was deemed obscene.

U.S. pieties regarding the Civil War are deflated as the troupe plays *Gone With the Wind* for comedy. The actors improbably recreate the film as a musical immediately after they and the villagers have seen it. Tom, who has not seen the film, must quickly assume the "role" of Clark Gable (which he plays as John Wayne) and several characters ask for their entrance cues from the wings.

This absurd conjunction of theater and cinema reflects more than a mixing of Irish drama and American film. Theater is a critical metaphor for Irish identity because of its historical associations with the nationalist politics of the Abbey Theatre and the theatricality of Catholic ritual. New media such as television and film, which enable international popular culture to invade this traditional village, might be assumed to readily displace indigenous forms of theatrical immediacy. Yet the film privileges neither the traditional Irish theatre nor these newfangled technologies of film and television. In *The Playboys*, they coexist and inform one another. Here, Irishness involves adaptation and creative response, neither relinquishing the past nor fetishizing the present. Irishness is not mired in backwardness, but, rather, recognizes the necessity of marrying continuity and change.

The players' version of *Gone With The Wind* makes this point evident. This American narrative is transformed by the Irish context, where a civil war and ongoing sectarian conflict also have bifurcated the nation. In the players' version, a male actor (Milo O'Shea) plays mammy in race and gender drag by donning blackface and sporting a dress.[7] Unlike the Selznick original, this mammy questions the logic of fighting for the South in the Civil War. She tells Scarlett that fighting a war would only secure the "freedom to be slaves." The performance privileges mammy over the putative heroine, who is reduced to a blubbering ninny, and forwards a critique of the plantation melodrama and its racist ideology.

In the midst of the play, in yet another public display, Tara's sister interrupts the performance because Tara's son has been taken by Sergeant Hagerty (Albert Finney), a representative of the law and a bureaucratically powerful but not well-liked member of the community. The secret of the child's paternity is revealed when, drunk and humiliated by Tara's rejection, Hagerty returns his son. Shortly thereafter, Tara, Tom, and the baby leave on the back of a motorcycle.

Throughout the film, Tara performs a socially improper pregnancy and maternity by refusing to name the Sergeant as the father, by refusing his offers of marriage, and by enacting an ironic identification with the Virgin Mary. Tara embraces maternity as a role, not a state of being. By connecting Tara's pregnancy to religion and theater, the film not only exposes the incongruities at the heart of the Irish Catholic reverence for Virgin Mary but also depicts gender and national identities as performances.

In *A Man of No Importance*, Adele Rice's problem pregnancy reveals the gap between narrow concepts of traditional Irishness and the actual diversity of Irish identities. The film features Albert Finney as Alfie Byrne, a closeted gay Dublin bus conductor whose identification with Oscar Wilde compels him to cast his ever-faithful passengers in amateur productions of Wilde's work. Like *The Playboys*, the film is set around 1960 and portrays an Ireland caught between the insularity of the previous decades and the increasing cultural openness that marked the period after 1960. Questions of Ireland's internal diversity are central to this film. Alfie's fondness for Oscar Wilde draws sexual pluralism, not simply women's sexuality, into debates about Irishness. Because Wilde was Anglo-Irish, and Alfie and his passenger-performers are Catholic, Alfie's identification with Oscar Wilde defies narrow nationalist prescriptions by asserting that national heroes need not be Catholic, or heterosexual.

As the play's director, Alfie engages in a variety of identifications with real and imagined characters. He selects Adele, a young newcomer to his bus route, to be the star of Wilde's *Salome* (1894). He encourages his recalcitrant driver friend, Robert (Rufus Sewell), whom he refers to as Bosie (the name of Wilde's lover), to play the role of John the Baptist. Alfie begins to treat Adele as an ethereal princess, and to share in her identification.[8]

Frequent rehearsals in a church annex draw Alfie and Adele together as director and protégé, but the local authorities become uneasy about the play's content. Thanks to Alfie's landlord, who reports the use of unsavory language (the word "virginity") to the parish council, rehearsals are brought to a halt.[9] The decision of the parish council expresses the regressive politics of church involvement in public events.

As Alfie explores his identification with Salome and Adele, he learns that Adele is in love with a man from her rural village. He is named John, further emphasizing the parallel with Salome's unrequited love for John the Baptist. When Alfie visits her boarding house and finds her having sex with John, he is crushed. Alfie must relinquish his naive and idealized vision of Adele (an ideal that is largely ironic, since Salome generally is presented as an evil sexual temptress). In addition, Adele is pregnant. Her sexual transgression fully captures Alfie's contradictory image of Adele as the ethereal yet erotic princess. Salome functions as a theatrical icon of female sexuality that stands in contrast to sanctioned Irish images of the Virgin Mary. Adele scandalously brings the two together.

If Alfie has used his heteropathic identification with Salome to get outside himself, then the corollary to Alfie's disillusionment is his desire to enact his own sexuality, as Adele has done. Not surprisingly, Alfie understands his sexuality as performance. Early in the film, Alfie visits the local gay bar, shyly hiding behind a partition, but leaves soon after being noticed by young men at the bar. Later, after the revelations about Adele surface, Alfie takes to the street dressed as Oscar Wilde.

Rather than living vicariously through Adele's performance as Salome, Alfie performs as Wilde and comes out, wearing Wilde's signature long cloak. He returns to the gay bar, but is lured into an alley and beaten. By (literally) assuming the mantle of gayness in his performance as Wilde, Alfie's desires, and his body, become public property.

Adele's and Alfie's transgressive sexualities exist within the Irish Republic yet are suppressed, in part because they serve neither marital nor reproductive purposes. Their sexual differences, however, carry far different consequences: sexually deviant women (Adele, Salome) and men (Alfie, Wilde) are not identical in this milieu. Adele decides to emigrate to England, which indicates the impossibility of her position in Catholic Ireland. She and Alfie part friends. By contrast, Alfie's community of bus riders welcomes him back the day he returns after his public trauma. He is reunited with Robert, who, while firmly acknowledging Alfie's homosexuality and his own heterosexuality, finally agrees to play the role of John the Baptist.

Alfie and Adele's parallel journeys diverge: there is no place for Adele to enact her sexuality, her pregnancy, or her maternity in Ireland, despite the legal and religious obsession with women as mothers. She is purged from her Irish Catholic village, from Dublin, and from the nation. Adele's path can be read as a cautionary reminder of the state's continuing interest in and control over maternity. Like the fourteen-year-old pregnant victim of incest in the much publicized X case, Adele cannot find what she needs "at home."

Performances of pregnancy and ironic identifications with the Virgin Mary in *The Playboys* and *A Man of No Importance* highlight the discrepancies between the idealized Catholic Madonna and the practices and processes of Irish women's sexuality and maternity. Tara and Adele are identified with the Virgin Mary and the Biblical figure of Salome, yet their performances destabilize iconographies of maternity. By linking problem pregnancies to theatricality, these pregnant women challenge essentialist concepts of national, gender, and sexual identities.

JUST ANOTHER GIRL ON THE IRT AND *HUSH-A-BYE BABY*: DISCOURSE AND DISAVOWAL

In stark contrast to the giddy theatricality of *The Playboys* and *A Man of No Importance*, two other problem pregnancy films, *Just Another Girl on the IRT* and *Hush-a-Bye Baby*, explore the experiences of teenaged girls who face unexpected pregnancies and hide their condition from everyone around them. Stylistically, the films favor documentary realism, evident in the use of young actors and non-actors, but they also incorporate popular music in ways that mark them as films for the post-MTV generation.

The music, clothing styles, and sexual politics of the films contextualize the girls' experiences within the popular culture and political climate of the 1980s. In *Just Another Girl*, African American teenaged girls who live in Brooklyn operate with insufficient information in a culture that defines their sexuality as their subjectivity. In the Derry of *Hush-A-Bye*

Baby, there is no language to discuss sexuality, aside from official church condemnation of contraception and abortion. In both films, the protagonists' coming-of-age process involves rejecting the figures of identification their cultures offer (the sexually charged "bad girl" and the sanctified Madonna) and resisting the political and religious discourses that attempt to define who they are.

In *Just Another Girl*, Chantel Mitchell's (Ariyan Johnson) direct address to the audience establishes her position as storyteller. That technique is important to the film's political project: to challenge the dominant representation of young African American women in the news. "Tomorrow you might be reading about this in the papers," Chantel says, "I'm gonna tell y'all the real deal." With this gesture, the film functions as a hip-hop revision of Ousmane Sembene's 1966 *Black Girl (La noire de . . .)*. Both films combat the anonymity of the "girl" of the title, which was, in Sembene's case, drawn from newspaper headlines. Both films employ voice-over narration to privilege the protagonists' subjectivities and to offer a point of audience identification rather than contribute to the objectification of young black girls.

Chantel is intelligent, ambitious, and responsible. She tells the camera, "I'm a Brooklyn girl. I let nobody mess with me and I do what I want when I want." She works at a part-time job, takes care of her younger brothers while her parents are at work, and plans to finish high school a year early, go to college, and become a doctor. Her intelligence and initiative are evident in classroom scenes where she challenges her white, male history teacher's Eurocentric version of history. This sequence reveals the expectations that define and circumscribe Chantel's ambitions. She earns no reward for her efforts. The teacher sends her to the principal as a troublemaker. The principal is a black man who tells her that she must learn how to behave like a lady.

Chantel and her girlfriends are immature in matters of sexuality. At work, Chantel embarrasses an obnoxious customer by asking her friend Natete (Ebony Jerido) for a price check on virgin olive oil. The film sounds a cautionary note when Chantel and Natete run into Denisha, a high school friend who has just had a baby. Though she clearly plans on being sexually active—she mentions with consternation that she will be having her period when their friend Lavonica's party takes place—Chantel cannot identify with Denisha. Instead, she is distracted by the possibility of enacting her identity through consumption: she focuses on purchasing high-top sneakers and a jacket she has seen in a store window.

Though their language is peppered with discussions of sex, Chantel and her friends manifest profound misunderstandings of sex, birth control, and pregnancy. Chantel, Natete, and Lavonica discuss the upcoming party. When Natete tells the other two she has been taking her sister's birth control pills in preparation for Lavonica's party, "just in case," Chantel, who plans to become a doctor, chastises her, telling her she must have her own prescription. They discuss their distaste for condoms, and agree that AIDS is a concern, although they mistakenly believe that one must be gay or an IV-drug user to become infected.

Their ignorance does not reflect their total insulation from public discourses on sexuality but instead is linked to the fact that the source of their information is television. When Lavonica points out that someone the girls might sleep with may be gay or a drug user, Natete accuses her of watching too many television shows like "20/20." Natete and Chantel agree, amidst peals of laughter, that they cannot get pregnant during menstruation or if they have sex standing up. Natete adds that a Coca-Cola douche is also effective contraception. While their laughter suggests they see the faulty logic and absurdity of such schemes, Lavonica's frown foreshadows the consequences of their playful and partial knowledge.

Chantel's ambitions are eclipsed by her sexuality, the attribute that makes her recognizable within her culture, but only as the "bad black girl" or as "just another girl" (Jewell 46). When she acts on her belief that she is not just another girl, Chantel draws criticism at school and at home. She is, effectively, instructed to divest herself of her identity except for her sexual potential.

Chantel's maternal and paternal identifications do not help her to challenge this troubling dynamic. In fact, her working mother, whose child-rearing duties Chantel has taken on, is rarely present. Her father becomes upset when she tells him Jerard is taking her to Lavonica's party. He doesn't want her to date someone from the projects. When she replies that they live in the projects, he slaps her and warns, "If you're not careful, you're going to end up like your mother." His statement implies that her mother's identity is illegitimate or undesirable.

The film's title suggests Chantel's identification not with another individual but with transport, with the act of moving, and with the subway line that takes her out of Brooklyn. When Chantel meets Tyrone, his new Jeep, a symbol of wealth and freedom, signifies a way out of the projects and off the subway line of the film's title. Chantel takes responsibility and begins a cycle of birth-control pills, but her effort is undermined by Tyrone's refusal to wear a condom. After two positive pregnancy tests, Chantel visits a clinic. She asks about abortion, but the counselor, named Paula, replies that, as a federally funded clinic they are not permitted to provide information on abortion, a pointed reference to the gag rule imposed on women's clinics during the George H. W. Bush administration.

Because she is not just another girl, Chantel falls back on her ingenuity as she plunges into denial. She refuses to face reality by identifying with herself at a moment in time prior to becoming pregnant. Chantel tells the camera: "For days and weeks it was business as usual. Maybe I'm not pregnant. Maybe it's just a dream." She lies to Natete, and her shame that she has not proven to be smarter than other girls is evident in her comment: "You didn't think I was stupid enough to get pregnant, did you?" When she tells Ty, he accuses her of tricking him into marrying her, and then gives her money for an abortion, which Chantel uses for a shopping spree with Natete. She embarks on a campaign to keep the pregnancy hidden from her friends and family, buying identical pairs of jeans and skirts and giving her mother the smaller-sized items to wash. Chantel throws food away at night so her family will think she is overeating and gaining weight. But denial cannot solve the problem of her pregnancy

The film's circular structure suggests the way the public transportation system cannot take Chantel beyond the city or beyond herself. The film opens with the birth of Chantel's child and her rejection of the baby. At the conclusion, it circles back to Ty's return to the dumpster to collect the abandoned baby girl. Structurally, the film interrupts the presumed climax—the baby's birth and abandonment. Then the story continues. In the final scene, Chantel tells the audience that she is raising her daughter at home with her family as she attends community college. Wiser and tired, Chantel exhibits some of the spirit of her earlier narration in her final monologue: "It's tough . . . but we are getting it together."

In her characterization of Chantel, director Leslie Harris clearly rejects the representations of black mothers as "welfare queens" as well as the lingering suspicions of African American women as the sexual bad girls that Jewell describes. Instead, a host of material circumstances that relate to Chantel's local situation and national culture conspire to produce this series of events. They include an educational system that constrains rather than nurtures intelligence, a youth culture that equates sexuality with self worth, the economic realities of working families, and government policies that disallow discussions of alternatives to teenage maternity. They all coalesce to produce the very girls who were vilified in national politics during the Reagan and first Bush administrations. Chantel's insistence that her story be heard above and beyond the din of those ideological discourses is a plea for intervention in conventional modes of cultural identification.

The denial of pregnancy is also at the heart of *Hush-a-Bye Baby*, a project of the Derry Film and Video Workshop, which was committed to developing indigenous Northern Ireland filmmaking. The film was broadcast in 1989 by Channel Four and achieved tremendous popular success. *Hush-a-Bye Baby* examines the plight of a pregnant Catholic girl whose life is bound by Catholic dogma and the continuing violence of the Troubles.[10] When Goretti (Emer McCourt) becomes pregnant and her boyfriend is detained for suspected Republican activity, she, like Chantel, resorts to denial. Catholic politics—in the form of Virgin Mary iconography and the Irish abortion referendum of 1983—establish the historical and political context for the narrative. Like Chantel, Goretti finds precious few figures with whom to identify except for the maternal-virginal Mary.

Goretti's pregnancy is linked to both Irish nationalism and to Catholicism. Goretti's name signifies her identification with Catholic ideals of womanhood. Maria Goretti was an Italian saint who witnessed a Virgin apparition and died rather than lose her chastity in an attempted rape. But the politics of nationalism are equally important to this film. Goretti is alone in her pregnancy because of repressive British tactics in Northern Ireland that resulted in the incarceration of thousands of "suspected terrorists" for an indefinite term without charges being brought against them. When Goretti writes to her boyfriend Ciaran (Michael Liebman), who has been detained, she writes in Irish so the British authorities cannot read the letters. When she looks up the word "pregnant" in Irish, she learns that it translates as "carrying a family." The phrase signifies her status as a vessel for the transmission and maintenance of family.

The relevance of contemporary Irish debates regarding sexuality and pregnancy are brought home in scenes of Goretti's sojourn in the Gaelic hinterland. Goretti and her friend Dinky (Cathy Casey) spend time in Ireland's Gaeltacht, the Irish-speaking region in the northwest of Ireland. They live with families in County Donegal in order to practice their Irish language skills. In a highly evocative scene, Goretti helps make dinner. While listening to a radio broadcast about the abortion referendum, she breaks an egg into a mixing bowl. The use of slow motion and an extreme close-up on the egg as it falls into the flour indicate the material realities and mythical resonance of her bodily state. On the radio, an anti-abortion activist states that the most dangerous place to be in Ireland is in a woman's womb (repeating a bishop's earlier statement). Her interlocutor's reply is that such attitudes provided small consolation to Ann Lovett, the young girl who died in childbirth at the foot of the Virgin Mary statue after keeping her pregnancy a secret. Goretti is offered clashing identifications in this scene: the disembodied radio voices, the traditional older woman of the family she is staying with, the memory of Ann Lovett, and, finally, the egg that tumbles into the bowl.

This emphasis on Catholic proscriptions on women's sexuality differentiates this film from male-centered Irish films. Megan Sullivan writes that the film presents Irish nationalism as just one among many ideologies that affects Irish Catholic women.

> When the pregnant Goretti walks by the "You are now entering free Derry" wall, the film signals these inconsistencies. Post-1969 and another generation later, as a woman, Goretti is still trapped by the same circumstances which would have oppressed her earlier: sexuality, religion, class and state intervention. (112–13)

In addition to the radio show and the public discourse of the Troubles in Derry, Goretti confronts the traditional iconography of the Blessed Virgin, which highlights the irony of her situation but also points to the continued influence of paradoxical expectations about women's sexuality. As Goretti and Dinky walk past a Virgin Mary Grotto, Dinky tells the statue "don't fucking move," a reference to the moving statues apparitions in 1984–1985, when individuals reported seeing statues of the Virgin move. In contrast to those mobile statues, Goretti is paralyzed by her predicament. Because of these political and religious discourses, Goretti's pregnancy is a public matter, despite her silence and her refusal to tell her family.

Back at school, Goretti experiences an alternative to identifying with the Virgin when she reads Irish poetry. The girls are assigned Seamus Heaney's "Limbo," a poem about a young unmarried woman who drowns her baby in the Donegal town of Ballyshannon. Among her peers, only Goretti recognizes the tenderness of the poetic language Heaney uses to describe the drowning. The other students are unable to empathize with the mother in the poem.

Goretti's entrapment by church and state is driven home in a scene where she sits on the beach alone, surrounded by egg-shaped rocks. She watches a blue fertilizer bag wash ashore. As Luke Gibbons contends, this image is laden with significance: the dead baby found on a Kerry beach had washed ashore inside a fertilizer bag. "This incongruous detail is not just a problem of ecology: to Irish viewers it represents a return of the repressed—the Kerry babies controversy" (1992 13). The significance is clear. Women in Ireland labor under religious strictures that deny them their sexuality but also fix their identities as mothers.

The film moves toward a conclusion without resolution, which emphasizes Goretti's pregnancy as a process that is difficult to capture through traditional dramatic structures. At home, she wakes up in the middle of the night crying out in pain as her parents open the bedroom door. The unresolved ending is suggestive of a miscarriage or other physical problem; but it may be simply that, like Chantel, she has gone into early labor.[11]

Goretti's physical reiteration of the Virgin Mary narrative is pointedly oppositional: the British authorities have incarcerated her Joseph, and no statues move on her behalf. She is bombarded with a traditional model of women's identity but finds a moment of identification that provides solace only when she reads the Heaney poem.

In *Just Another Girl on the IRT* and *Hush-A-Bye Baby*, Chantel and Goretti deny their problem pregnancies, seeking to stop time and remain in a state of pre-lapsarian suspended animation. Both are intelligent, responsible young women who know the "facts of life" on a number of levels. Yet few models or symbols of sexual women exist. For Goretti, the Blessed Virgin becomes a figure of ironic rebuke rather than identification. Chantel's intense need to differentiate herself from the public image of African American girlhood leaves her without options for identification. Both films locate the crisis of problem pregnancy not in the maternal psyche but in women's material circumstances and the political and religious ideologies that inform them.

MORE LIKE A VIRGIN? *THE SNAPPER* AND *BLESSED FRUIT*

The two Irish films in this final pairing of problem pregnancy films take Irish women's religious identification to an extreme, presenting an ironic perspective on the Virgin Mary as a symbol of gender and national identity. They do so by examining two contemporary Madonnas against the backdrop of the story of the virgin birth.

In *The Snapper*, based on a Roddy Doyle novel, protagonist Sharon Curley (Tina Kellegher) conflates Catholic and contemporary Madonnas in a comic manner. Visibly pregnant and obviously drunk, she sings Madonna's "Papa Don't Preach" for her friends at a karaoke pub, identifying with American popular music's most egregious bad girl. As the whole of Dublin's Barrytown jeers at Sharon, the public nature of her problem pregnancy is clearly evident. As a spectacularly pregnant woman channeling Madonna, Sharon is a figure of exotic fascination. But when the secret of the baby's paternity leaks out, Sharon becomes just another young woman made pregnant by a specific man, and is suddenly viewed as a brazen jezebel.

Sharon's pregnancy assumes the status of a public performance, from the sexual act that produces the child to its birth. The pregnancy was the result of Sharon's drunken vulnerability. A flashback portrays a drunken encounter between Sharon and her neighbor Mr. Burgess on the hood of a car in a public parking lot. It is difficult to imagine how Sharon could have conceived a child in a more transgressive fashion. The public nature of the event, the obvious lack of any emotional connection and the hint of coercion, the generational difference, and the fact that Mr. Burgess is married and the father of Sharon's friend Yvonne all compound the fact that he is an unappealing character.

As Sharon spins tales for her friends of an imaginary encounter with a Spanish sailor, the film makes clear that Irish notions of sexuality and family are at the root of her difficulties. She is called "slut" and "whore," only after the rumor circulates that Mr. Burgess is the culprit. The community disparages her, despite the fact that Sharon would prefer that Burgess stay completely out of her life. Sharon is taunted openly when Burgess temporarily takes leave of his family. The community, it seems, blames Sharon not for her pregnancy but for the existence of a disappointingly human, rather than a divine (or foreign) father for her child.

Sharon redefines the Madonna as a young woman without need of a Joseph to sanctify her sexual and reproductive history. She also challenges the social disapproval typically accorded unmarried pregnant women; on the DART train, she responds to the smirks of two young boys with a swift kick to the shin. Certainly, Sharon's close-knit, if somewhat chaotic working-class family provides a basis for her challenge to the status quo. Her parents are troubled by her pregnancy, but, ultimately, welcome the child rather than dwelling on social morality.

The comedy's final punch line is Sharon's usurpation of paternal power. After her daughter is born, Sharon announces her decision to name the child after the father, but not in traditional fashion. In her Hiberno-English, Sharon laughingly proclaims, "I'm after calling her Georgina," converting the given name of the child's father (George Burgess) into feminine form rather than using his surname. With this gesture, Sharon recognizes the earthly father of her child, but appropriates the function of cultural, in addition to biological, reproduction.

In *Blessed Fruit*, a short comedy, filmmaker Orla Walsh blends emotional intensity with humor as she mocks the Irish Catholic obsession with virgin birth. Walsh's protagonist Molly (Sheila Feehily) spends much of the film's sixteen minutes in a Catholic Church, praying to a statue of the Virgin because she thinks she is pregnant. Her name and predicament evoke Joyce's Molly Bloom as much as they call up associations with the Blessed Virgin: Molly does not know whether the father of her child is Jason, her longtime lover, or Robert, a married actor with whom she had a brief affair.

The film intersperses Molly's golden-hued, candle-lit supplication to the Virgin with scenes of confrontation and reconciliation with the two men that Molly conjures up in her imagination. Molly questions whether either man would welcome fatherhood, especially under these uncertain circumstances. In one scene, Jason accepts the news of impending fatherhood with joy; in another, he rejects her and calls her a slut; in a third, Robert keeps Molly waiting outside on his doorstep while making excuses to his off-screen wife. A comic scenario of accidental reunion brings together Robert and his son—a visual double for Robert, reading Stanislavski at the tender age of ten—after Molly and Jason have raised him as their child. In the penultimate scene, Molly's period begins and she dances her way out of church, accompanied by a "Hallelujah" chorus. This unmoving virgin has answered Molly's prayers.

A third visual and narrative strand frames Molly's session in church. Shot in digital video in steely blue-gray tones, this parallel narrative depicts the Virgin explaining her predicament to Joseph. But, in this contemporary version, a suspicious Joseph works as a carpenter at a building site, and his Mary wears traditional blue robes and the latest running shoes. She eventually convinces him that she is pregnant with God's child. This secondary story line achieves equal status with Molly's tale because the film returns to Mary in its conclusion. In the grainy, digitized world of the postmodern Holy Family, Mary whispers into a telephone, telling her off-screen interlocutor that "[Joseph] fell for it, the gobshite."

Using the most contemporary film technology, Walsh restages the sacred story of Jesus's conception as yet another performance. The blasphemy of the virgin's deceit is expressed in saucy Dublin vernacular ("gobshite"). Whereas Molly prays to, identifies with, and reconsiders the figure of the Blessed Virgin as she conjures up her own potentially unpleasant future, the film goes on to rewrite the virgin birth as a joke played on Joseph, the cuckolded boyfriend.

By layering reality and fantasy, Walsh's film accentuates the psychological and institutional power of the Catholic Church over women's lives in the Republic of Ireland. Molly tries out a number of possible scenarios; truth telling, withholding the truth from Robert and Jason, and life as a single mother. The fact that thoroughly modern Molly seeks refuge in the church as she imagines these multiple scenarios of impending motherhood, however, reiterates the reality that (hetero)sexuality and reproduction are governed by religious practices that assume the force of law in Ireland. Walsh's film, along with other contemporary reconsiderations of the Virgin (most notably, Neil Jordan's *The Butcher Boy* (1997), have contributed to the refunctioning of Catholic iconography in contemporary Irish culture.

The comic twist given to identifications with the Virgin Mary in *Blessed Fruit* and *The Snapper* present a distinctively postmodern response to the enforced identification between women and mothers. By reframing the terms of representation of the virgin birth, and of women's sexuality more generally, Molly and Sharon explore gender, sexuality, and maternity not as a fixed states of being, but as constantly evolving narratives, susceptible to re-vision.

CONCLUSION

Irish and African American problem pregnancy films address the fact that women's sexuality, pregnancy, and reproduction are not "private" matters, but are, in fact, cornerstones upon which the larger community defines and perpetuates itself. Using various strategies that place the pregnant body at the center of a community's crisis, the films intervene in traditions of maternal representation that reify mothers and blame women for their part in biological reproduction, while refusing women a role in cultural reproduction. They articulate women's circumscribed possibilities for identification, while also poking fun at maternal pieties. They implicate a number of gendered assumptions that underlie racial and national identities. Because they characterize pregnancy and motherhood as social processes, they highlight a model of identity as performance that individuals construct and disrupt within the context of their various communities.

CHAPTER FOUR

Culturing Violence: Masculine Identification in Irish and African American Gangster Films

The problem pregnancy films of chapter 3 take aim at troubling maternal identifications, rejecting essentialist notions of gender by calling attention to pregnancy and maternity as disruptive performances. During the 1980s and 1990s, another focal point for social disruption arose within Irish and African American cinemas: the figure of the gangster.

A spate of gangster films focused on the performance of gender in the context of social crisis, only this time masculinity was the identity under scrutiny. While hearkening back to the classical gangster genre, these films also addressed the recent histories of violence associated with the Troubles in Northern Ireland and gang culture in urban America. African American gangsters revived the traditional gangster narrative so familiar from the films of the 1930s and 1940s, including *The Public Enemy* (William Wellman 1931), *Scarface* (Howard Hawks 1932), and *White Heat* (Raoul Walsh 1949). They reconsider those tales of meteoric rise and inevitable downfall within the context of contemporary black urban communities, often adopting documentary and neorealist techniques such as handheld cameras to convey a sense of immediacy and authenticity.

By contrast, Irish gangster films tended to emulate a variant of the genre that developed within British and American films about political violence in Ireland: the tale of the isolated individual who attempts to break free from the cycle of violence. That subgenre is epitomized by films such as John Ford's *The Informer* (1935) and *Odd Man Out* (Carol Reed 1947).

Regardless of their allegiance to different traditions within the gangster cycle, all five films examined in this chapter emphasize the role that masculine identification plays in perpetuating violence. In their focus on characters who perform their gangster identities through identifications with various role models, the films reveal the instabilities that underlie race, gender, and nationality. A brief discussion of a scene from Jim Sheridan's *In the Name of the Father* (1993) serves to introduce the genre's focus on identification.

In the Name of the Father recounts the experiences of Gerry Conlon (Daniel Day Lewis) and his father Giuseppe (Pete Postlethwaite), two Irishmen who are unjustly incarcerated as terrorists for a 1974 IRA pub bombing in Guildford, England, that killed four people.[1] Five years into Gerry and Giuseppe's internment, the inmates in their South London prison gather on the main floor to watch a film. Unbeknownst to Gerry or Giuseppe, Joe McAndrew (Don Baker), a recently imprisoned IRA operative, has organized an attack on the chief of the prison staff, a man named Barker.[2] During a film screening, several inmates douse Barker with lighter fluid, and McAndrew sets him on fire. But Gerry intervenes, throwing a blanket over the flaming man and saving his life. The backdrop to Barker's dance of agony is the prison's makeshift movie screen, a white sheet on which an image of the film burning in the projector is visible. This moment thus captures two flaming objects: a man in agony with whom Gerry identifies and the violent destruction of a film that has channeled and contained Gerry's empathetic sentiments until the moment of the attack.

This startling breakdown in the image recalls the scene in Ingmar Bergman's *Persona* (1966) when the film appears to jump in the gate, break, and then burn. This self-reflexive moment takes place immediately after a scene in which Alma (Bibi Andersson) intentionally leaves broken glass on the ground for Elisabet (Liv Ullman) to step on. The connection between Bergman and Sheridan's films is apt. Alma and McAndrew's aggressive acts inflict pain, indicating their willingness to disavow their connections with others. Their separatist logic causes film representation, which depends upon the spectator to invest emotion in the screen image, to break down. Both directors force viewers to witness a body in pain in order to demonstrate the way cinematic identification bridges the distance between self and other, between "you" and "me." Both films stage dramas of confused identification that precisely implicate cinema's "identificatory lure" (Silverman 65). Yet, at these moments, they step back to reveal such identifications to be illusory relationships.

In Sheridan's film, the scene marks a rupture in identification within the narrative as well because it depicts a turning point at which Gerry begins to reject the IRA man Joe and to acknowledge his connections to his long-suffering father. In both *Persona* and *In the Name of the Father*, form and content call attention to characters whose identities are based on their ability to acquire the identities of others. The former concerns the merging of feminine identities whereas the latter focuses on masculine difference, examining the father-son relationship.

In Sheridan's film, Barker's attack plays out in front of Francis Ford Coppola's self-consciously patriarchal gangster film *The Godfather* (1972). The scene that is visible at the moment of the attack is one in which an aging Don Vito Corleone (Marlon Brando), who has returned home after a long hospital stay occasioned by an attack on him by rival gangsters, counsels his son Michael (Al Pacino). Like Giuseppe Conlon, Corelone is old and sick; like Joe McAndrew, Vito remains a master strategist, a gangster emeritus as it were. The appearance of *The Godfather* at this crucial moment when Gerry's fascination with violence is tempered by his sympathy for and identification with the prison guard is not coincidental.

The Godfather citation crystallizes one central theme of *In the Name of the Father*: the role paternal identification plays in the perpetuation of violence. *The Godfather* and *In The Name of the Father* are films that organize violence around the father-son dyad. Michael Corleone and Gerry Conlon's actions are shown to be determined by their relationships with their fathers. Young Michael Corleone kills in the name of his father and, ultimately, assumes his place as Don Corleone. In Sheridan's film, Gerry Conlon is a petty criminal imprisoned with his tuberculosis-stricken father, a man he has spent his life rejecting as a figure of identification.

In prison, Gerry initially admires the outlaw heroics of the IRA operative. But, after the attack, he rejects Joe McAndrew's inhumanity, in part because the prison guard Barker has been kind to Giuseppe. That Gerry's two father figures—Joe McAndrew and Giuseppe Conlon—share the same first name is a fictional device of the film that further underlines the importance of the paternal theme. But this privileging of fathers is not merely a cinematic embellishment: Gerry Conlon dedicated himself in his 1990 memoir, *Proved Innocent* (later changed to *In the Name of the Father*), to clearing the name of his father, who died in prison in 1980.

With its explicit references to the gangster genre, Sheridan's film resembles a number of Irish and African American films such as *Danny Boy* (discussed in chapter 2), *Cal* (Pat O'Connor 1984), *The Crying Game* (Neil Jordan 1992), *Boyz N the Hood* (John Singleton 1991), and *Menace II Society* (Albert and Allen Hughes 1993).[3] The genre's significance to African American and Irish film cultures rests partly on the way it foregrounds divisions of ethnicity, race, and class that are internal to a national body. Unlike other male-centered action genres like the combat film, which celebrates skill, sacrifice, and male bonding against the backdrop of national belonging, the gangster film explores fissures that undermine the idea of univocal national identity.[4] Gangsters are outsiders in their own culture; they are made so by circumstance and, arguably, by choice. Implicitly, the gangster genre forwards a critique of national narratives by focusing on the social and economic disenfranchisement of these internal others. The gangster figure seems to be the perfect vehicle for stories of violent behavior that grows out of long-term economic distress, political disenfranchisement, and social alienation.

In the cinema's representation of the gangster, one consequence of his utter alienation is that he becomes a master of self-creation. He crafts and consciously performs an identity. Rather than bowing to dominant culture's marginalization of him, the gangster fashions an image from that culture's fears and fantasies, including the imaginative realm of cinema.[5] John Baxter calls the cinema "the criminal's university," noting that gangsters and actors have a great deal in common. "Both in the public eye, both dependent on the protection of their charisma to survive in an uncertain world, both doomed to short-lived careers, gangsters and actors seem too close for true separation" (14). The premium the gangster places on his screen image, writes John McCarty, suggests his arrested development and immature sexuality. McCarty calls the gangster "a gun-toting Peter Pan, a perpetual adolescent living in a world of fantasy whose style has been shaped, in part, by decades of gangster movies" (230).

From the gangster's first appearance on screen, which is conventionally associated with D. W. Griffith's *Musketeers of Pig Alley* (1912), his persona has been shaped by a reciprocal process involving cinematic images and cultural acts. Griffith derived his film's plot from newspaper headlines and shot the film in New York locations where rival gangs were actually engaged in turf wars. He supposedly employed real gangsters as extras. These facts were exploited in Biograph publicity materials, just as, two decades later Warner Brothers—the "gangster studio"—would advertise that its plots were "snatched from today's headlines."

That tradition of self-conscious image creation lives on in the post-*Godfather* gangster. In Brian DePalma's *Scarface* (1983), Cuban gangster Tony Montana states: "I watched guys like Humphrey Bogart, James Cagney. They teach me to talk." In Mario Van Peebles's *New Jack City* (1991), gangster-entrepreneur Nino Brown watches scenes from De Palma's *Scarface* and invokes the names of Cagney and Raft. In F. Gary Gray's *Set it Off* (1996), a gang of four women reprises the meeting of the Dons scene from Coppola's *The Godfather*.

Acknowledging the tradition of the gangster as a self-made man, recent Irish and African American films emphasize the gangster's self-fashioning through practices of identification. Acts of identification are aimed at an array of figures, from rock musicians to film characters; often, they involve paternal and fraternal figures and generally they are enacted within groups of men. Within the gang family, paternal identifications—like that between Vito and Michael Corleone—are highly prized. Fraternal bonding is less important, and identification across gender is virtually nonexistent. The social reproduction of gangster culture is linked to a specific (and ambiguous) masculine ideal: the gangster as a man's man and an unambiguous authority figure.

In their emphasis on character identification, contemporary Irish and African American gangster films also reexamine the causes of violence. More specifically, they reject dominant representations of Irish and black cultures as inherently violent. As John Hill has shown, British and American gangster films often treat violence as an innate quality: "a manifestation of Irish 'national character'" (1988 149). Hill has criticized the way the gangster genre depoliticizes violence, shifting the focus from politics to criminal psychology. Similarly, Hollywood films have long reinforced a dominant perspective that black men are "the very embodiment of social transgression per se" (Harper 143). Cinematic gang culture resonates with historical representations that venerate and vilify black culture as "an internal threat to dominant American culture and social order" (Rose 144).

Yet the films in this chapter suggest that violence is a *cultural*, not a biological inheritance, passed from one man to another through acts of identification. They attempt to counter racist and essentialist paradigms of innate violence by showing that acts of masculine identification, which give rise to performances, enable the transition from young man to killer. Masculine identifications are not merely private, psychological matters in these films. Moments of heteropathic identification, when identity is suspended, are shown to be commonplace practices within postmodern film and music culture.

Whereas the films in chapter 3 countered maternal essentialism by foregrounding the public status of the pregnant body, contemporary Irish and African American gangster films highlight male bodies that are fractured by violence. The loss of physical wholeness offers a metaphor for the decentering of the subject. All five films in this chapter depict men experiencing extreme body states of pain and pleasure (generally related to violence or sex). These states suggest a loss of physical integrity that parallels the lack of stability of racial, sexual, and national identities.

Before proceeding to readings of individual films, I briefly discuss the gangster as an ambiguous figure that embodies, but never resolves, cultural contradictions involving class, race, and gender. These ambiguities make him an especially appropriate figure for replacing essentialist notions of identity and embracing identity as performance.

AMBIGUOUS BODIES

The cinema's century-long love affair with the gangster has been predicated upon his versatility. An example of Robert Ray's composite hero, the gangster has proven his ability to absorb contradictions relating to race, nation, and gender. The classical gangster cycle of the 1930s situated the ethnic male within industrial monopoly capitalism during Prohibition, the Depression, and the rise of the labor movement—political and economic events that suggested the American notions of equality were incompatible with capitalism. The gangster rejected the laborer role that white capital allotted to immigrants and African Americans and mastered the dynamics of capital accumulation on his own terms. The successful gangster earned loyalty from allies and respect from enemies, but ultimately he thrived only if he challenged and replaced his superior or mentor. Recreating a hierarchy outside mainstream culture, the gangster nevertheless prized street smarts and hard work over lineage and good "breeding" (notions derived from the very nativist ideology that prevented him from pursuing legal avenues to success). His rags-to-riches story mirrored the Horatio Alger myth that ratified the capitalist system.

The gangster's class-mobility narrative influenced notions of race and national identity far beyond the confines of the cinema. According to David Ruth in *Inventing the Public Enemy*, the gangster alleviated early twentieth-century nativist anxieties by channeling ethnic difference into class mobility.

> As the gangster rose in crime and in society he came into his own as a consumer and usually shed the obvious markers of his ethnicity. [. . .] Observers saw him less as a member of an outside group than as a successful American. [. . .] Ironically, the ethnic gangster, partly through his smooth style, contributed to the replacement of complex, progressive-era racial taxonomies with the emerging conception of a monolithic white race. (73)

For Ruth, the ethnic gangster's capacity for conspicuous consumption signified success, which, in turn, contributed to a rethinking of racial hierarchies (for Jewish, Irish, and Italian gangsters) and helped to create a category of white American-ness.

Similar ambiguities inform the gangster's gender and sexuality. The gangster's body exudes a hypermasculine aggression and an equally melodramatic dandyism. (In the parlance of the twenty-first century, he might be called a metrosexual.) His mother may serve as an object of desire rather than, or in addition to, his moll, as is the case in *The Public Enemy* and *White Heat*.[6] Yet his milieu is populated almost exclusively by men: sidekicks, cronies, underlings, and representatives of the law.

The gangster's ambiguous masculinity, which is linked to his love of conspicuous consumption and display, is also connected to fact that he prefers the homosocial cameraderie of the all-male gang to both the bosom of his biological family and the tainted love of the untrustworthy moll. Robyn Wiegman writes that the homosocial "locates the contradiction in patriarchal organization between the primacy accorded to relationships among men and the compulsory imperative of heterosexual reproduction" (1997 50). The gangster circumvents the imperative of heterosexual reproduction by reproducing his own all-male society. This is one reason for the critical importance of paternal identification in gang culture: only gangsters can produce other gangsters.

Leadership of the gang is tied to, or at least enhanced by, an ability to attract beautiful women but is reinforced through competitive, violent encounters with men. The gangster's relationships with his sidekick, rival, and lawman/counterpart are more important to him than relationships with women. In the alternative family unit of the gang, women are superfluous: they are inadequate to the task of performing the gang's labor and also unnecessary for the gang's continued existence. The gang perpetuates itself without recourse to heterosexual reproduction.

The gangster is a complex manifestation of instabilities that trouble national, gender, and racial identities. The gangster moves from ethnic outsider to off-white big shot, from humble origins to wealth and fame. He rises, only to fall, often betrayed by his gang cohorts. He is ethnically marked but has the potential to become quintessentially American. A masculine exemplar, his personal and business affairs revolve exclusively around the ritualized activities of men. An idiosyncratic urban dandy, his power depends upon the sadomasochistic physicality of gang culture. Bursting with Machiavellian ambition, he pursues sensual, sartorial, and sexual gratification with excessive zeal and conspicuous consumption.

The gangster embodies and contains contradictions: his center cannot hold. For these reasons among others, he is an attractive figure of identification for both film spectators and for characters (who often become the gangster's spectators within the narrative). The readings below examine Irish and African American films that use identification to draw out the multifarious quality of the gangster persona and, in doing so, expose the way in which he circumvents essentialist race, national, and gender identities.

NAMING TWO FATHERS

Judging from his memoir, Gerry Conlon experienced his arrest and incarceration by British authorities as a cinematic nightmare. He cites *The Godfather* when he describes the prosecution's junior barrister, Michael Hill, at his committal hearing on St. Patrick's Day in 1975.

> He scared the daylights out of me. He looked like Al Pacino in *The Godfather*, another Michael, and he was very impressive, very compelling. Here, I thought, is a man who can really make a cock-and-bull story sound like gospel. (118)

When he conflates Michael Hill with Michael Corleone, Conlon suggests that the former's mastery of language rivals the latter's ruthless use of violence. Furthermore, the sacred and profane aspects of mafia justice, evident in the closing moments of *The Godfather*, are hinted at in Hill's ability to preach the "gospel."[7] Conlon goes on to discuss his defense team in terms of romances and Westerns: "they would be my knights in shining armor, or the U.S. cavalry charging over the hill just before the Indians scalp me" (121). Later, when Gerry is imprisoned at Wandsworth Prison, he writes that he resembles "this Charlie Chaplin character" (138) because the prison-issue clothing is too large. At Wormwood Scrubs, he describes a group of guards in riot gear as "a battalion of Darth Vaders" (187).

In his memoir, Gerry describes himself through a camera lens. In the film adaptation, paternal figures loom larger than the film characters Gerry mentions in the book, however. As the title's religious overtones suggest, *In the Name of the Father* presents a prodigal son who must choose between the moral and the immoral, the violent and the righteous. As a young man, Gerry is depicted as exceedingly immature: as a petty thief in Belfast, Northern Ireland, he and his friends repeatedly bring down the wrath of the British army on their neighborhood. Gerry seems incapable of understanding the deadly consequences of such actions: his unruliness poses a challenge to the British and the Irish Republican Army alike.[8] Gerry strays from the path to becoming a man, the film suggests, largely because he rejects his father Giuseppe's insufficient masculinity in favor of youthful pranks and rebellious hi-jinks.

After leaving Belfast for London—a move encouraged by Giuseppe because the IRA has grown increasingly impatient with the youth's antics—Gerry moves into a commune ("Xanadu") with his friends Paul Hill, Patrick Armstrong, and Armstrong's girlfriend Carole Richardson.[9] He steals money from a prostitute, spending the windfall on sartorial excess in the form of afghan coats and platform shoes for himself and Paul.[10] The Kinks' song "Dedicated Follower of Fashion" accompanies a scene of Gerry returning to Belfast for a visit. In the next scene—as if in response to Gerry's appropriation of their music and money—British troops storm the Conlon home and arrest Gerry under the Prevention of Terrorism Act, which empowered the British to hold suspects for seven days before charging them. Gerry is taken to England, tortured, and brought to trial for the Guildford bombing. There his youthful jauntyness dovetails with the surreal events. Gerry fidgets during the trial, relieving his discomfort and boredom by playing hangman with his co-defendants.

Gerry's innocent childishness—a stereotypical trope of Irishness, as Martin McLoone and Diane Negra have pointed out—is linked to his utter disenfranchisement as a Belfast Catholic growing up in a family of "passive nationalists" (23).[11] Though Gerry avoided learning Irish in school, he cannot properly be said to have a mastery of juridical English, either: "The clerk of the court read out the charges against us, in language I only half understood" (124).[12] When he is about to testify, he knows that his language and appearance work against him: he approaches the witness-box "trembling in every limb, knowing that my accent will be hard for them to understand, knowing I was wearing jeans. I was totally intimidated" (127). His sense of otherness is palpable. But he hopes that the identification between disenfranchised Irish and black men will eventually work in his favor:

> Then the jury was sworn in. It was all male, and there was nothing much else to read into them except that there were two Black guys among them. I saw this as a wee gee, a tiny sign of hope, because in prison the Blacks and Irish have good relations and you could be sure, at least, they wouldn't be best friends with the police. (125)

In the film, Gerry encounters that solidarity firsthand. In prison, he cheers the West Indian teams in cricket matches against the English. Gerry forms an alliance with a Jamaican inmate, Mackie, who shares his marijuana along with his anticolonial sentiments.

In a stunning metaphor for resistance that has become mired in escapism, Gerry, Mackie, and their Jamaican friends swallow pieces of a map of the British Empire that have been saturated with LSD. When Gerry and Mackie appropriate the Imperial map, they douse it with a consciousness-expanding drug associated with political and psychic liberation—this was the 1970s after all. They identify with one another as victims of the colonial process and attempt to transcend their physical imprisonment with psychic liberation. Martin McLoone has argued that this moment casts only a fleeting glance at politics:

> There is a clear reference here to a kind of post-colonial solidarity among peripheral and marginalized cultures. [. . .] However, like the film's treatment of the IRA, this political notion slips out in an unguarded moment in the film's otherwise controlling moral vision. (73)

McLoone is correct in observing that Sheridan's film is more interested in morality than politics. I would suggest an additional reason for

Mackie's marginalization, however: Gerry's coming of age depends upon his identifications with the paternal figures of Joe and Giuseppe. Gerry can't grow up, the film implies, by identifying with his brothers, whether they are Jamaican or members of the IRA.

Masculine identifications shape Gerry's journey from rebellious punk to responsible adult, but paternal identifications are presented as the most important factor in his transformation from would-be gangster to private citizen. After he and his father are sentenced, they enter a shared cell, a device of the film that places the men in close proximity. (In reality the Conlons were housed in different jails.) Gerry unleashes a diatribe about his father's simultaneous omnipresence and insufficiency. According to Gerry, Giuseppe's excessive criticism, his obsession with Gerry's failures, and his physical frailty have contributed to Gerry's irresponsibility and self-loathing. His father's insistence that Gerry fouled the ball in a football match ruined the victory for Gerry: "You could only see what I was doing wrong," he tells his father. Gerry remembers riding on the handlebars of his father's bicycle as a child in the most nightmarish of terms; he knew even at an early age that Giuseppe's health was too delicate for such activities. "Why did you have to be sick all your life?" Gerry mutters in disgust. "You've been a victim all your life."

When Joe McAndrew enters the prison, he immediately earns Gerry's respect and that of the other prisoners because he is willing to fight. "He's the real thing," Mackie remarks. Explicitly comparing Joe with Giuseppe, Gerry tells his father, "at least he fights back, which is more than you ever did in your life." Joe's tactics are not limited to inciting protests; they also include threatening the most powerful prisoner. Warning him not to harm any Irish prisoners, Joe tells him he will bomb the man's home with his family in it. "I don't make threats, I just carry out orders." Joe organizes a peaceful protest which is met with a full-scale assault by the prison guards in riot gear. These events precipitate the attack on Barker during the screening of *The Godfather*.

Caught between two fathers, Gerry is forced to choose. He has rejected his father and idealized the IRA leader, and he has also participated in the fraternal, but ultimately futile, anticolonial gestures of the Jamaicans. When he sees the IRA's cruelty in action during the attack on Barker, Gerry makes the transition from cinematic identification—and his hero worship of McAndrew—to actual empathy. Gerry mocks Joe, disgusted by him: "You're a brave man," he intones, "A very brave man." He also reconsiders his father's supposedly emasculated pacifism.

FIGURE 4.1. Gerry's father looms in the background as a figure of identification in Jim Sheridan's *In the Name of the Father*. Courtesy of Photofest.

By definition, of course, Gerry's coming-of-age process must involve a transformation. Gerry gradually rejects violence as a result of his identifications with fraternal and paternal figures. His ultimate embrace of Giuseppe reflects not only his maturity but also his rejection of the ruthless, narrow nationalism of McAndrew.

As McLoone implies with his observations on the film's controlling moral vision, there are few positions of ambiguity or compromise in this film. One possible alternative to the paternal dynamic—the fraternal postcolonial perspective of the Jamaicans—is presented only briefly. In keeping with the lack of ambiguity at the thematic level, the film's visual patterns emphasize stark oppositions by dividing space into inside and outside. During Gerry's interrogation and torture, there are several cuts to the hallway outside, where the torturers' co-workers carry a birthday cake with flaming candles down the hall and sing "Happy Birthday." Later, when tea is served to the guards, straight cuts exaggerate the discrepancy between the human rights violations occurring inside the holding cells and the imperial civility outside.

Ultimately, however, the film undermines the distinction between interior and exterior when the inmates learn of Giuseppe's death. Alone in his cell, Gerry hears the other inmates calling him to the window. In a poetic sequence that visually rhymes with the scene of Barker's attack, the inmates reclaim the vast empty space outside the prison walls by setting pieces of paper on fire and throwing them out the window into the darkness. The memorial to Giuseppe transcends the private experience of individual mourning; it is an act of identification shared by the prison community and by those outside of it. The flaming slips of paper—burning bodies—allow the inmates to briefly colonize the space beyond the prison walls. The solidarity among the prisoners—Irish, British, and Jamaican—creates a community despite a physical context (the prison) that militates against the forging of bonds.

Sheridan's film establishes stark oppositions of politics and personality that it only partially dismantles. Gerry must choose between two father figures: the sacrificial Giuseppe or the avenging Joe.[13] Gerry rejects the arbitrary violence of the IRA (which is likened to the British military and the ordinary gangster) and continues his father's work by seeking legal means of redress for their wrongful imprisonment. The film is most interested in the fact that Gerry comes of age, evolving from a boy-rebel without a cause to a man who fights by the rules. But the film also suggests that masculine identification is critical to that ongoing process of identity formation. Gerry's identifications with Mackie, Joe, and Giuseppe imply that possibilities do exist beyond an either/or model. But the film's strict focus on Gerry's paternal associations (which include Joe, Giuseppe, and the Heavenly Father of the film's title) forecloses many of those possibilities and mitigates the degree of complexity with which Gerry might contemplate and enact his Irish identity.

BOYZ N THE HOOD: IDENTIFYING ANY FATHER

In many ways, 1991 was a critical year for African American cinema: twelve films directed by African Americans were released and Whoopi Goldberg won the Academy Award for best supporting actress for *Ghost* (Jerry Zucker 1990). John Singleton's *Boyz N the Hood* was released to great acclaim and became one of the highest-grossing black-directed films in history.[14] At the time, a *New York Times Magazine* referenced Spike Lee's breakthrough feature, *She's Gotta Have It* (1986), when a cover story announced that white Hollywood "had to have" more up-and-coming black filmmakers like Singleton. Deborah McDowell responded: "what it's 'gotta have' more urgently are more profits like the $55 million that Columbia Pictures earned on its $6 million investment in *Boyz N the Hood*" (375). Two years later, Albert and Allen Hughes's debut film *Menace II Society* grossed $28 million on a budget of less than $4 million.

Whereas McDowell views the African American gangster film as one of the "leading signifers of an aggressively heterosexual Black masculinity" (375), Michael Eric Dyson emphasizes the film's claim to realism. He called *Boyz* "the most brilliantly executed and fully realized portrait yet of the coming of age odyssey that black boys must undertake in the suffocating conditions of urban decay and civic chaos" (210).

Drawing heavily from the gangster rap idiom through its soundtrack, Singleton's male coming-of-age story renders a community in the midst of economic, educational, and drug-related crises and probes one symptom of this mayhem: gang violence. The gang is a metaphor for family and community even as it disrupts those structures; within the gang, men come of age or die trying. There are no intact nuclear families in the film, and black communities are fragmented by poverty, drugs, gang violence, and gender divisions. The boys of the film re-create the family unit through fraternal relationships. But unless they are able to embrace paternal identification as Gerry did in *In the Name of the Father*, they are fated to succumb to the ubiquitous violence that devastates the community.

In the South Central L.A. landscape of *Boyz N the Hood*, there is a glut of young men and a pronounced absence of father figures. The family of Tre Styles (Cuba Gooding, Jr.) is an exception to this rule. The story recounts the period in Tre's life when his father, Furious Styles (Lawrence Fishburne) takes over the primary parenting duties because his ex-wife Reva (Angela Bassett) wants Tre to learn how to be a man. Like Chantal in Leslie Harris's *Just Another Girl on the IRT* (1992), Tre resists the Eurocentric bias of his school and repeatedly gets into trouble. He goes to live with his father and befriends Ricky (Morris Chestnut) and Dough Boy (Ice Cube), two brothers who live on his street. The film chronicles the boys growing up amidst the burgeoning gang culture in Los Angeles.

Boyz emphasizes the critical importance of masculine identification for African American men coming of age. One way that identification defines young black men's sense of themselves is through practices of policing. Manthia Diawara associates the intensive monitoring of the black community in the film, evidenced by traffic signs, helicopters, police cars, and sirens, with the contest over media images in African American communities.

> It is by making the gang members and other people in the hood accept this stereotype of themselves that the community is transformed into a ghetto, a place where Black life is not worth much. (22)

In *Boyz*, a punitive and paternal African American police officer enforces these stereotypes. The officer abuses his position of authority and hurls epithets at Tre and Ricky. As Diawara writes, this police officer views every young black man as a gang member, just as the British authorities saw Gerry Conlon and his Belfast cronies as IRA operatives. In Ed Guerrero's words: "Singleton's tale makes it clear [. . .] that in occupied territory all paths are closely intertwined, for Black people are not seen for what they aspire to; rather, what they are suspected of" (185). Robyn Wiegman argues that the police officer represents "the structures of discipline turned inward by the African American subject, whose defense against racism is often, paradoxically, a reiterative devaluation of Black life" (1993 184). His paternalistic authority reflects the authoritarian structures of law enforcement and institutional racism. The policeman enacts his overidentification with dominant white culture: by virtue of that alignment, he is vested with the authority to act with impunity on the stereotypes he has internalized.

The policeman exemplifies the way identification reinforces the hegemony of a dominant white culture that criminalizes black men. The policeman's identity is mediated through his occupation, a supposedly lawful "fraternity" that can be likened to a gang because of its rites of passage, its routine practice of violence, and its codes of secrecy.[15] This dominant fraternal identification leads to his misrecognition of the young African American men he encounters as inherently violent. He perpetuates what Dyson calls a "culturally reinforced self-loathing and chronic lack of self-esteem" (211).

The only hope of circumventing "stunted, wasted lives" (Guererro 184) seems to be to avoid these annihilating identifications with dominant culture images. The film offers two options to Tre, Ricky, and Dough Boy: paternal and fraternal identification. Singleton defines the former as a relation of normalcy, while the latter is pathologized both within Ricky and Dough Boy's family and as part of the gang's irredeemable abnormality.

The paternal role is constructed as a familial and social role. For Tre's father, Furious Styles, the personal is political, and that includes his approach to fathering. Professionally, Furious works on behalf of his community, lending money to small businesses. He preaches the importance of black economic self-determination, championing a market-oriented solution to persistent structural problems. During a speech where he rejects the claims to brotherhood of the "Seoul Brothers" (a Korean business planning to establish itself in Furious's neighborhood), he makes clear his belief in the importance of black economic nationalism.

Sexual dynamics within the families in the neighborhood determine the young men's practices of identification. In the Styles household, Furious adopts the role of disciplinarian, castigating Tre for not using a condom during a sexual encounter that, unbeknownst to him, Tre has fabricated for his own self-aggrandizement. Despite the disciplinary character of their interactions—or, perhaps because of it—their relationship clearly advantages Tre relative to his fatherless friends Ricky and Dough Boy, whose family is hopelessly fragmented.

One source of the boys' problem is Brenda, Ricky and Dough Boy's mother. Brenda introduces an improper, possibly even sexual, investment into the parent-child relation, which poisons the family. Brenda prefers Ricky to Dough Boy—identifying her sons with their fathers, her former lovers. When Brenda tells the disfavored Dough Boy "you're just like your father," the comment is both damning and significant. First, the comment is meant to be derogatory, as Brenda is in the midst of telling Dough Boy that he "ain't worth shit." Second, Brenda offers to Dough Boy a paternal identification that is an absence; his father's name is never mentioned and thus he functions as a black hole or blank screen. Dough Boy is presented with a model of a devalued and absent father, reviled on both counts. (If he were so absolutely useless, his absence should be welcomed.) Dough Boy's nickname symbolizes the doom that surrounds him; he is encased in a childish, powerless existence. Dough Boy turns to his friends on the street—the only brothers he is able to form a bond with—becomes involved in crime, and is sent to jail at a young age.

Brenda reserves her affection for Ricky, the football star whose opportunities for identification are not as limited as those of Dough Boy. Though his father is absent and his brother abjected, Ricky is able to identify with his own image. Ricky watches videos of his football games with a talent scout and imagines his future as a football star, a role that is sanctioned by dominant white culture. He also develops fraternal ties with Tre, as his relationship with Dough Boy has been irrevocably harmed by Brenda's differential treatment.

Clearly, Brenda does not function as a figure of identification for the boys, nor can they look to one another for masculine mutuality. The film suggests that, partly due to the fact that Brenda elicits and exacerbates competitive feelings between the brothers, fraternal bonding can never serve as a substitute for the father-son relationship each boy lacks. In the film more generally, women are linked to a problematically assertive sexuality—Brenda and the other single mother on the street hit on Furious Styles—and associated with the disturbance of bonds between men.

In a world marked by the absence of fathers, one might expect brothers to occupy a central place of importance. Brotherhood signifies familial, spiritual, and political affiliations as well as egalitarianism. But in *Boyz*, young brothers are shown to lack the knowledge and maturity necessary to avert violence and death. Tre is unable to convince Ricky he is in danger; he decides to go to the store after a fight with Dough Boy and believes he can outrun the gang members who follow him in a car. He is killed in a drive-by revenge shooting. The implication is that Ricky has paid for Dough Boy's gang activities; the sins of the brother are visited on his sibling. After Ricky is killed, Dough Boy and Tre plot revenge, but Tre does not follow through. His grief and anger are tempered in a scene with his girlfriend Brandi, where he cries in her arms and they have sex for the first time. For Tre, sexual initiation, not a perpetuation of violence against other young black men, signifies his passage to manhood.

The film alludes to the potential for meaningful fraternal relationships after Ricky's death when Dough Boy tells Tre he understands his decision not to participate in the killing of the gang members. Telling Dough Boy that he has one brother left, Tre acknowledges that the fraternal connection is important to their survival. But an intertitle in the epilogue (another of the film's bows to documentary realism) informs the audience that Dough Boy was killed two weeks after he avenged Ricky's death. In short, brothers are insufficient in comparison to fathers, and women are completely unavailable as figures of identification for young men. Tre, who successfully matures, thanks to the presence of Furious, leaves for college in Atlanta with Brandi.

Although Michele Wallace recognizes that the film encouraged dialogue about social conditions, she cautions against equating *Boyz* with the reality of black communities, in large part because of its prescriptive paternalism.

> The boys who don't have fathers fail. The boys who do have fathers succeed. And the success of such a movie at the box office reflects its power to confirm hegemonic family values. (1992 125)

While my discussion has focused on the dynamics of paternal identification, Manthia Diawara emphasizes the film's social critique:

> *Boyz N the Hood* blames the rise of crime and the people's feeling of being trapped in the hood on a conspiracy among the gang members, the police, the liquor stores, and Reagan. (22–23)

The film clearly explicates these causes of African American marginality, yet it also presents a private and personal solution to entrenched and systematic problems: a single mode of identification. Young African American men survive if they are able to identify with their fathers; there are few tangible benefits from pursuing identifications with brothers, mothers, sisters, wives, or girlfriends. The possibilities of flexible identification—for example, the potential for building a resistant African American masculinity in the context of the African American community—remains unexplored. The gang cannot function as a community of

FIGURE 4.2. In John Singleton's 'hood, father knows best. Courtesy of Photofest.

resistance, aimed at the economic and social causes of oppression, because its fraternal bonds are understood as being inadequate to the task of cultural reproduction. This would seem to be the analogue of matriarchal mythologies, wherein African American maternity has been figured as inherently illegitimate. Here, paternity is the only solution, yet it is wholly unavailable. So, despite the fact that the film attempts to characterize violence as a social process, not an innate feature of African American-ness, it presents the hierarchical father-son relationship as the primary means of intervention.

Like *In the Name of the Father*, *Boyz* presents a paternal ideal that virtually disavows the possibility that some forms of identification—fraternal, maternal, and sororal—might provide fruitful avenues for psychological restitution and political commitment. Singleton has returned to these questions of family structure and paternal identification in *Baby Boy* (2001) and *Four Brothers* (2005), both of which attempt to counter essentialist ideas linking African American masculinity to criminality and aggression. Only the latter film, which depicts four adopted brothers—two white and two Black—who avenge their mother's death, suggests that Singleton has tempered his insistence on the paternal ideal.

Ironically, the privileging of the paternal over the fraternal in *Boyz N the Hood* clashes with the gangster rap music that underwrites the film's African American ghetto aesthetic. Rap music celebrates the bond among brothers. In rap, the posse and the homeys are lauded as central to the survival of urban male communities.

MENACING SELF-IMAGES

Like Singleton and Sheridan's films, Albert and Allen Hughes's *Menace II Society* looks at the rise and fall of a ghetto gangster, emphasizing his masculine identifications. The film defines the relation of young, African American would-be gangsters to their world not only through fathers but also in relation to popular culture icons of masculinity. The film follows the exploits of a young man named Caine (Tyrin Turner) as he grows into adulthood in the gang culture of South Central L.A. in the 1980s.

The context for the Hughes Brothers' male coming-of-age saga—as it was in the Belfast of Sheridan's film and the South Central L.A. of Singleton's—is an atmosphere of social unrest and a physical environment akin to a war zone. In the film's hallucinatory opening scene, shot with a wide-angle lens and saturated color, Caine accompanies his friend O-Dog (Larenz Tate), to a Korean grocery, where O-Dog kills the proprietor and his wife and steals the surveillance videotape. After a fade to black, the film quickly shifts to another visual register: black-and-white footage that reenacts the Watts riots of 1965. After scenes of extreme police brutality, fires, crowds, and mayhem, another fade-out spans the years between these riots and the late 1970s, when Caine grew up. In true gangster and *film noir* fashion, Caine narrates the next scene in first person, describing the entry of drugs into South Central Los Angeles and his parents' immersion in drug culture. "After the riots, then came the drugs." The collapse of political protest coincides with the defeatist self-absorption of drug culture.

In the next sequence, the documentary realism of the riots gives way to scenes of private interiors, which are shot in an expressionistic style with vivid red lighting, loud music, and low camera angles. Caine, who is a small child, wanders through his parents' wild party in pajamas and takes an initiatory drink of beer from the bottle held by Pernell (Glenn Plummer) a friend of his father's. Caine's father Tat (Samuel Jackson) is a drug dealer who physically abuses Caine's mother Karen (Khandi Alexander). The three-scene exposition culminates in a poker game during which Tat kills one of the other card-players. Tat dies in prison and Karen dies of a heroin overdose, so Caine goes to live with his grandparents.

Despite Tat's absence as a role model (or, perhaps, because of it), Caine follows in his footsteps, becoming a drug dealer. A critical part of this process is the importance of popular culture identifications, and, particularly, the cinematic icons with whom Caine and other characters forge identifications. When Tat pulls a gun on his poker crony, the man jokingly accuses Tat of acting like the hero of the popular Blaxploitation film *Superfly* (1972): "Who do you think you are, Ron O'Neal?" Tat's story departs from Superfly's narrative, however, which underscores the illusory nature of such linkages. In *Superfly*, Youngblood Priest, a drug dealer and user, defies the odds, and genre conventions, by successfully leaving a life of crime after one last score.

At a critical turning point in the film—his first wounding—Caine engages in an overt act of identification that cements his outlaw persona by linking him to a gangster culture that exists beyond his father's realm. Waiting in a hospital room after being treated for a gunshot wound, Caine watches a scene from *He Walked by Night* (Alfred Werker 1948), a film about a dangerous cop killer. His moment of fascinated spectatorship, along with his initiating wound, signify Caine's transformation. In the violence that led to the death of Caine's cousin Harold, Caine and Harold were both innocent bystanders. But Caine's body has been damaged, revealing its vulnerability and instability. In the context of a violation of his body, Caine reformulates his identity based on his admiration for the film gangster's cool demeanor. He takes his cues from the white gangster as much as he does from African American father figures, including his grandfather, the imprisoned Pernell, and his teacher, Mr. Baker (Charles Dutton).

As noted in the book's introduction, Caine, his father Tat, and Grandpapa (Arnold Johnson) are all associated with popular culture identifications that suggest the historically contingent character of masculine identity. Caine models himself on the mid-century gangster, whereas Tat favors the Blaxpolitation hero, and Grandpapa admires the Hollywood heroes of Frank Capra films. These screen identifications attest to the historically variable construction of black masculinity rather than an essentialist ontology. They also point to the way that the process of identification might be used to both secure and to call into question racial and national identities. Grandpapa's fondness for George Bailey ratifies his apparent acquiescence to the status quo, whereas Caine's gangster identification pushes him further outside the law and mainstream culture.

Far more dramatic, however, is the fact that Caine's friend O-Dog, the convenience store killer, epitomizes the inability to identify with others, whether on screen or off. O-Dog and his gang watch the surveillance tape of the Korean convenience store robbery incessantly, as if it were a music video or beloved action flick. O-Dog absorbs the tape and is absorbed by it on psychic and physical levels. At the climax, he screams and shouts at the Korean grocer. The short piece of tape is O-Dog's claim to fame, providing him with the opportunity to identify with himself as a larger-than-life celebrity. His only access to narcissism is through this movie—which reiterates a dominant cultural stereotype of the rage-filled, irrationally violent black man—and it annihilates him.

This wholesale commitment to his screen identity destroys O-Dog, much like a drug addiction would. The repeated screenings limit his access to the actual event and to the world around him. He becomes the most solipsistic and alienated character in the film. Early in the film, Caine tells us that O-Dog represents America's "worst nightmare" because he is young, black, and "doesn't give a fuck." Yet O-Dog's monstrosity fully emerges only during this process of obsessive spectatorship and overidentification. He is unable to distinguish the fantasy of himself—as a violent movie star on the tape—from the reality. He claims he will become a "big-ass movie star" who is "larger than that Steven Segal." In

Lacan's terminology, O-Dog is trapped in the mirror stage, admiring the coherent image of himself that is, fundamentally, a misrepresentation. But psychoanalysis and politics coincide here. That misrepresentation is indeed America's worst nightmare: a black male aggressor. O-Dog performs that stereotype, then fully embraces that misrepresentation as evidence of his authentic black masculinity.

O-Dog's narcissistic obsession contributes to the film's systematic representation of dead-end identifications. Together with *He Walked by Night*, *Superfly*, and *It's a Wonderful Life*, the robbery film demarcates the limited choices available to young African American men and the danger of investment in popular culture images.

Caine seeks the counsel of one additional father figure: Mr. Baker, his history teacher. But it is already too late.[16] As gangster film fans know, those who choose to live by the sword must die by the sword, and Caine has become a successful gangster and player. Caught in a cycle of drug selling and using, he makes a young woman named Ilena pregnant and abandons her. Caine has decided to leave Los Angeles to start anew with Ronnie (Pernell's girlfriend), who has found a job in Atlanta. Ilena's cousin confronts Caine and is beaten by him, but later exacts his revenge in a drive-by shooting that kills Mr. Baker's son Sharif and Caine. Caine's recklessness bears generational repercussions: he is responsible for destroying the only intact father-son relationship in the film, that between Mr. Baker and Sharif, his clean-living Muslim son.

The film's didactic narration from a character whose corrupt lifestyle has caught up with him offers a case study in the problematics of identification. From beyond the grave, Caine espouses a "self-help" approach to gangsterism, to use Adolph Reed's term (1999). Caine counsels spectators who have enjoyed his gangster exploits (much as O-Dog had reveled in his own) and encourages them to reject those identifications. Against the backdrop of the Watts Riots, which suggests an underlying historical analysis of urban African American communities, Caine urges the audience to make choices, to resist the pull of gangsterism, and to reject the racist vision of aggressive black masculinity. Yet the film articulates the difficulty of resisting that vision: it feeds the pathology of a culture that obsessively fantasizes about black men like O-Dog who kill.

Although the film has been compared to Martin Scorsese's *Mean Streets* (1973), *Menace*'s "dead-end" sensibility and its narration-beyond-the-grave device more directly recall the earlier morality tales of classic gangster films.[17] To identify with the protagonist and narrator Caine is to identify with an already-dead man. This circular device of pre-destination depoliticizes violence along the lines that John Hill has described (1988). Despite the Hughes Brothers' attempt to complicate the viewer's understanding of urban violence in *Menace*, the inevitable result of Caine's identification with cinematic gangsters is violent death at the hands of another young African American man. No possibility exists for resisting dominant culture, and, as was the case in *In the Name of the Father* and *Boyz N the Hood*, fraternal bonding is a virtual impossibility.

CAL AND *THE CRYING GAME*: GENDER, SEXUALITY, AND NATIONAL IDENTITY

Two Irish gangster films reiterate the distinctive focus of John Ford's *The Informer* and Carol's Reed's *Odd Man Out* by depicting male characters who desperately want out of the violent gang lifestyle but are helpless to accomplish that feat. They resituate these earlier nationalist tales within the context of the Troubles in Northern Ireland, a guerrilla war waged by the Irish Republican Army against the Royal Ulster Constabulary, Protestant paramilitary groups, and British military forces that has claimed several thousands of lives.

Pat O'Connor's *Cal*, based on the novel by Bernard MacLaverty, opens with young Cal McCloskey (John Lynch) as he is drawn into sectarian violence by serving as the driver for an IRA operative who assassinates a wealthy Protestant man named Morton. The narrative traces Cal's guilt over the killing, his withdrawal from his father Shamie (Donal McCann), and his romantic relationship with Marcella Morton (Helen Mirren), the victim's widow. The schizophrenic, polarized politics of Northern Ireland are channeled through Cal's psyche, in the form of his multiple identifications. In many ways, the film's focus on guilt and redemption, and its unconventional identifications across gender, set the stage for Neil Jordan's *The Crying Game*, made nearly a decade later.

Joe Cleary considers both *Cal* and *The Crying Game* emblematic of the dominant narrative of the Northern Irish conflict because they suppress political conflict.

> [In these films] a political tale of the 'national romance' kind and an apolitical tale of escape into domestic privacy are often combined or overlapped—with the former usually being superseded, overwritten, or finally cancelled out by the latter. (1996 241)

Cleary argues that these narratives are conservative because they offer up only two extreme positions: militant nationalism or a repudiation of politics altogether (1996 265). *Cal* depicts characters who fail to see political solutions to the Troubles, but both the novel and film present this stalemate as the lamentable effect of the extremist ideologies that permeate life in the north, not as a reality. Skeffington (John Kavanagh), the local IRA leader, tells Cal, "Think of an Ireland free of the Brits. Would we ever achieve it through the politicians?" Cal replies "no." And Crilly (Stevan Rimkus), Morton's killer, adds "too damned right." (24). But Cal is under duress in this scene; he parrots what he knows the men want to hear. His confused involvement with the IRA allows Brian McIlroy to persuasively argue that the film critiques both British and Irish nationalisms. "O'Connor appears to be earnestly searching for a middle path that is not snared with political traps" (2001 85). Refusing to endorse a specific political stance, the film uses Cal's multiple identifications to reject polarized identities of all kinds.

Like the protagonists of *In the Name of the Father*, *Boyz N the Hood*, and *Menace II Society*, Cal's engagement with violence is mediated through identification. Like *In the Name of the Father*, the film makes linkages between father figures and political action (McIlroy 85). The film's first scene, which depicts the murder, establishes the importance of Cal's identification with his victim, Morton, and with his father, Shamie. Opening with a series of tight shots inside the getaway car, the film reveals no faces until Robert Morton opens the front door of his home to his assailant. Close-ups alternate between Cal's hands on the steering wheel of the car, his partner Crilly's hands on a gun, Crilly's boots walking across the yard, and the gun in Morton's face. The sound of the first gunshot is matched with a shot of Cal's hand on the steering wheel, initiating a motif in which hands signify guilt. Crilly and Cal flee the scene of the killing. In the next scene, Cal visits his father, Shamie, at an abattoir where he works. Cal must reach around Shamie's bloody apron, bloodying his own hands in the process, to take money from his father's pants pocket. The dirty work of killing, which bloodies the men's hands, has now become a family affair.

After Morton's death, Cal refuses further IRA activities, withdraws to his room to listen to music, and becomes obsessed with Morton's widow, Marcella.[18] Cal meets Marcella Morton at the library where she works when he borrows cassette tapes. He later takes a job at the Morton estate. The elder Mrs. Morton hires Cal to split logs and then offers him more work, under the supervision of Protestant Orangeman Mr. Dunlop. The Mortons begrudgingly allow him to stay in an abandoned cottage on the estate when his father's Belfast home burns to the ground after a sectarian attack. The family accepts Cal. When the elderly Mr. Morton is taken to the hospital, he grants Cal a fatherly gesture, calling him "a very good boy."

In town to buy Christmas gifts, Cal is picked up by Crilly and informed that his father, who has been depressed since their house was burned down by Protestant paramilitaries, has been taken to an asylum. Cal may have abandoned his father, but he has inherited some of his vulnerability. Crilly and Skeffington, the IRA's teacher-terrorist, attempt to run a British army roadblock, and Cal escapes from the car, only to be turned in by Crilly, who has been captured. Cal has only enough time to return to Marcella to tell her he was involved in Robert's death before the police come to arrest him.

Throughout the film, Cal identifies with the victim Robert Morton. He repeatedly returns to the scene of the murder, eventually usurping Morton's place. His attachment to the dead man is marked by frequent glances at photographs in the Morton home. Marcella offers Cal her dead husband Robert's clothes when she learns that Cal has taken up residence in the abandoned cottage. That exchange of identities is realized in Cal's flashbacks of the night of the murder when he makes love with Marcella for the first time. Cal experiences temporary impotence as images of the killing are intercut with his sexual encounter with Marcella: guilty memories aroused by guilty sex. At this moment, however, Cal identifies with Marcella, not Morton, through the motif involving his hands. The film makes this connection explicit through editing, whereas the novel elaborates it through a descriptive passage that compares Cal and Marcella's acts of touching.

> He saw himself again touching the back of the steering wheel lightly with his fingers, heard again the incessant barking of the dogs and Crilly trying to get sound out of the bell. Marcella touched his back with her fingernails descending his spine, all the time staring unblinkingly at him. (138)

Cal associates Morton's violent death—"an originary act of symbolic parricide" (Cleary 247)—with his lack of masculinity, which reverses the traditional symbolism of Oedipal violence as a male rite of passage. "He feared that, as far as Marcella was concerned, he had gelded himself that dark winter's night" (138). The murder seems to have emasculating effects on Cal: it "does not release Cal from the tyranny of the Father or the Law, but rather confirms his castration, his abjection before the Name-of-the-Father" (Cleary 252).

Cal identifies with both Marcella and Robert, and he bears responsibility for the destruction of their union. Cleary argues that "*Cal* is structured so as to invite us to identify with the Catholic couple's desire for sexual union, which can be read metonymically as the desire for a united Ireland" (Cleary 254). The couple Cleary refers to is Cal and Marcella (who was raised Catholic), but it might be more appropriate to consider the union in light of the nationalist desire for a Catholic Ireland. The doomed nature of Cal and Marcella's romance seems to highlight the problematic exclusivity of this nationalist vision.

Cal engages in a variety of paternal identifications in addition to assuming Morton's place. IRA cronies insinuate themselves into the family. Crilly brings Shamie a gun to protect himself after the McCluskeys are threatened by Protestant paramilitaries, and then asks for favors in return. Crilly repeatedly refers to Cal as "sonny boy," and he takes over Cal's job working with Shamie at the abattoir when Cal quits. Although they have been friends since childhood, Cal studiously avoids Crilly after the Morton killing.

Cal temporarily staves off his fascination with Morton and his obsession with the killing by retreating into music, taking advantage of the opportunity to transport himself beyond his grim, local reality. Music fills a void for Cal, functioning as a fetish object to both obscure and stand in for what he lacks. Early in the novel and film he listens to a blues-inflected Rolling Stones LP, which he sings to in an "American voice" (11). When the Rolling Stones record has ended, "[t]he silence made him want to play another record" (11). During a meeting with Crilly and Skeffington, he moves his fingers to "the wailing guitar sequence from 'the Dark Side of the Moon'" (23) as the music plays only in his head. In church, he remembers his dead mother by conjuring up an image of her singing "rebel songs" like "Roddy McCorley," "The Croppy Boy," and "Father Murphy" (37).

Cal's wide-ranging musical tastes furnish him with various possibilities for identification across race and national identity. Cal "[chants] a negro work song in a thick American accent, striking the wedge at the end of each line" (43). After he is attacked by a Protestant gang, "there were some scratches from the hedge and both his lips were beginning to swell visibly. He pursed them out and spoke to his image in a negro voice" (47). Lauren Onkey has argued that, through these musical associations, the film draws parallels between Irish Catholics in Northern Ireland and African Americans in the United States. Yet the music ultimately fails to move Cal beyond his isolation.

> His feelings of "white negroism" do not evoke the feelings of community central to *The Commitments.* He shares neither his passion for music nor his love of dirty labor with his contemporaries. So his "Blackness" is associated with his feelings of isolation within the Northern Irish war. (156)

Cal's musical recourse to blackness reflects his status as an internal other, a Catholic in the North, and one who has repudiated the Republican cause.

The act of translating music into his own idiom by singing along speaks to his desire to break down social and linguistic boundaries. In the context of Irish culture, with its prominent oral tradition, Cal's linguistic play must be carefully considered. He listens to the Rolling Stones, practices French, and blends foreign phrases in a form of language play that recalls James Joyce's experimental word games in *Finnegan's Wake*:

> He had learned very little French at school but he had retained enough of it to mutter to himself, "*Cochon merde,*" and twist his head. It was as if his mind had stuck. The phrase would come up again and again. He even fretted as to whether or not it was grammatically correct. Not that it mattered because he even made up phrases of his own which were a mixture of French and English: "Dirty *vache.* You big *crotte de chien.*" (10)

Later, Cal uses this self-castigating language again, in reference to himself: "*Merde. Crotte de chien.* Merderer" (14). Here, the dirty work Onkey refers to encompasses excrement and murder.

Ironically, Cal's musical interests and verbal acrobatics—two attributes stereotypically associated with Irishness—reveal his alienation from Irish national identity. Cal is more familiar with foreign tongues than he is with the Irish language. "For the sake of the Movement he had tried to teach himself some Gaelic out of a book he had just bought at a jumble sale but he never knew how to pronounce the written form of the words. How did you say 'bh' and 'dh'?" (10).

For Cal, the process of developing an Irish identity involves translating visual symbols into spoken language, moving from static text into the performative, oral, and aural realm of music. "The [Irish] words remained as printed symbols locked inside his head and he gave up the notion soon after. Some day he might go to a class and hear the words spoken" (10). Performing the words brings the Irish language, and, perhaps, the nation, into reality. But Cal's linguistic and musical tastes remain eclectic: by combining elements of French and English, with his "negro" voice, he draws together several national, cultural, racial, and linguistic traditions.

Cal resists opportunities for masculine identification in his Catholic Belfast community (Shamie, Crilly) and instead privileges associations with African American and English musical cultures. Onkey writes that Cal's identification with foreignness allows him to transcend the impossibly polarized opposition between the IRA on one side and the Protestant paramilitaries on the other:

> It seems that an alliance with a group *outside* Ireland, like African Americans, is one of the few ways Cal can find a place for himself in Northern Ireland. Both the immediacy of Cal's political situation and Mac Laverty's more nuanced use of the Irish and African American alliance make that alliance more credible and potentially productive. It functions as a small way that Cal can find solace rather than the key to his essential Irish identity (or the ticket to rock stardom). (157)

Cal's identification represents an escape from reality and also provides another mode of engagement with his circumstances. The music takes him beyond Belfast's polarized streets and yet also clarifies his impossible position within them.

Cal's cross-race and cross-gender identifications are unusual in that they challenge his claims to whiteness and masculinity. Despite this fact, Jack Boozer argues that *Cal* fails to fully "illuminate the way in which basic assumptions about gender might already play a key role in the configuration of larger political-economic beliefs" (174). Assumptions about, and practices of, gender emerge more fully as a point of critique in a later film that closely follows *Cal*'s narrative pattern: Neil Jordan's *The Crying Game.*

One of the best-known Irish films of the 1990s, Neil Jordan's *The Crying Game* grossed $6 million in forty-seven days. Eventually, the film made more than $60 million and appeared on more than 100 critics' lists of the top films of the year (Bell-Metereau 1993). With a plot that combines elements of *Cal* and Hitchcock's *Vertigo* (1958), *The Crying Game* traces the personal awakening of IRA Volunteer Fergus Hennessy (Stephen Rea) as he repudiates nationalist violence and leaves Ireland behind. This, too, is a coming-of-age story. But this film focuses on the way that masculinity and violence are mediated by performances of gender and sexuality.

A stint performing guard duty for a captured British soldier precipitates Fergus's crisis of confidence. In defiance of his orders, he befriends the black British soldier named Jody (Forest Whitaker). The men discuss sports, women, and colonial politics. Jody, like Fergus, is an abjected British subject, hailing from Antigua. As a result, Fergus finds it nearly impossible to carry out the ordered assassination when the time comes. Jody flees, but Fergus witnesses his death when a British Army Saracen tank kills him as it makes its way to the IRA hideout.

Fearful of both the British authorities and his former IRA comrades, Fergus escapes from Ireland. (The only paternal figure in the film is Tommy, the old man who enables his passage across the water.) His flight from Ireland to Britain suggests Fergus's lingering identification with the British soldier: he moves to London, where Jody lived, to start a new life as "Jimmy." Fergus seeks out Jody's lover Dil (Jaye Davidson), which he promised Jody he would do. Fergus becomes attracted to Dil. When he discovers Dil is a transvestite living as a woman, Fergus rejects a sexual relationship but becomes Dil's protector. In the meantime, IRA operatives Jude (Miranda Richardson) and Peter (Adrian Dunbar) track Fergus to London and assign him a suicide mission. When he fails to appear—Dil, who has learned that he was involved in Jody's death, now holds him hostage—Jude shows up at Dil's apartment with her gun drawn. But Dil shoots Jude with the gun Jude had provided Fergus for the job. The final scene depicts Fergus's incarceration in a modern British prison: he has taken the rap for Dil and assuaged his guilt for his violent past. In a comic coda, Dil visits Fergus and establishes her intention of carrying on their love affair.

The Crying Game has been the subject of numerous critical essays, many of which focus on the film's sexual and racial politics, its potential misogyny, and its political equivocation. Amy Zillax notes that identification is central to the film, and particularly, that its "identificatory flexibility [. . .] could be positively liberatory" (33). Although fluid identifications might provide "a way out of the ideological stratification [the film] presupposes," Zillax argues that the film's focus on the unveiled spectacle of Dil's body and on Fergus's homophobic response to it emphasize that the characters resist the narrative and identificatory flexibility the film tries to propose (35). In Zillax's view, the film defines political agency as "dependent upon a murderously coherent identity" (45). Yet, I think it's fair to suggest that the film characterizes political *violence* as dependent upon a "murderously" coherent identity, not political agency altogether.[19]

In the opening sequences in Northern Ireland, the film restricts its universe to a limited visual landscape where Jody's color, more than anything else, signifies that he is out of place. Jody confirms this fact when he tells Fergus that Northern Ireland is the only place where people call him "nigger" to his face. This visual homogeneity offers a metaphor for the nationalist image of Ireland. Jody's difference—which is racially and sexually marked, but ultimately has more to do with his rejection of an us/them model—connects him to Fergus, who is something of an outsider in his IRA unit because he finds it difficult to objectify others. It is Fergus's identification with the captive Jody that initiates his process of reorientation and causes him to repudiate the official nationalist vision of a monolithic and united Catholic Ireland.

In contrast to the Northern Ireland scenes, the early sequences in the bar in London where Fergus meets Dil, reveal a world that thrives on difference. Patrick McGee correctly notes that the Metro "could never be mistaken for a utopia" (154). "[N]evertheless," he continues, it "captures in microcosm the multicultural, multisexual *nation* that is postcolonial Britain. This would not be the official nation but the sublimated nation" (154). Fergus exchanges his narrow nationalist community for that diverse, sublimated nation, of which Jody and Dil are citizens.

The Crying Game is more insistent than *Cal* that gender and sexuality are intimately related to national identity and to practices of violence. Whereas Jack Boozer believes that "Peter and Jude [Fergus's IRA comrades] fit together in a category of ideological extremism that surpasses sexual difference" (174), I would argue instead that they represent an awareness that sexuality may be performed in the service of the nation. After Jody's kidnapping, Jude makes a remark to Fergus about what she will, and will not do, for her country. One implication is that she would not have sex with Jody merely for the Republican cause. But another interpretation is that Jude is conscious of performing as a seductive woman for her country.

Both Jude (the "real" woman) and Dil (the "imposter") occupy positions and perform identities that confound the idea of natural sexual differences. Jude revels in her sexuality and aggression, which are defined by and, in turn, inform her IRA activities. At the time of the kidnapping, she is sexually involved with Fergus and has no qualms about physically abusing Jody. In London, Jude performs a different role. Visibly decked out as a femme fatale, she orders Fergus to take the suicide mission, and commands him to have sex with her (an injunction he silently declines).

Finally, however, Jude's female body—defined in surprisingly biologistic terms by the grief-stricken, gun-wielding Dil—pays the price for the inflexibility of IRA nationalism. Although *The Crying Game* redefines identities through characters like Fergus and Dil, who negotiate differences of race, nation, and sexuality, the film finally reasserts a masculine imperative. Patrick McGee notes, "If sexuality is inextricably bound to the historical constructions of national, racial and gender differences, it is the hatred of women that continues to support these binary economies even after the system of patriarchal-imperialist representations has entered into a state of crisis" (155). Once again, a woman stands in for Ireland, but now that national construct represents a narrow essentialism that the protagonists seek to destroy.

In response to critics who complain that the film is apolitical, Jack Boozer writes that private and sexual registers are precisely where the politics of the film lie: "seemingly private sexual and emotional desires are constantly intruded upon by the larger social symbolic of political positioning" (172). In other words, national imperatives—to be soldiers or volunteers, for example, or to police Northern Ireland or to kill a stranger—are indistinguishable from the "private" realms those frameworks of identity construct, including sexuality.

Fergus's odyssey from volunteer to prisoner—a sacrificial trajectory to be sure—is enabled by his identification with Jody. "Dil's act of bondage effectively snares Fergus [. . .] into a masculinity that abjures phallic demonstrations of superiority" (Boozer 173). But it is earlier, during Jody's bondage that Fergus first learns to refuse those phallic demonstrations. Jude pistol whips Jody for example; whereas Fergus leaves his hood off and engages him in conversation. In defiance of IRA procedures, Fergus meets Jody as an equal, a fraternal figure, perhaps, and an object of sexual interest. Several moments in the early scenes establish the playful sexuality developing between them—when Jody tell him that he has nice eyes, or when Fergus tells Jody "the pleasure was all mine" after he has helped him to urinate.

After Jody's death, Fergus is as obsessed with images of Jody as he is protective of Dil. He repeatedly dreams about Jody, which signifies the soldier's continuing importance as a figure of both identification and, potentially, desire. Fergus's bond with Jody makes possible his alliance with Dil. Finally, transforming Dil into Jody—ostensibly for her protection—reveals that Fergus is able to clearly distinguish between the rigid view of the Irish nationalists (where men can't become women) and his evolving perspective. Fergus has rejected the Irish nationalist precepts of ethnic homogeneity, binary sexual difference, and phallic masculinity and he uses those ideological blinders against his former comrades.

Patrick McGee argues that *The Crying Game* presents a model of reciprocity that does not rest upon identification but "acts of symbolic exchange between points of incommensurable difference" (152). In fact, he writes, the film "expresses [. . .] the impossibility of identification as the condition of social kinship and exchange" (150). Yet, acts of symbolic exchange occur precisely because of Fergus's identification with Jody. In befriending Jody and keeping his promise to look after Dil, Fergus's act of masculine solidarity becomes a process of identity transformation, where the assumptions he has made about gender are revealed to be as faulty as those he has made regarding national identity.

CONCLUSION

The films in this chapter explore the role identification plays in the cultural reproduction of violence by focusing on the figure of the gangster and his practices of self-fashioning within communities of men. These films propose that violence is reproduced through masculine identifications, emphasizing the importance of paternal identification in films like *In the Name of the Father*, *Boyz N the Hood*, and *Menace II Society*. The paternal position seems to overshadow possibilities for fraternal bonding.

In these films, acts of identification do not consolidate and reinforce traditional ideas about national or racial identity. Instead they complicate them, revealing that masculine identities are both constructed and historically situated. In *Menace II Society*, identifications with gangster figures across race and generation seem paradoxical in that they fix the gangster identity itself rather than opening up possibilities for new performances of masculinity. In *Cal* African American music offers an estranged IRA soldier a sense of identity beyond the oppositional rhetoric of Protestant versus Catholic or British versus Irish. *Cal* and *The Crying Game* focus on gender identities, and the protagonist of the latter film moves beyond race and gender as he questions racial, national, and sexual essentialisms.

The films in this chapter take pains to establish the immediate historical, economic, and political causes of violence. They attempt to counter previous film representations that imply there are "natural" proclivities toward violence. Oddly enough, however, they reiterate the notion that personal, private solutions are adequate to stemming the violence they depict. Whereas the classical gangster film generally called upon the social body to condemn the gangster's acts, these films ultimately locate the social dilemmas within the psyches of gangsters themselves, positing masculine identifications as the source of, and solution to, antisocial violence.

CHAPTER FIVE

"Both Sides of the Epic": Identification and the Nonessentialist Western

> Who better than an Irishman could understand the Indians, while remaining enthusiastic about the fable of the U.S. Cavalry? We are on both sides of the epic.
>
> —John Ford, Interview with Eric Leguèbe

Mike Newell's *Into the West* (1992), written by Jim Sheridan, reconsiders the Western from a contemporary Irish vantage point. Seated astride a magical white horse in a public housing high-rise apartment in Dublin, young Ossie and Tito Reilly (Ciarán Fitzgerald and Rúaidhrí Conroy), Irish travelers, imagine they are in the Wild West like their heroes Butch Cassidy and the Sundance Kid. "Was there a wild west in Ireland?" Ossie asks his older brother, Tito. Tito replies, "There still is, on the other side of the mountains." Seeking to locate himself in the Irish west, Ossie asks Tito to define their relationship to frontier icons: "Then, are we travelers Indians?" Ossie wonders. "No," Tito admonishes, "we're the cowboys." Elizabeth Butler Cullingford argues that the remainder of the film discredits Tito's view that travelers are "on the winning side," because the settled Irish people of Southern Ireland treat the traveler boys with racist hostility (2001 180–81). Yet, in terms of their behavior, the boys actually continue to harbor affiliations with both sides of the conflict. They mimic both the cowboys and Indians they've seen in videos, cooking tinned beans and whooping it up around the campfire.

It is no coincidence that Ossie and Tito identify with the genial and dynamic American duo of Butch and Sundance. Rugged and courageous outlaws, they are insiders and outsiders in their own culture. They join a number of anti-heroes of New American Cinema: men and women who paradoxically embody American-ness through acts of rebellion against official culture. But beyond their affinity for Butch and Sundance, the boys' double identification with cowboys and Indians offers a method for moving beyond either/or formulas for identity. Ossie and Tito fall outside of the system of difference established by oppositions of Celt and Anglo-Saxon, Catholic or Protestant, cowboy or Indian. As Irish travelers, the boys are defined by their geographical mobility, which serves as a literal counterpart to their desire for fluid identities.

The benefits of the booming Celtic Tiger economy have not trickled down to the Reillys or to their poor Dublin neighbors. This fact is made explicit in the opening scene. John Reilly (Gabriel Byrne) has settled his family in Dublin after the death of Mary Reilly, John's wife and the boys' mother. John orders Tito and Ossie to claim to be members of the expansive Murphy brood (there are fifteen children in the family) in order to secure the Murphys a government flat. The urban poor and the travelers are equally impoverished, yet early scenes of the film reveal important differences between the Reillys and their neighbors. The Reilly children bring a horse up the elevator into their apartment, indicating their direct link to a rural and nomadic existence that seems incompatible with modern life.

Unable to assimilate into modern, settled culture, the travelers (known derogatorily as tinkers or Irish gypsies) represent a pre-modern community displaced by industrial capitalism. In the opening scenes, the grandfather's traveling life seems vastly preferable to settled Dublin life. But the perils of traveler culture are presented as well—Mary Reilly died in childbirth because no hospital would treat a traveler. By linking travelers to the discourse of the Western genre, *Into the West* expresses the complexity of cultural and national identities in an Ireland divided not by North/South or Catholic/Protestant axes, but by regional, class, and ethnic differences. In exploring the boys' multiple identifications, the film suggests a way out of binary models of identity and reminds audiences of the radical pluralism embedded within Irishness.

This chapter examines the way Irish and African American films have reinterpreted the Western genre and exposed the fraudulent nature of its underlying principle: the essentialist division between winners and losers in the national contest. *Eat the Peach* (Peter Ormrod 1986), *Into the West*, *Posse* (Mario Van Peebles 1993), and *The Disappearance of Finbar* (Sue Clayton 1996) seek to dismantle the genre's nationalist rhetoric of identity, and, particularly its stark contrasts between winner and loser, colonizer and colonized, and self and other.

These films investigate the ideological origins and constructed nature of national identity. In doing so, they engage in what Richard Kearney describes as a postnational project of historical reinterpretation. "Post-nationalism is not Pol-Potism," he writes. "It does not solicit a liquidation of the past but its reinterpretation or *Aughebung*" (59). Because these films go beyond critiques of nationalism and call attention to underlying models for conceptualizing identity, I refer to them as nonessentialist Westerns.

Processes of identification are central to the way Irish and African American Westerns reinterpret colonial and neocolonial histories. Ossie and Tito engage in both cowboy and Indian activities, rejecting the idea of exclusive identification. When, at the film's conclusion, John Reilly states, "there's a little traveler in everyone," he projects the internal otherness associated with the travelers onto everyone in Ireland, and, indeed, beyond Ireland to the world at large. John Reilly's utopian vision rests upon a new model of difference. He constructs an imagined global community defined by the otherness that everyone shares.

Before moving to the readings of these films, I briefly examine the manner in which the Western genre merges colonial history, racial essentialism, and nationalist ideology. It is for these reasons that the genre represents an ideal vehicle for contemporary Irish and African American filmmakers to explore the constructed nature of identity.

CONQUEST, THE NATION, AND THE WESTERN

A central theme of the Western is that violence is necessary in order to establish a microcosm of the national community on the rugged and empty frontier west of the Mississippi. Until the late 1960s, Hollywood rarely disputed European-Americans' territorial claims or questioned the necessity of the elimination of indigenous American people. Colonial privilege fell under the rubric of manifest destiny, even in a number of postwar Westerns that treated Indians as noble savages, such as John Ford's *Cheyenne Autumn* (1964).

The white entitlement to the American West has been a frequent subject in American literature and films. That implicit claim to possession of the continent's geography is often signified through spatial metaphors of emptiness. Since the mid-nineteenth century, popular representations of the West depicted the region as an unpopulated vacuum: a sepia-toned landscape haunted by "vanishing Americans" whose decline was inevitable. As John Lenhian writes, the inhabitants and their claims to the space of the West were written out of existence.

> At worst, the Indian was considered a brute savage and represented the antithesis of civilized respectability and Christian virtue. [. . .] At best, he was natural man living the free, primitive life, until civilization intruded upon his Garden of Eden and rendered him tragically obsolescent. (58)

Unlike nineteenth-century still photographs, which depicted contemporary Indian life, filmmakers tended to treat the West as "a museum piece, a reconstruction of the past" (Buscombe 43). Edward Buscombe, Brian Henderson, Steven Neale, and others argue that the idea of "pastness" is one way the Western genre has suppressed America's history of genocide.

The Western reflects American ideologies about race. Richard Abel, Richard Dyer, and Virginia Wright Wexman show that the genre was a distinctively American product that helped to establish a white nativist American identity in the early twentieth century. Abel argues that the discourse surrounding the Western was critical to the film industry's attempt to create a uniquely American film genre and to marginalize rival "foreign" film producers such as Pathé. Contemporary commentators in *The Saturday Evening Post* and *Harper's Monthly* extolled westerns as "wholesome," "national," "patriotic" and "educational," replete with values of Anglo-Saxon masculine dominance associated with "white supremacist entertainment" (Abel 81–84). By 1910, one-fifth of American films were Westerns (*BFI Companion* 24).

The Western's foremost means of expressing those values are mise-en-scène and point of view. The movement westward signifies that characters are released from the restrictions of civilized society "back East" and are vulnerable to a greater danger linked to the immense scale and savagery of the natural world. The genre conveys the pleasure and danger of being lost in a vast and inhospitable landscape. Vulnerable individuals huddle together against the elements (which, in the classical Western, includes Indians), forming motley frontier communities. Whereas John Cawelti argues that the Western landscape restates ideological conflicts through strict dichotomies (wilderness versus civilization, mountains versus plains, openness versus enclosure, and desert versus garden), Jane Tompkins notes that those oppositions constantly threaten to break down (48). In defining the whole nation on the basis of its vast frontier, the Western overwhelms viewers with images of a landscape that is clearly impervious to human activity but which must, nevertheless, be "conquered." Western narratives privilege the perspectives of the white settlers, which validates the concept of western territory as property. Yet, the monumental landscape, and its ability to dwarf and swallow up the individual, undermines the settler belief that nature can be possessed and tamed.

The importance of geography—and, more particularly, the implicit threat to identity posed by emptiness—influences the dynamics of character identification within the genre. In the Western, the character most aware of the potential for annihilation, the cowboy, ensures his survival by learning and incorporating Indian knowledge. But neither the cowboy nor the Indian can acknowledge such identifications. "Going Indian," which refers to a process of incorporating Indian otherness into a white identity, becomes synonymous with insanity or death.

"GONE INDIAN": WESTERN IDENTIFICATION

According to Robert Baird, the process whereby a white settler identifies with the native other—or "goes Indian"—is a historical legacy and a wish-fulfillment dream central to American culture from Thoreau through liberal Westerns like *Little Big Man* (Arthur Penn 1970). This slippage of identity appears in the testimonies of settlers and captives in colonial American literature and in the recurrent theme of Indian parentage or adoption in both literature and film.

In cinema, John Ford's films inherited these racial dynamics of identification. Charles Ramirez Berg argues that in Ford's films, Native Americans act as a "social and racial boundary" (80) against which Irish and

European Americans who are presented as racially ambiguous are pressed by the "ever advancing colonizing Mainstream" (81). Thus, conquest involves choosing sides and forging identifications. According to Joan Dagle, Ford's postwar Westerns reject the narrative of conquest altogether. She writes that *The Searchers* (1956) "turns the Western narrative inside out to reveal its racism" (102). Dagle attributes *The Searchers*'s revisionism in large part to its treatment of identification across the white-red divide.

The Ford Western remains an important paradigm for the study of identification in the Western in part because Ford's own identification with American Indians—on screen and off—is the frequent subject of Ford biographers and film critics.[1] Tales abound regarding Ford's personal relationship with the Navajo: "He's been taken in the Navajo tribe," reports Henry Goulding in Peter Bogdanovich's *John Ford*. "They have a special name for 'im, the Navajos. Natani Nez. That's his name, only his. Natani Nez. It means the Tall Soldier" (15). Peter Bogdanovich relates that late in his career Ford told him that he made *Cheyenne Autumn* because "I've killed more Indians than Custer, Beecher, and Chivington put together" (104). Ford recognized the racist double standard of the Western.

> Let's face it, we've treated them very badly—it's a blot on our shield; we've cheated and robbed, killed, murdered, massacred and everything else, but they kill one white man and, God, out come the troops. (104)

The transition from classical to postwar Western—from manifest destiny to postwar pessimism—can be traced in the changing point-of-view structure and strategies for identification in John Ford's *Stagecoach* (1939) and *The Searchers*. In *Stagecoach*, a group of white settlers grapples with domestic and national crises while under attack by Geronimo. The resolution affirms white property ownership, heterosexual coupling, and the possibility for redemption. In *The Searchers*, the potential for cultural mixing between whites and Indians overwhelms the outlaw hero and the narrative itself.

The Ringo Kid of *Stagecoach* (John Wayne) is an outlaw-hero in search of revenge. His actions—breaking out of jail, planning to avenge his brother's murder—cannot be sanctioned by the official representatives of the United States, a nation of laws. The narrative focuses on Ringo and Dallas (Claire Trevor), who symbolize hardy frontier individuals able to establish a middle ground between the overly moralistic town of Tonto and the lawless, raucous, and inaptly named Lordsburg. At the end of the film, after Ringo slays the men who killed his brother, and after Dallas has proven her commitment to domesticity by assisting in the birth of Lucy Mallory's daughter, Ringo and Dallas are free to pursue the American dream on his ranch just across the border.

In *Stagecoach*, characters do not identify with Indians. Instead, Indians are elements of the hostile environment. Their numbers and their savagery contribute to the vulnerability of the stagecoach and its passengers. Their attacks offer a lesson to the white community on the folly of magnifying the white nation's internal divisions between North and South (symbolized by Hatfield, still loyal to the Confederacy) and East and West (symbolized by Gatewood, the corrupt banker who is apprehended by western authorities in Lordsburg). The conflict between the stagecoach riders and the Indians (as others) unifies the white community. The fact that Ringo and Dallas flee across the border to Mexico suggests the overly restrictive boundaries of the national community. In the film's rhetoric, Ringo's double homicide is ethically justified, just as Dallas's prostitution is explained by her socio-economic circumstances. But they must leave the country to make a new start.

In *The Searchers*, the conflict between settlers and Indians manifests itself within the psyche of the reluctant protagonist Ethan Edwards (John Wayne). Ethan's obsessive search for his niece Debbie (taken hostage by Comanche chief Scar after a raid on the Edwards homestead) is motivated by his unchaste love for his sister-in-law Martha. Those feelings are revealed to the audience through Ethan's point of view shots—the primary means of establishing Ethan's humanity.

Ethan knows a great deal about the Comanche Indians, but he uses that knowledge to destroy them, not to identify with them. As is often observed, Ethan is not a sympathetic figure. He is socially awkward and a perpetual loner; he refuses allegiance to any nation, but is associated with the white supremacist beliefs of the Confereracy. Like Ringo Kid, he seeks revenge, but his motives are mixed. He may be searching for Debbie in order to kill her because she has been tainted by her assimilation into the tribe.

The Searchers complicates the dynamics of identification relative to *Stagecoach* in two ways. First, it draws a parallel between Scar's thirst for vengeance and Ethan's. In other words, the film alludes to the costs for all concerned, not merely the white settlers, of the genocidal drive west. The audience realizes Ethan ought to be able to identify with Scar, but that he refuses to.

Second, the film alludes to a settler perspective other than Ethan's. Martin Pawley (Jeffrey Hunter) is Ethan's adopted, part-Cherokee nephew, who accompanies his uncle on the search, despite the fact that Ethan rebukes him as a "blanket head." Martin's first person voice-over narration of a letter to Laurie (Vera Miles), who waits impatiently for him at home, establishes a voice that counters Ethan's. Martin's perspective is continually overshadowed by that of his uncle, even when he narrates his own letter. Ethan, it is clear, has understood the exchange that resulted in Martin's marriage to a young Indian woman named Look, when Martin did not. Ethan's superior knowledge and his intense, relentless search dominate the film.

Douglas Pye contends that *The Searchers* fails in its critique of racism in the Western because it cannot transcend the genre's conventions. He writes, *The Searchers*

> probably goes further than any other Western in dramatizing and implicating us in the neurosis of racism. But in wrestling as a Western with the ideological and psychosexual complex that underlies attitudes toward race, it is working *within* almost intractable traditions of representation. Much of what is fascinating about *The Searchers* lies in the resulting struggle to control point of view—in fact, its multiple forms of incoherence. (229)

Whether it is read as a parable of the actual historical situation of Indians (or, as some have argued, African Americans) in the United States, the film is clearly a meditation on the nation's ability to expand its notion of Americanness to include "others." As Brian Henderson argues, the film is rife with the rhetoric of the adoption and assimilation of ethnic others. Figures of otherness—Martin and Debbie—are made acceptable by Ethan's ultimate grudging acceptance. Yet Ethan, the white patriarch, refuses to acknowledge, much less endorse, his own internalization of otherness—evident in his vast knowledge of the Comanche—and he withdraws from the frontier community.

Obsolete, like the Indians he detests, Ethan chooses the frontier, his prospects unclear. If the sparse locations the white community occupies are already overly civilized for Ethan and require too much compromise of self, where can he wander off to, if not the locations occupied by the equally nomadic Indians? Rather than cope with the loss of self implied by assimilation into the frontier town, he chooses to surrender his identity by melting into the landscape which, paradoxically, visually equates him with the Indians.

The shift in Ford's emphasis on identification from *Stagecoach* to *The Searchers* shows that racial essentialism underlies the national narrative. Yet the latter film's ambivalent critique of national identity lays the groundwork for the nonessentialist Western. Contemporary African American and Irish Westerns begin from the premise that racial categories underlie the rhetoric of national identity. They emphasize acts of identification that both lay bare those racial dynamics and destabilize them.

NONESSENTIALIST WESTERNS

The nonessentialist Western emerged from within New Black Cinema and Irish Cinema for two reasons: first, the genre directly addresses questions of race and national identity. All of these films draw from the revisionist Westerns of the 1970s, including *Little Big Man* and *Buck and the Preacher* (Poitier 1972) and share common elements with the Western revival films that followed on the success of *Unforgiven* (Eastwood 1992). The second reason for the interest in the Western as a genre relates to the social upheavals of the 1970s and 1980s, which encouraged artists to revisit the meanings of Irishness and blackness. The Western was adapted to Irish and African American contexts because the genre depicts "a point in history when the project of the creation and settlement of a new society was underway" (Dyer 33).

Nonessentialist Westerns like *Eat the Peach, Posse, Into the West,* and *The Disappearance of Finbar* begin to address, with some trepidation, what postnational identities might look like in a globalized world. In all of these films, identifications that disrupt and diversify conventional racial and national identities are played out through mise-en-scène and point of view. These films also make ironic references to the Western genre and depict frontierism in terms of entrepreneurship, which provides a cautionary link to the late twentieth century global economic system.

Below I examine four films: *Eat the Peach, Posse, Into the West,* and *The Disappearance of Finbar.* In each film, character identification contributes to the erosion of the frontier narrative and to the dissolution of rigid ideas about race and national identity. They make evident Jane Tompkins's observation that the genre "signals a powerful need for self-transformation" (4). They also indicate a powerful desire on the part of filmmakers to transform notions of self. *Eat the Peach* uses metaphors of motion to consider the nature of the contemporary frontier, especially for characters buffeted by the effects of globalism. *Posse* and *Into the West* rewrite the Western by introducing other "others" (African Americans and travelers) into Western landscapes. *The Disappearance of Finbar* chronicles the disappearance of the Western subject altogether.

LINEAR LANDSCAPES, CIRCULAR DESTINY: *EAT THE PEACH*

Filmed on the Bog of Allen in County Kildare and titled after T. S. Eliot's poem "The Love Song of J. Alfred Prufrock," *Eat the Peach* offers its viewers a mise-en-scène mired in visual oppositions, as John Cawelti's characterization of the Western as a genre concerned with dichotomies would predict. In this film, the linear openness of the bog is contrasted with circular enclosure. Recurrent images of trains that rumble through a rural-industrial wasteland suggest the openness of unfettered geography and unobstructed views. A nearly uninhabited landscape grows out of the black bog, the fossilized repository of Irish culture.[2] By contrast, the Wall of Death built by the film's main characters, Vinny (Stephen Brennan) and his brother in law Arthur (Eamon Morrisey), is a wholly enclosed structure whose contours hint at the circular motion it contains. These contrasts between openness and enclosure, and linearity and circularity, do not lend themselves to easy interpretation, however. The circular Wall of Death is associated with speed, abandon, and transcendence, whereas the trainscape scenes simply remind viewers of the vast nothingness that the characters call home.

Cowritten by director Peter Ormrod and producer John Kelleher, *Eat the Peach* incorporates elements of the Western and the road movie, and especially its biker subgenre. Because of its motorcycle-crazed protagonists, *Eat the Peach* might well be compared to *The Wild One* (László Benedek 1953) and to *Easy Rider* (Dennis Hopper 1969), cult films that recreate the American cowboy as hippie biker. In referencing and revisiting the Western, *Eat the Peach* suggests that ethnic nationalism is no longer viable in 1980s Ireland. It nevertheless sounds a cautionary note regarding the identities that may replace those predicated upon ethnic nationalism: there is both optimism and uncertainty in the film's conclusion. The film sheds light on the economic forces at work on the contemporary frontier, the new global village. These tensions are expressed in the identifications practiced by Vinny and Arthur as they build their Wall, and by Boots (Niall Toibin), an entrepreneur/con man and "Amerophile" who assists them (Byrne 153). In this plucky tale of survival, Irishness as a national identity disintegrates in the face of economic and social forces, leaving the characters to construct and perform identities out of available objects, the same way they construct the Wall of Death. The Wall is an apt symbol of contemporary Ireland's economic prospects, since Vinny and Arthur intend to market it as a tourist attraction. Between 1990 and 2000, the number of overseas tourists to the island doubled.

In the opening scene, Arthur is fired from his job at Nagushi, Inc., a multinational corporation run by Japanese managers. In solidarity, Vinny stops going to work repairing farm equipment. After watching a scene from the Elvis Presley film *Roustabout* (John Rich 1964) at the local pub, an inebriated Vinny decides to build a Wall of Death. Arthur agrees to help build the structure adjacent to Vinny's house on the bog. Through their quirky friend Boots's connections, Vinny and Arthur take jobs driving a truck for a powerful underworld figure named Boss Murtagh; they smuggle liquor and petrol to Northern Ireland to earn the money for construction materials.

The Wall enjoys a healthy attendance on opening day—even the parish priest gives his blessing. A government minister, who is Boss Murtaugh's brother, dedicates the structure. Soon after Vinny's skillful performance begins, however, the audience grows fearful that the shaky viewing platform will collapse. They abandon the structure. No investors come forward to finance Vinny and Arthur's next project: to re-build the Wall in sections to take on the road as a traveling act. Frustrated, Vinny sets fire to the Wall and lets it burn, telling his wife Nora, "It's mine and I can burn it." In the meantime, Arthur visits Boots, who is in the hospital after being beaten by Boss Murtagh's thugs for stealing from the Boss.

The final scene takes place several months after the climactic fire when a recovered Boots visits Arthur, Vinny, and Nora at their newly rebuilt home. Vinny has built a garden near the ruins of the Wall and now farms tomatoes. Arthur runs a shop in town. In the film's concluding moments, Vinny and Arthur unveil their newest project—a homemade helicopter—to an admiring audience of Boots, Nora, and Vinny and Nora's two children. The makeshift helicopter never leaves the ground, but low camera angles frame Vinny and Arthur at the controls against the sky, as if they are airborne.[3]

In keeping with the Western's visual treatment of individuals as tiny figures dwarfed by a hostile and empty landscape, the film establishes a visual contrast between modern and traditional, and between progress and stasis, by juxtaposing shots that emphasize the empty, linear bog (traversed by the trains that Vinny races against on his motorbike) and shots that highlight the circularity of the Wall of Death.

That conflict between linear and circular motion (the latter associated with transcending the bog) is also evident in scenes that directly address the role of foreign capital and culture in contemporary Ireland. The multinational corporation that fires Arthur and shuts down without apparent regard for its Irish workforce is a Japanese firm. After a speech given by the company's CEO, who announces the plant closing and mentions a "provision for redundancy payments," the CEO and his wife leave the site in a helicopter that flies past an array of international flags adorning the entrance to the plant. Contrary to logic, the circular motion of helicopter blades, which rhymes with the circularity of the movement inside the Wall of Death, seems to be the only way to escape the economic collapse of this outpost on the globalizing frontier.

But the film repeatedly undermines these oppositions of circle versus line, and movement versus stasis. Although a conflict is established between Irishness and foreignness when the company CEO cites communication problems as a reason the plant closed, soon after the closing that intercultural tension is attenuated. Bunzo (Takashi Kawahara), a Japanese co-worker who has befriended Arthur and Vinny, rides off with the two of them to watch Japanese sumo wrestling videos. They play-act as samurai warriors with Bunzo. Soon, however, Bunzo is summoned by yet another helicopter that looms ominously over the three men. Although Bunzo envies their life in Ireland—he tells Arthur and Vinnie "you're free here, you have a good life, good air"—he must leave. Bunzo's comments thwart any presumption that Ireland, because of its apparent economic dependency, is backward in relation to Japan, an industrial superpower. He presents the two Irish men with a videotape player; "a present from the Japanese people." The gift symbolizes the destructive economic impact of the Japanese company and yet it also remains a source of pleasurable access to popular culture—including the Japanese sumo genre and familiar Western films. Whether the three men's lives are better as a result of Japan's exploitation of Ireland's new openness to the industrialized world remains a poignant question.

After the Japanese depart, Vinny and Arthur pursue an alternative identification with American popular culture. Vinny and Arthur idolize Elvis Presley. This identification proves to be just as ambivalent as their immersion in Japanese popular culture. Identifying with Elvis's Americanness does not translate into motion, progress, or a liberating escape from the Irish bog, despite the fact that Elvis's biker film *Roustabout* is the inspiration for building the Wall. Whereas Vinny serenades his friends with a one-guitar rendition of "Heartbreak Hotel," Arthur watches the film and mouths lines of dialogue along with Elvis as the latter delivers a lesson on style and international trade to the college boys who challenge him.

> ELVIS: "Cycle" is out; it's either a bike or a motorcycle.
>
> MAN: Made in Japan, huh?
>
> ELVIS: That's right. Made in Japan.
>
> MAN: What's the matter, aren't American cycles good enough for you?
>
> ELVIS: You don't dig world trade, college boy? After all that economics they tried to shove into you?

The scene ends when Elvis dismounts and dispatches two of the three men with karate moves; he claims that his martial arts prowess "goes with the 'cycle.'" Arthur impersonates Elvis, copying the karate gestures, just as he had with the Japanese samurai. (Not surprisingly, like Elvis, Arthur and Vinny ride Japanese motorcycles.)

Vinny doesn't pay much attention to the *Roustabout* video until the scene in which Elvis watches a stunt rider on the red, white, and blue Wall of Death. Vinny literally becomes mesmerized, silently watching the scene in the pub and later at home. He rewinds the tape several times to hear the expert tell Elvis that "the takeoff point is 40"—the speed at which the motorcycle begins to climb the Wall. Whereas Arthur imagines himself as Elvis the street fighter, Vinny pushes the fantasy further, imagining himself variously as Elvis, as the motorcycle rider Elvis watches, and as the engineering expert who understands the physics of the death-defying Wall. Vinny's ability to fluidly transcend culture and location in pursuit of the ideal ride on the Wall of Death is comically questioned, however as he realizes late in the construction process that the "40" of the film means 40 *miles* per hour, not 40 kilometers per hour.

Elvis's image as a virile American singer, actor, and motorcycle enthusiast offers an appealing masculine identity for men like Arthur and Vinny, who have been downsized in the new economy. In his analysis of the white working-class male fascination with Elvis, Eric Lott finds that the purpose of impersonating Elvis is "to provide 'magical resolutions' to [the] social pressures confronting contemporary white working-class masculinity" (1997 197). White men perform Elvis for a number of reasons: through him, they become fetishized erotic and exotic objects because Elvis is the signifier of white male ventures into black culture (1997 200–04). Elvis impersonation "is an extension of a working-class male dynamic of social puissance through physical assertion" (1997 216).

Elvis mimicry allows Vinny and Arthur to promote themselves as performers, to push their physical limits, and to imagine transcending their luckless bog existence. They adopt his swaggering physicality and street-wise masculinity. Their Great Wall of Death becomes the theater for their own "enlarged and fantastical embodiment" (Lott 1997 213), a fact made evident when they buy mail-order costumes with their names emblazoned on them for opening day. Yet the men are not merely hapless comic impersonators of Elvis's hybrid hypermasculinity. Vinny does sweep his wife Nora off her feet after singing Elvis songs to her. He rides her into the house on the motorcycle and carries her off to bed. During the night, however, the motorcycle leaks fuel. When the fuel is ignited by a space heater, the explosion destroys their house. Apparently, Elvis's energy cannot be contained within a humble Irish home.

Vinny and Arthur's performances of identity are a source of comedy as well. Their Wall of Death, based on a principle of repetitive motion, requires that they head for the Ireland-Northern Ireland border in order to finance its construction. Like their *Easy Rider* predecessors, Arthur and Vinny smuggle contraband. But their dangerous cross-border runs are treated comically. In one scene, Arthur navigates the "unapproved roads" into Northern Ireland on his motorbike, communicating with Vinny, trucker-like, through a CB radio. Arthur's absurdly small motorized tricycle is framed against the truck, rendering their communication system, which pays homage to *Smokey and the Bandit* (Hal Needham 1977), laughably incongruous.

These border escapades raise the specter of another dimension of Irish identity that Arthur and Vinnie flout, namely the violence associated with the IRA. On their final run, Vinny and Arthur must drive a farm tractor covered with bales of hay that mask an enormous petrol tank. When their vehicle runs out of fuel across the border, they enter a pub in search of diesel fuel, but are ostracized by the insular crowd gathered there—a group of men whose secretive manner and style of dress link them to the IRA. Outside the pub, British troops inspect the abandoned tractor with a high-tech robot. They "detonate" it, believing it to be a bomb. The men from the pub shake Arthur's hand, telling him, before beating a hasty retreat, "I don't know who you are, but I'm glad to have met you." This scene not only undercuts Vinny and Arthur's claims to Elvis-like outlaw masculinity, but it also shows that the very same notion of powerful masculinity has already been claimed by the insular, backward IRA, the overeager British military, and the gangster Boss Murtagh. Vinny and Arthur do not readily conform to any of these masculine models.

The scene also emphasizes that the border between Northern Ireland and the Republic functions only ironically as a national boundary. In fact, it enables a thriving smuggling business in a number of fairly innocuous products like fuel and liquor. When Vinny tells Nora about the job, he tells her he is engaged in "truck haulage; International truck haulage, sort of."

Despite Arthur and Vinny's hero worship of Elvis, the character with the greatest investment in American identification is Boots. Clad in cowboy boots, a ten-gallon hat, and a string tie, Boots personifies the cowboy wanna-be. According to Terry Byrne, an Irish connotation of the term "cowboy" is "someone who bluffs his way through life [. . .] [and] Boots is a cowboy in both meanings of the word" (153). He tells a local waitress that he helped promote a young female singer in Memphis. He similarly advocates on behalf of Vinny and Arthur and signs on as the Wall's manager-promoter. Speaking with the twang of a Texas oil man—which he alternates with an Irish accent—Boots tells them: "Amigos, it's great to see somebody in this crazy goddamned country get off their ass and show a bit of enterprise." Boots lures the television reporter to the Great Wall's opening day, though, of course, he himself misses the opening because his greed and recklessness has landed him in the hospital with a severe beating (he has been watering down Boss's liquor). When he confesses to Arthur that he has never been to the United States and that his rugged American persona is a cowboy performance, Arthur replies, "Everybody knows that." No one expresses surprise at Boots's performed identity.

The tension between identification with other cultures—with their crass commercial values and seductive popular culture—and the characters' "authentic" Irish roots is never resolved. Reinventing themselves at the film's conclusion as a shopkeeper and a farmer, Arthur and Vinny choose solidly Irish occupations, rooted in their local community and in the land. They have not, however, relinquished the aspirations developed through their identifications with others.

Their refusal to limit their ambitions to the local cultural context—or to the geography of the bog—is signified in the return of the helicopter, previously associated with the Japanese corporation. The helicopter reiterates the dynamics of circular and upward motion that Vinny and Arthur experienced through riding their motorcycles on the Wall of Death. The film's closing images of linearity versus circularity question the viability of the frontier metaphor itself. How does the notion of the empty frontier, and vast space, translate to the present day circumstances of these characters? That question remains unresolved amidst these images of equilibrium and movement.

Although it is not yet fully functional, the helicopter, which is a notoriously unstable machine, promises to fulfill Vinny and Arthur's desire for both speed and containment. The Wall of Death and the helicopter blades should not be viewed as symbols of a defeatist attitude; the motorcycle must "take off" and leave the ground when it spirals up and around the Wall. The helicopter is a device that depends on the rotation of blades, but that rotation functions in the service of lifting the vehicle off the ground. The circular, inward-looking Wall and helicopter are apparatuses that permit Vinny and Arthur to transcend the physical limits of their everyday lives—including economic and geographical constraints. The spiral motion contrasts with the oblivious progress of forward motion (characteristic of the train), but it also endows circular motion with an external goal.

In *Eat the Peach*, Vinny and Arthur choose to become innovators and *bricoleurs* rather than be defeated by the international economic forces that buffet the Irish economy. They innovate not to fix their identities—as Japanese samurai or American cowboys or Elvises—but to continue to adapt the lessons of their performed identity for their local context. The open ending refuses to mire Arthur and Vinny in their bogland (now also a garden), but, instead, leaves them in a state of suspended animation. The film's conclusion is an ambivalent image of two men who are not entirely in control, which provides a metaphor for Irish identities during the massive social upheavals of the 1980s. The conclusion also reflects a desire to transcend the limitations of the Irish geographical and social landscape.

POSSE AND *INTO THE WEST*: POPULATING THE WESTERN WITH OTHER OTHERS

Mario Van Peebles's *Posse* and Mike Newell's *Into the West* are contemporary Westerns that reassess the genre by populating its landscape with "other others." By situating African Americans and Irish travelers in the West, and in the Western, they complicate the racial dynamics of conquest as well as essentialist notions of race and national identity.

In *Posse*, Mario Van Peebles writes African Americans into the historical landscape of the U.S. West and projects them into the cinematic space of the Western. Van Peebles's restorative project should be examined not only in relation to the genre, but also in light of the representation of the American West within African American culture.

An important difference between African American and European American geopolitics is that, for African Americans, geographical movement often is linked to cultural theft or seen as necessary for survival, not as an opportunity for a new beginning. In African American literature and film, the North American continent possesses no frontier; the enforced act of re-creating a civilization away from home was already an aspect of the experience of enslaved Africans. Furthermore, setting out for a frontier is not necessarily synonymous with an erasure of the past: the history of enslavement cannot be repressed, and racial difference generally remains an issue in the American context.

In African American literature, opportunity, hope, and freedom often are figured through a migration North (out of slavery into freedom) or a movement east (in the form of a mythical return to the African continent). The North American continent embodies great ambivalence. Whereas slave narratives imagine the North as a locus of freedom, twentieth-century authors like Ralph Ellison, Ann Petry, and Toni Morrison counter the image of the industrial North as the Promised Land with depictions of the harsh realities of racism. The American South represents a place of trauma and dispossession in novels like Morrison's *Beloved.* But it can also represent home (which is brought to the foreground in Ellison's *Invisible Man* and Morrison's *Song of Solomon*), and a place where there are tangible links to ancestors from Africa (evident in Julie Dash's *Daughters of the Dust*).

African American interventions in the Western genre span the twentieth century and encompass literary and film representation. Oscar Micheaux's *The Homesteader* represents an early consideration of frontier imperialism from an African American perspective, as Michael Johnson has argued. Micheaux published the novel in 1917 and adapted the story as the first African American feature film in 1919. Johnson contends that the protagonist, Jean Baptiste, is a complex Western hero because he embodies Micheaux's belief in the contemporary doctrine of racial uplift. Influenced by the ideas and activities of Booker T. Washington, Micheaux felt that African Americans needed heroes to look up to. Thus, Micheaux's project "neither condemns nor critiques the dominant culture myth of manifest destiny but rather claims a share of the spoils for the enterprising Black man" (Johnson 362).

African American Western films that emerged later in the century were influenced, in turn, by the civil rights movement, the slow integration of Hollywood cinema, and the powerful imagery of the Blaxploitation hero. During the 1960s, actor Sidney Poitier achieved great success as an iconic figure for white audiences during the civil rights era—he played an educated, upper-class black man in film such as *A Patch of Blue* (Guy Green 1965), *In the Heat of the Night* (Norman Jewison 1967), and *Guess Who's Coming to Dinner* (Stanley Kramer 1967).

In 1972, Poitier directed and starred in the African American Western *Buck and the Preacher*. The film departs from Micheaux's saga of the enterprising black man on the frontier by emphasizing wagon train leader Buck's (Poitier) political commitment to the black community. The film depicts the westward migration of a group of former slaves after the Civil War and the actions of a murderous gang of nightriders who are intent upon returning them to slavery. Even the Preacher (Harry Belafonte) abandons his wicked ways and joins the struggle, helping Buck and Ruth (Ruby Dee) thwart the racists and marshal the wagon train of former slaves to freedom.

The influence of the black action film is similarly apparent in the comic western *Adios Amigo* (1976), directed by Fred Williamson and starring Williamson and Richard Pryor. Williamson was a former football hero who made his name as an actor by appearing in Robert Altman's *M*A*S*H* (1970), and in Blaxploitation films such as *That Man Bolt* (1973) and *Black Caesar* (1975). Williamson established his own production company, Po' Boy Productions, in 1974.

Buck and the Preacher and *Adios Amigo* are source texts for Van Peebles's *Posse*. The former presents a plot that is similar to that of *Posse*: Buck is determined to help a wagon train of former slaves to a safe location on the frontier. White supremacists are equally intent upon returning these people to slavery; at several points they lament the dying way of life in the agricultural South, where black bodies are sorely needed to plant and harvest the crops. The Indian chief who charges Buck eight dollars per head to guarantee safe passage eventually comes to the rescue of Buck and the Preacher (a good-bad man turned good), as they fight the white supremacists.[4] In a similar vein, *Adios Amigo* depicts greed and racism as intertwined: a white man pays a gang one hundred dollars to hound Williamson's character from his land.

Stylistically, these two 1970s African American westerns lay the groundwork for Van Peebles's film. A visual device links all of these films to conventions of historical representation, as scenes end in still images that are converted into grainy, sepia halftones (*Buck and the Preacher*), or Western action paintings (*Adios Amigo*), or black and white photographs (*Posse*). All three are indebted to Sergio Leone's Westerns, particularly in the visual style and the costuming of the main character. In his wide-brimmed black hat with silver concho shells and tightly fitted black clothing that leaves his chest exposed, Williamson's Big Ben seems to take a cue from both Melvin Van Peebles's Sweetback and Leone's Man with No Name. Ben, in turn, establishes the sartorial standard for Mario Van Peebles as Jesse Lee.

Thematically, the films vary in important ways, however. The two 1970s films focus on male action heroes to the virtual exclusion of their membership in a community. Buck works on behalf of the wagon train that came from St. Anne's Parish, Louisiana, yet he is a loner rather than a member of the community. Like Jesse Lee, he will enlist the support of Indians in the area: their tribal chief delivers a diatribe against white colonialism that aligns the Indians with the dispossessed African Americans. In *Adios Amigo*, Williamson's Big Ben is primarily out to save himself (often from Pryor's Sam) but manages to assist Pryor's scheming crook from time to time. By contrast, *Posse* manages to both single out the exceptional figure of Jesse Lee, clearly a reluctant hero, and to embed him within diverse communities that include his posse and Freemansville.

Several African American films of the 1990s do not share *Posse*'s focus on the Western genre, yet they reiterate the contradictions implicit in the idea of the Western frontier from an African American perspective. Films by Charles Burnett (*To Sleep With Anger* 1990) and Carl Franklin (*Devil In a Blue Dress* 1995 and *One False Move* 1992) are set in post–World War II Los Angeles, and they all depict the way that the corrupt underpinnings of the racist Deep South (the region from which the main characters have migrated) remain a force to reckon with. In short, in African American views of the West, the frontier is inevitably informed by the history of slavery in the American South.

Posse addresses the implications of slavery for the concept of national identity by tracing the westward journey of a group of African Americans who have escaped military conscription in Cuba. They travel first to New Orleans and finally to Freemansville, a town located in the Western Territories. The saga of Jesse Lee and his posse begins in 1898 during the Spanish American War. The film opens with Jesse and his cohorts serving the United States in an imperial war as part of a segregated battalion. The Tenth Cavalry, under the Custeresque dandy Colonel Graham (Billy Zane), has been suffering a war of attrition. Black soldiers on the front lines bear the brunt of enemy attacks as well as their commander's capricious sadism. Sent on a suicide assignment, Lee's men ambush the enemy and find a cache of gold coins, the true object of Graham's mission. The men take the gold and flee Cuba for New Orleans with Graham in hot pursuit. Eventually the former soldiers (and several friends they acquire in New Orleans) follow Jesse into the Territories. Consistent with his outlaw-hero status, Jesse has a score to settle there: his father, King David, was murdered in the midst of establishing the town, the victim of a group of violent white racists from nearby Cutter's Town. Like the African American novels and films cited previously, *Posse* poses the movement west not as a new beginning but as a necessary step in order to right past wrongs.

Alexandra Keller describes *Posse* as a postmodern Western that is highly self-conscious about its generic heritage (2002), and R. Philip Loy places the film in a category of racially conscious contemporary Westerns (2004). *Posse* does more than show the purposeful westward migration of African Americans, of course. First, like *Buck and the Preacher*, it reminds audiences about an episode in African American history that has been all but erased in the dichotomous racial configuration of the Western: African Americans who served in the Civil War often moved west to become the Buffalo Soldiers fighting the Indian Wars.

Second, the film charts the important population movements of Western culture in the form of an allegory. The Cuban setting and the capture of Spanish gold establish the posse's exploits as a counter-conquest; their path retraces those of European conquerors from Columbus to Cortez. Their movements highlight the existence and significance of the African Diaspora, represented in key locations such as Cuba and New Orleans and retrace the triangular geometry and geography of the Atlantic slave trade. In their escape from Cuba, Lee's men hide in coffins that they have emptied of the remains of men from the Tenth Cavalry. The symbolism of their plight—they, like enslaved Africans before them, are "dead" passengers en route to the American South—becomes apparent when, during this re-enactment of the middle passage, Lee reads a narrative recounting the struggles of Nicodemus, a slave. The name has complex resonances, but clearly signifies new beginnings: the Biblical Nicodemus was a follower of Christ who questioned the ability of a human being to be born again. Nicodemus was also a legendary slave, an African prince who was brought to the Americas in 1692 and who later purchased his freedom. The 1864 song "Wake Nicodemus" by composer Henry Clay Work recounts another story of Nicodemus, a slave who prophesied a Black Exodus out of slavery. Nicodemus, Kansas, was a town founded in 1877 by former slaves from Kentucky called "Exodusters." (Interestingly, the town went into decline after the railroad passed it by, which parallels the plot of *Posse*.)

Posse self-consciously asserts a different history of western expansion than the one offered by most of its antecedents, including the works of John Ford and Sergio Leone that it cites. This history of an African American Western experience is based upon the internal diversity of the growing nation as well as the central role of an African American oral tradition that is based upon identification and memory, rather than official history. The film's frame device of direct narration drives this point home through the words of a character who claims to have been an eyewitness to the events depicted in Freemansville (a fact revealed only at the end of the film).

Posse opens with the reminiscences of an elderly African American man played by Woody Strode, a veteran actor who appeared in more than seventy films, including John Ford's *The Man Who Shot Liberty Valence* (1962). When Strode castigates people for forgetting the past, he is not blaming them for cognitive deficits but, rather, chiding those who may have political motivations for memory lapses and reminding all viewers of the repercussions of forgetting. This assertion validates his narration, as the opening scene moves between verifiable facts and the narrator's acts of remembrance. The narrator—who is referred to as the storyteller in the credits—notes that nearly one-third of cowboys were former slaves and that there was a large contingent of black people among Los Angeles's first settlers: 50 percent of the population. "Never hear their stories," he observes pointedly. For him, history must include those stories. He presents the story of Jesse Lee as fact, a claim bolstered by his presence as a young boy at the time of Jesse's return to Freemansville.

Even though he was not privy to the experiences Jesse and the men had in Cuba and New Orleans prior to their exploits in Freemansville, the storyteller identifies with Jesse Lee and his posse's activities. This imaginative frame encompasses all the events of the film. His expansive identification with Jesse guides viewers through the film. In the opening scene, he fuses oral history and silent photographic artifacts, stating that pictures don't lie and implying that words do. He introduces a series of photographs of black cowboys that culminates in a picture of "the original posse." Strode directs the audience to a staged tableaux of the characters that appears in the film's diegesis: they are now subjects of his memory and of cinema.

In other words, the film visualizes and enacts the storyteller's imaginative reconstruction of events. Acting as a go-between for the audience, the narrator urges viewers to use his identification with Jesse to imagine a different history of the West. Using actual photographs of Buffalo Soldiers and cinematic fictions to re-construct official history reiterates the lesson of John Ford's *The Man Who Shot Liberty Valence*: history becomes inseparable from legend. However, in Ford's film, when the newspaper printed the legend of Ranse Stoddard, it established a name, a set of events, and a figure of identification for the historical record. Here, the narrator must do the same things outside official history. His storytelling works through different media. His contributions as a version of the African griot (a tribe's historian and storyteller) are both aural and visual.

According to Douglas Pye, this self-conscious attention to historiography is one way that *Posse* deviates from the classical Western. The classical Western must remain unreflective, suppressing the relation between the historical West and present-day circumstances because "the condition of its viability is not to know the present" (Pye 111). Another indication of the film's historical self-consciousness is its title. Donald Hoffman points out that the title not only recalls the 1975 film of the same name, but also cites "the use of the word in rap to denote a close-knit group of intensely loyal friends, somewhere between a clique and a gang" (49). Hoffman writes that this conflation of past and present represents "naïve historiography" (49) and hints at the film's "suspiciously mixed purpose" (48). The plot invites a reading of Jesse Lee as a man

FIGURE 5.1. As Jesse Lee, Mario Van Peebles reprises his father's role as Sweetback and references classic Western figures. Playing Papa Joe, Melvin Van Peebles has Jesse's back. Courtesy of Photofest.

whose time has not *yet* come: for instance, Hoffman notes direct reference to the 1991 Rodney King beating (51). Hoffman conjectures that, in creating Jesse Lee, Mario Van Peebles is responding to criticism of his father's film *Sweet Sweetback's Baadasssss Song* (Melvin Van Peebles 1970).

Although I differ with Hoffman's claim that *Posse*'s historiography is naïve, he makes a useful point when he compares the film to *Sweetback*. *Posse*'s broad temporal and geographical scope reflects a desire to not only connect past and present (drawing attention to subjects that official history has erased) but also to link various forms of otherness within a global context of colonialism. Whereas Mario Van Peebles's casting of recognized figures from 1970s film and television such as Pam Grier, Nispey Russell, Issac Hayes, and Melvin Van Peebles signals the survival and continuity of African American artists, the appearance of the Hudlin brothers and Aaron Neville suggests the emergence of new generations. *Posse*'s broader historical connections are sweeping and sometimes obvious: for example, several characters, including Jesse's lover Lana (Salli Richadson), possess African and Native American ancestry. But, I would argue, these attempts to link diverse histories represents a desire to tell a story with the epic appeal of the traditional Western and its saga of survival against all odds.

Returning to Hoffman's comparison of *Posse* and *Sweetback*, an examination of the point-of-view structures and modes of character identification in the two films reveals the ways that *Posse* seeks to move beyond traditional ideas about national identity, including those associated with black nationalism. In *Sweetback*, Melvin Van Peebles's badman hero follows in the tradition of Br'er Rabbit, Slave John, and Stackolee. Initially, he lacks a political consciousness. He lives within a community of sex workers because he has been raised in a brothel. Sweetback allows himself to be taken to the police station as a formality: the sex club owner regularly does the police the favor of supplying a black male body as a "usual suspect." When Sweetback witnesses the police beating of Moo Moo, a black activist, he defends Moo Moo and they escape, but Sweetback immediately abandons any pretense toward organized resistance, rejecting Moo Moo's inclusive "we."

During these early scenes, Sweetback is rarely a figure of identification for the audience or for other characters. Women look at him with desire in mind, not identification, and the boss and police officers merely see him as a black body serving their purposes. The extent of Sweetback's alienation from the world around him is suggested in the dearth of point-of-view shots. The scene of his arrest is shot from the interior of the police car; the images blur into a montage of city street life and neon signs. Over the course of his flight from the police, however, Sweetback becomes politicized. In this section of the film, the camera depicts Sweetback's actions but still limits his optical point of view: viewers are presented with a fragmentary perspective on the triumphs he enjoys and the betrayals he suffers.

What provides unity amidst this fragmentation is the sense that Sweetback is a symbol for the African American community. Like Buck in *Buck and the Preacher*, Sweetback is not shown to be a member of that community, but, instead, its icon. Sweetback functions as a heroic figure of identification for the characters in urban Los Angeles who circulate stories about his legendary exploits, and who give mock interviews to the camera. They refuse to tell investigators whether they have seen him or not. They don't know him personally; their solidarity is race-based. In the parlance of the film, like Sweetback, they have "had enough of the Man."

As Sweetback makes for the Mexican border, a chorus sings, urging the injured warrior on. At this moment, the point-of-view structure, which has emphasized the way characters identify with Sweetback, finds its counterpart on the soundtrack. The powerful voices encourage and praise their hero; through the music the audience shares the perspective of the African American community, not that of Sweetback. His goal of escape may be clear, but his emotions and psychology remain opaque. Thus, the chorus solidifies the importance of the identifications practiced by one star of the film—listed in the credits as "The Black Community."

Although Mark Reid, Ed Guerrero, and Jesse Algernon Rhines situate this film in the black action or Blaxploitation genre, *Sweetback* can also be read as a black nationalist Western. Along these lines, Manthia Diawara writes, "[Melvin] Van Peebles thematizes Black nationalism by casting the Black Community as an internal colony and Sweetback, a pimp, as the hero of decolonization" (1993 9). Rhines notes that the Blaxploitation hero's ethos of individualism defied contemporary political practices: his "super-cool individualism was the antithesis of what contemporaneous Black political organizations, like SNCC, the NAACP, or SCLS supported for Black people" (46). These contradictions reflect an ongoing tension among the desire for heroic icons (in the vein of filmmaker Oscar Micheaux's early-twentieth-century works), the community orientation of African American political organizations, and the box-office draw of the black action hero in the era of the New American Cinema and its plethora of radical antiheroes.

Balancing these contradictions, Mario Van Peebles's *Posse* explicitly creates a community context for his Western hero, the good-badman Jesse Lee, whose name invites comparison with Jesse James, a legendary and historical white "Robin Hood" outlaw. Initially Lee and his cohorts are the victims of Graham's state-sanctioned violence against African Americans and Cubans; then they must thwart the extralegal white supremacist violence of the Cutter's Town gang to protect the citizens of Freemansville.

In joining forces with Jesse, the men of the posse, perhaps unwittingly at first, chart a course that moves them beyond the oppositional politics of self-defense to a constructive identification with Freemansville's diversity. "Posse" itself is an ambiguous term, signifying a group representing official interests of law enforcement or, alternately, a group alliance or outlaw gang. In this film, the posse's position changes: first it represents a group of opportunistic thieves in American uniforms, then it becomes a populist band akin to *The Magnificent Seven* (John Sturges 1960) or to Robin Hood's merry men, as defenders of the oppressed. The double meaning of the word connotes that their values are righteous, despite their lack of official status.

Jesse functions as a figure of identification for all the men in his posse, ranging from those who served with him in the military in Cuba to the low-life denizens of New Orleans they pick up along the way. The white member of the group, Jimmy (Steven Baldwin), convinces fellow gambler Father Time (Big Daddy Kane) to follow Jesse because the journey offers excitement and action. The childlike Obobo (Tom Lister) follows Jesse like a dutiful son. Unlike the others, who drink liquor and enjoy the services of prostitutes in New Orleans, Obobo drinks only milk and does not consummate a heterosexual relationship until he reaches Freemansville, when Jesse himself is reunited with his childhood friend and lover, Lana. In *Posse*, men identify with Jesse as a leader and a comrade who is present and working among them, not as a larger-than-life mythic fugitive like Sweetback or the distant but caring wagon master Buck.

Scenes that suggest that Jesse is a mature adult but that the men of his posse are immature underline the importance of the men's identification with Jesse. Two scenes involving swimming holes attempt to draw a sharp contrast between the youthful homosociality of the gang and Jesse's mature heterosexuality. Before their arrival at Freemansville, the posse hides out in Diablo Pass. Jimmy playfully kicks Father Time—a paragon of sartorial style—into the swimming hole. The revelry begins as Father Time's sputters, "your ass is mine" to which Jimmy responds, "here it comes" and leaps into the water. A montage of naked torsos and behinds follows. A partially naked Jesse remains respectably out of the fray. Later, after reuniting with Lana, Jesse visits another swimming hole with her. Afterward, they make love and Lana highlights the reproductive implications of their coupling by telling him that the potential creation of new life, can drive "Mr. Death" away. Significantly no one in Jesse's posse forms a relationship with a woman; only he seems preordained to take the place of the film's absent patriarch, his dead father King David.

These relationships of identification modify the relationship of leader to the community seen in earlier African American Westerns like Micheaux's and Poitier's and the Blaxploitation Western of Melvin Van Peebles. Jesse is a hero and a member of the community; in contrast to these earlier figures and to his father, he is an outlaw-messiah figure who exists as a legend and a historical figure at the same time. This embodiment of Jesse as hero and human is signaled at the most important moment of identification in the film: when Jesse hands the Nicodemus narrative to the young boy who becomes the storyteller. This moment of identification with Jesse Lee as a historical human being is the truth claim and the impetus for the film's challenge to official history and offer of an alternative history.

Choosing Woody Strode to narrate a film concerned with the tensions between African American identities and the claims of U.S. citizenship presents another historical critique, one aimed at Hollywood.[5] With this casting choice, Van Peebles indicts Hollywood's effacement of African Americans as historical actors and as film actors. *Posse* identifies the Western as a purveyor of colonialist history. Film references reinforce this theme. When pursuing Lee's men, Graham's counter-posse emerges from a train car, reminiscent of *Butch Cassidy and the Sundance Kid* (George Roy Hill 1969) and *The Wild Bunch* (Peckinpah 1969). Merging signature devices of other directors, such as the fanning of the gun, drawn from Sergio Leone spaghetti Westerns, and the use of John Ford's framing, creates a visual palimpsest of Western conventions. These influences suggest that, far from being a separatist black nationalist project, reconstructing an African American West involves incorporating the legends and visions of European and American cinematic history.

In its alternative history, the film offers complex communities of resistance. Unlike *Sweetback*'s "Black Community," no racially monolithic community exists in *Posse*. Lee's inner circle includes white, African American, and Native American comrades. Freemansville, established by

King David as a haven, is home to African Americans and Native Americans. It also harbors Carver, a black entrepreneur who identifies with the European Americans of Cutter's Town and actively works to undermine Freemansville's self-sufficiency. Carver has been working with the Cutter's Town men to drive out African American residents. The acts of terror that have been driving the townspeople out are part of an elaborate plot to buy up land to sell at a profit to the encroaching railroad.

In keeping with its depiction of harmonious, diverse communities such as the posse and Freemansville, *Posse* blames capitalism and individualism for the racist violence that haunts Freemansville. This explanation resonates with the defining features of slavery: an economic system that enriched a few (primarily but not exclusively white Europeans and Americans) by appropriating and trading in the labor and lives of Africans and African Americans. The film also expands the notion of community beyond racial essentialism, including the black nationalism of earlier black Westerns. The posse contains a trusted white member, who, in a reversal of the tradition of black sacrifice—still evident in Eastwood's *Unforgiven*—is killed.

The forces that threaten Freemansville's survival emanate from within the community, not only from the hostile white supremacists. This plot line offers a materialist analysis of racism, since an important underlying motive for the racist acts is mercenary. The film equally indicts black and white characters engaged in greedy speculation. Furthermore, this plotline links the conquest of the American West to the economic basis for all New World conquests: gold.

Mario Van Peebles's *Posse* recreates the cowboy loner as a man defined by his involvement in the community. However, this community has little to do with the official nation (the men of his posse leave Cuba as fugitives), nor does it uphold an essentialist notion of black community. Finally, the importance of identification for individual and social transformation is driven home when viewers learn that the storyteller witnessed the posse's defense of Freemansville and that Jesse himself—both a fact and a legend—chose him to be the recipient of the Nicodemus narrative.

COWBOYS AND INDIANS: *INTO THE WEST*

Like *Posse*, *Into the West* places other others into a Western context to pose questions about the conquest narrative. Written by Jim Sheridan and directed by Mike Newell, the film uses magical realism to tell the story of two Irish traveler boys who venture from their Dublin housing estate into the west of Irish legend and American cinema. The film opens on the beach on the west coast of Ireland where a mysterious white horse trails an old traveler (David Kelly) who makes his way to Dublin to see his son-in-law John Reilly and grandsons Tito and Ossie. This magical white horse—associated with the boys' dead mother Mary Reilly and with Celtic legend—takes a particular liking to Ossie and carries the boys westward. They journey across Ireland on the back of the white horse, tracked by John/Papa Reilly, who has availed himself of the help of the travelers, and by the police. In the film's concluding moments, the horse carries Ossie out to sea near the beach where the film opens. Miraculously, he does not drown but is rescued by a vision of his mother, who died in childbirth. Reunited, the family burns Mary's caravan in order to free her spirit.

As with most Westerns, landscape and geography are essential. At the film's opening, the open beachscape and bucolic scenes predominate, as the old man takes his caravan and the horse to Dublin on narrow, empty roads. As he nears Dublin, a jumbo jet appears on the horizon (out of nowhere, it seems) swooping over the prancing horse. The jarring moment violates the peaceful pastoral aesthetic and introduces a theme of interpenetrating modes of apprehending reality.

The scene also introduces a motif implicit in the film's subject matter: *Into the West* foregrounds travel and modes of transport, juxtaposing the primitive and the postmodern. The main characters walk, ride horses and trains, use elevators to carry horses to apartments high in the sky, and are tracked by airplanes and helicopters. Each mode of transportation is successively more modern, industrial, and sinister, until finally the helicopter represents a militaristic technology of surveillance. (The helicopter assumes a darker meaning here than it does in Ormrod's *Eat the Peach.*)

The film's mise-en-scène functions according to the Western's framework of opposition: countryside versus cityscape. The film's visual style alternates between the magic realism of traveler culture and the realism of urban Dublin. Stanley Orr writes that

> Newell incorporates a grittily Realistic presentation of Dublin's poor with a highly Formalistic treatment of Irish myth and legend. At the same time he synthesizes the generic conventions of fantasy with those of the American Western, ultimately reclaiming a genre traditionally complicit with imperialist expansion. (4)

FIGURE 5.2. A primitive form of transportation whisks two Irish traveler boys away into a not-so-wild west in Mike Newell's *Into the West.* Courtesy of Photofest.

Orr and Joe Cleary, both of whom offer acute, incisive readings of the film, distinguish between the west of the Irish Literary Revival—the Irish-speaking west of Ireland—and the west of American film—the Wild West. They agree that the Wild West engulfs the Irish west in a familiar form of cultural imperialism, of which the boys' identification with cowboys and Indians is a symptom:

> It is as if the reality of the American western has colonized the Irish imaginative and cultural landscape. *Into the West* therefore recognizes a central problem in Irish Cinema [. . .] the conflict between foreign and indigenous representations of Ireland certainly lurks behind Tito and Ossie's propensity to see their native landscape through the filter of the American western. (Orr 15)

According to Cleary, however, the Western's absorption of Irish mythology is complicated by the fact that cinema becomes the only means of escape from contemporary industrialized culture.

> [T]he journey "into the west" [is] a desperate quest for the very conditions that make romance possible in a world that seems continually to extend the conditions that make it impossible [. . .] in the world of advanced capitalism the simulacra of escape which is cinema itself is the only "escape" that remains. (Cleary 1995 157)

The point that neither Orr nor Cleary addresses is that the escape—whether it be into the Wild West, into the Irish West, and/or into cinema—is represented both as desirable and possible because the two boys have developed their empathic resources and their skills at hetopathic identification through a lifetime of watching films. This mechanism ensures the continued role of cinema as an escape into the West.

In this film, cinematic identifications affect the world of the present day. As I discuss in the opening of this chapter, while the boys are on the lam, after reclaiming *Tir na N'og* from the unscrupulous County Meath businessman who steals him, the boys enact their Western fantasy, at several times crying out "heigh-ho, Silver, away!" They are delighted to learn they are wanted criminals. Tito buys a newspaper and finds a published reward notice, which confirms that they are "real cowboys, wanted dead or alive!" In search of a bed for the night, the boys are turned away from a hotel proprietor who asks if they are travelers. They respond, "No, cowboys!" The hotel manager retorts, "we don't take cowboys." They also perform an "Indian" dance around their campfire when they learn they are wanted men. Subsisting on chocolate and beans, they mix the codes of victor and vanquished.

They again identify with Indians during a scene in which they take cover from the rain at the Savoy, a small-town movie theatre, and screen *Back to the Future III* (Zemeckis 1990), a film that shares *Into the West's* penchant for juxtaposition and fantasy. On their third night on the road—the first is spent in a railroad boxcar, the second in sleeping bags around a campfire—they duck into the Savoy at closing time and proceed to make it their shelter for the night. They watch, and later re-enact with the authorities, "a sequence of Indians chasing time-travelers across the Monument Valley desertscape" (Orr 17). Their subsequent actions render the boys not passive consumers of Hollywood fantasy but "active textual poachers who con-script the Western genre" (17). In doing so, they rewrite the positions of winner and loser.

Lance Pettit sees Ossie and Tito's use of fantasy as bewilderment, not reappropriation. He finds the boys' confusion regarding their identity troubling: "the film seems to present the Travelers as being outlaw cowboys, but this blurs into attributes of Native Americans" (2000 128). This blurring leads to a problematic overgeneralization.

> The Travelers are represented as the "Other" of mainstream Irish society and its contemporary culture, but the film works to humanize and reclaim them in a liberal gesture as somehow representative of Ireland's postcolonial status, of its confused identity in a postmodern world. (2000 129)

Because the film opts for a "universal" representation of cultural dislocation, Pettit concludes that it exacerbates the problems that arise from comparing Irish, Native American, and African American experiences with colonization (129).

But, the point may be precisely that the film exposes the ways that the Western is not a universal representation of anything, no matter how hard it tries. The Western is exposed as the national narrative of European Americans in the United States, disseminated on a global scale by Hollywood. That fantasy cannot work in translation: the travelers finally absorb the myth of the Western into their own myths. The intervention of an all-too immediate Irish reality forces Ossie to complain about the tedium of playacting. The temporary acquisition of identities offers little comfort when they are chased by helicopters through a small town. Ossie complains, "I'm tired of being a cowboy. We'll be cowboys tomorrow."

This self-consciousness about identities as performances is simultaneously a recognition that the boys are not able to "conscript" the genre to whatever their needs might be. Throughout the film, Ossie has immersed himself in pretense and in identifications with others, both by choice and under duress. He turns in a performance as one of fifteen Murphy children, he performs the "bad breathing" rendition of "Danny Boy" at Tito's behest when they beg for money in Dublin, and he dons the initially pleasurable cowboy role. Ossie finally sloughs off the Western fantasy, an indication that he understands the limits of cinematic identification.

Furthermore, the cinema's iconic figures of cowboy and Indian are replaced by the continually evolving identities the boys have fashioned for themselves through various performances. The police track them because they are horse thieves, having reclaimed *Tir na nOg* from Hartnett, and having interrupted a nationally televised equestrian event. They have committed a property crime and were filmed in the act. While their identification with Butch, Sundance, and the Indians may signify an overly general notion of Irish postcoloniality and the cultural imperialism of American film, the boys also confront the particular, internal schisms in Ireland. Those divisions depart from stereotyped representations of Catholics versus Protestants to focus on the tensions between settled culture and the travelers, as representative of those who have benefited from Ireland's entry into the global economic system (Hartnett) and those who have not (The Murphys, the Reillys). For audiences outside of Ireland at least, this shift complicates notions of Irish national identity.

A materialist critique of Irishness as a monolithic national identity is apparent in the links between Dublin law enforcement officers, who coerce John Reilly into signing away the horse, and the wealthy businessman Hartnett, who represents his privileged position as that of all of Ireland by naming his (stolen) property "National Security." The state wields the power to assign the property of others to the wealthy classes, who are then able to represent their private bounty as the nation's safety and equity (drawing on a second meaning of "security"). Although the Reillys' return to the extended family of the travelers may be utopian (Cleary 159–60), the film's analysis of contemporary economic relations is anything but naïve. Like *Posse, Into the West* suggests that the differences between the wealthy and the exploited can be explained by differential access to the political and economic system, not to essential racial identities.

The second way the film critiques the nation is through the figure of Mary Reilly. Cleary writes at length of the function of figure of the Great Mother in *Into the West*, concluding that the film's invocation of a supernatural spirit-mother masks the political regressivity of the return to traveler culture. For Cleary, the use of Mary represents a "dissatisfaction with modernity" and "a sign of a utopian desire for some alternative to the world as it presently exists" (1995 150). The loss of the mother, Cleary argues, represents a "loss of confidence in the possibility of realizing a world radically better than the present" (1995 167). In this view, the film's return to the west is a retreat into the past, one facilitated by the nostalgia of the Western genre.

Cleary's arguments are persuasive. Yet the mother figure permits at least one other reading, one associated with the more conventional link between mothers and Ireland, as discussed in chapter 3. The renegotiation of national identities during the 1980s and 1990s has elicited a reconsideration of the woman as a national symbol. Ossie's inability to remember or imagine his mother indicates the dispossession of the travelers—as the nation's orphans—or, perhaps, of all children of his generation. It suggests a need to renegotiate national symbols so that they encompass a traveler vision, and that of the most recent generation.

The possibility that a community might be created from a diversity of images arises from John Reilly's assumption of shared experience of otherness. When John Reilly claims "there's a little traveler in everyone" the gesture is all encompassing; but rather than gathering all the dispossessed under one umbrella, the statement posits an appropriately decentralized and organic postmodern metaphor: a kernel of internal dissent. Connecting with others is not seen to evolve from a commitment to a totalizing system, as required by a national ideal but, rather, a postmodern decentralization of hybrid identities that overlap in small ways, and in small narratives.

FADE TO WHITE: *THE DISAPPEARANCE OF FINBAR*

A film concerned with the contemporary implications of frontier mythologies, *The Disappearance of Finbar* makes explicit the importance of its Western motif in the opening scene. The film's protagonist Danny Quinn (Luke Griffin) is a four-year-old child, called to the stage with his friend Finbar Flynn (Jonathan Rhys-Meyers) to help sing "The Roscommon Cowboys," the signature song of Finbar's father's country-and-western band. The camera pans across an audience filled with people wearing ten-gallon hats and western shirts as they drink and sing along. This scene of self-conscious performance would be at home in Robert Altman's *Nashville* (1975).

Directed by Sue Clayton from a screenplay she co-wrote with Dermot Bolger (based on his novel, *The Disappearance of Rory Brophy*), *Finbar* blends the obsessive search narrative of John Ford's *The Searchers* with Danny's coming-of-age saga. The 1990s, as presaged by *Eat the Peach*, witnessed the increasing influence of global capital on Irish culture. This small town's residents, including Danny, vicariously invest their hopes of transcendence—or, at the very least, their fantasies of leaving for a better life elsewhere—in favored son Finbar. Thus Finbar's strange disappearance at about eighteen years of age not only produces a great outcry but also leads to a cult of Finbar celebrity worship that begins locally but eventually becomes a global phenomenon. Three years after Finbar's disappearance, Danny receives a phone call from him and sets out on a geographical and psychological quest that rivals that of Ethan Edwards. Danny travels to Sweden, Finland, and the Arctic Circle in search of his friend. (The film's unexpected use of Swedish locales reflects its status as a "Euro-pudding" project, financed through a number of sources including The Irish Film Board, Channel Four, the Swedish Film Institute, and the Eurimages fund.) As in Ford's classic Western, the search reveals more about Danny and his identity than it does about the object of his search, Finbar.

The film uses music to establish Finbar as a figure of identification for other characters. "The Roscommon Cowboys" is a repeated motif, as is "The Ballad of Finbar Flynn," and finally, the tango. The cowboy song, performed in the film's first scene, indicates Finbar's celebrity status in his community and among his friends: from earliest childhood, he is a lightning rod for their fantasies of heroism. Despite a few voice-overs by Danny, Danny's own identification with and attraction to Finbar is so overwhelming the audience may find Danny's identity obscure. Even his dreams revolve around the moment when he joins Finbar to sing "The Roscommon Cowboys." After Finbar's disappearance, he dreams that Finbar falls off the stage during the performance. Unable to relinquish his own emotional connection to Finbar—Danny cannot disentangle his quest for Finbar from a search for his own identity.

Finbar embodies the small town's fantasies of escape, their desire to be elsewhere, even their dreams of being someone else. Early on, however, Finbar rejects this role. A talented football prodigy, Finbar is sent home in disgrace from a team trip to Switzerland, to the dismay of his parents and Danny. Finbar's mother, washing his clothes as she sings "Roscommon Cowboys," cries in disappointment. Reunited, Danny and Finbar mock the adults by singing a parody of the same song in exaggerated American accents. Finbar asks Danny, "Have you been faithful?" and Danny denounces Finbar for not taking advantage of his opportunity to "get out of this hole." But Finbar rebels against his obligation to play the hero for the benefit of others.

In fact, Finbar consistently resists the expectations that others have for him. At school, the boys and their schoolmates prepare for exams. But Finbar makes the case that doing so is pointless: remaining in Roscommon and leaving for somewhere else are both dead ends. He challenges the teacher, asking, "What makes you think there's any point to this?" The chronically unprepared Finbar defiantly questions bothering with taking exams, since the process represents "the chance to be unemployed in six different languages." Fleeing the school after the teacher calls him a "self-opinionated intellectual pygmy," Finbar escapes to a virtual reality game at the video arcade, losing himself in a simulacrum of a frontier shootout. Finbar's adolescent existential crisis is thus linked to the internationalization of Ireland. He rejects the frontier mythologies that see promise in geographical relocation and new beginnings.

Finbar and Danny's bond is ruptured when Danny discovers that Finbar has been sexually involved with Katie (Lorraine Pilkington), the girl Danny cares for. Worse still is the fact that Finbar doesn't care about Katie; he uses her to get Danny upset. He expresses his boredom with "trivial women" and then tells Danny he can have her in the most insulting way: "She's all yours, Danny; doggy style's her best."

Finbar's disappearance after a rowdy night with his friends stirs up emotions in his small town and ultimately the event becomes an international cause célèbre. Finbar literally fades into the night as he walks on a motorway flyover as if he is walking on a tightrope. His body is never found. A group of family and friends forms the Finbar Flynn Action Committee (FFAC). Becoming internationally famous because of his absence, Finbar becomes what Douglas Pye calls a "fantastic impossible figure."

> At the heart of the Western, too, is the figure of the transcendent hero—most common in juvenile Westerns and dime novels [. . .] often a point of reference even when he is absent. At his simplest he is something like the Lone Ranger [. . .] unencumbered by most human limitations. (121)

Over the course of the next three years, the FFAC faithfully holds vigils and collects information about Finbar sightings. On the third anniversary of the disappearance, a dance is held. Decorations include balloons marked "Finbar phone home," a reference to Spielberg's *ET* (1982), another element that establishes Finbar's magical and alien status. (To bring the reference full circle: ET the extraterrestrial watches John Ford's *The Quiet Man* [1952] on television during his brief sojourn on planet earth.)

As with "The Roscommon Cowboys," music comes to define Finbar, but this time *as* an absence. Tellingly, "The Ballad of Finbar Flynn" becomes an international hit. A music video takes a country-and-western ballad structure, adds comical new-age lyrics, and embellishes it all with an edgy, Goth-style singer and production design. The film's ironic stance on the commodification of Finbar's absence is clear in the humorous send-up of the shallow music industry. Danny views the finished product in a setting that itself suggests the unmooring of national identities: he sees the video as he stands in the small Irish town's Vietnamese restaurant, the Lucky Star.

The other-worldliness of the space marks the moment when Danny sees the video as extraordinary. The restaurant's modernist interior is unlike any other setting in the film and does not appear in the film until this scene. Unadorned blank walls enclose emptiness, spatializing loss and foreshadowing Danny's journey into an empty, white landscape in search of Finbar. Leaving the restaurant, Danny sees the video on five monitors in a store window. Contemporary technology and musical fashion transmit the community's mourning process, in commodity form, to the world.

The formal emphasis on space strengthens a narrative motif in which Danny develops an awareness of the political significance of spatial organization. Danny has been working in construction and has learned that shaping empty space is a political matter that is tied to the issue of cultural and national boundaries. The British Empire's geographical reach is expressed through architecture, which is made evident when Danny ponders aloud a colonial snafu: "a hospital down the road, built like an Indian barracks and, in India, a barracks that resembles an Irish hospital."

In contrast to these situated structures, Finbar's song transports his persona along new, global nodes of connection: he moves from being a local figure of identification to that of transnational celebrity. Finbar emerges as a postmodern wanderer, an emblem of loss, and a locus for religious and supernatural beliefs. The song recounts the fact that Finbar never waved goodbye and mentions Finbar sightings around the world—from Tralee to a Greek monastery. In a hilarious merger of belief systems, the lyrics question whether he was taken into heaven or abducted by aliens.

The video and song catapult him (or, more precisely, his absence) into international fame. Like Pye's "fantastic impossible figure," Finbar enters the realm of myth on a global scale. Whereas his Roscommon neighbors cast him (and themselves) as cowboys, the youth culture that creates and responds to the song casts him as world, or even galactic, traveler.

After the video goes global, Danny receives a phone call from Finbar; he is in Stockholm and tells Danny he has seen the pop video. The remainder of the film charts Danny's journey out of Ireland to the Arctic Circle, an eastward trek through and to a hostile and empty landscape. Hitching rides to the northernmost, frozen expanses of Sweden, the musical motif shifts again. This time, Danny and his fellow travelers engage in a running joke regarding the tango.

The tango, a musical style closely associated with Argentina, becomes a hotly disputed cultural possession in a most unlikely place: the contested (but visually indiscernible) border between Sweden and Finland. At a truck stop, a Swedish man asks Danny if he dances the tango. Danny is puzzled and replies, "Isn't it unusual?" The man continues, "No, my wife, we dance. We, the Swedes make the tango." The next driver Danny rides with guffaws over this mistaken attribution of the tango to the Swedes, stating that: "Even a child could tell you it was a Finn invented the tango."

The drastic reconfiguration of geography—Danny's unsettling blend of Ireland, Sweden, Finland, and Argentina—is underscored by visual images of an increasingly empty landscape. The transnational tango and the white landscape seem to render the notions of culture and nationality moot.

As Danny moves farther north, certain foundations for identity, such as language and music, are exposed as unreliable tricks. Danny thinks he is communicating with the Swedes and Finns, only to be taught that linguistic signifiers are duplicitous. The joke regarding the tango's provenance points out that, on this frontier, culture doesn't seem to function as a point of origin or as a possession. Although there seems to be an intense rivalry between the Swedes and the Finns, Danny can't tell the difference between them. A number of characters seem to be foreigners passing through, which is emphasized by Danny's experiences as a hitchhiker. The Stockholm apartment Finbar once lived in now houses a Chinese couple. Everyone seems unexpectedly out of place, as evidenced in the exchange Danny has with one of his drivers.

DRIVER: English?

DANNY: No, Irish. Swedish?

DRIVER: No, Finnish.

Each one mistakes the other's national origin, assuming they are from the neighboring, and dominant, country (England, Sweden). On the Sweden/Finland border, the driver assures him that he will find Finbar in the nearby town of Pavovayarvy. Danny tells him he is looking for an old friend, and the driver repeats the phrase "Finbar/tango/famous." The connection with a bar and music seems perfectly in keeping with Finbar's history—he is associated with yet another musical performance. Jumping on a truck with workers from an oil rig, Danny learns that they all know of the Finbar–tango connection. After they drop him off, and he reaches the crest of a hill, he discovers that they have led him to the "Finn Bar," a remote, western-style outpost where the tango is the music of choice.

Culture and geography thwart Danny's search. Rather than finding hostile others on the frontier, he must confront his desire for and identification with Finbar. The mise-en-scène externalizes Danny's inner landscape. The blindingly colorless terrain offers him nothing but self-reflection.

That is, until a young Laplander named Abbi (Fanny Risberg), takes him in. He befriends her grandmother Johanna (Sif Ruua), a kindred spirit whose identifications tend toward classical Hollywood: she obsessively watches Hollywood musicals such as *The Great Ziegfeld* (Robert Z. Leonard 1936), *Damn Yankees* (George Abbot and Stanley Donen 1958), *Call Me Madam* (Walter Lang 1953), and *Porgy and Bess* (Otto Preminger 1959).

Surprisingly, Danny finally encounters Finbar at the Finn Bar. Finbar has become an electricity farmer, building windmills to generate power. He tells Danny he left Ireland because, when he fell off the motorway and landed in a truck of beets, "I felt so completely free." Like *The Searchers'* Debbie Edwards, he is not thrilled to have been found. He is surprised that "in three years you couldn't find anything better to do than to find me." When Finbar tells Danny, "it's time to get your own life," the latter replies, "I sure wouldn't want yours," a statement that contradicts everything the film has revealed thus far. Danny has indeed appropriated Finbar's life—traveling to Sweden, finding the tango bar, and even falling for Abbi, who previously had been involved with Finbar.

Finbar abandons Danny a second time, vanishing in the early hours of the morning. But this time, Danny decides to settle down, to stay with Abbi and Joanna on the frozen frontier, defining his home far from his geographical origin. He announces in a voice-over that he feels "a deep inescapable sense of home" but that he imagines Finbar finding the same sense of peace: "I like to think he went home."

Danny comes of age by relinquishing his attachment to Finbar and by leaving Finbar to the role of the wandering Western hero. In rewriting the *Searchers, The Disappearance of Finbar* shifts the focus from the drama of recovering a lost loved one to the underlying desire for that recovery. Danny learns to construct an identity around an absence. But that seems to be consistent with the age he lives in, with its shifting national identities and global youth culture. He finds only emptiness in the escapist frontier identity associated with Finbar. He no longer identifies with the Roscommon Cowboy because, in all that whiteness, there is nothing there with which to identity.

CONCLUSION

The films in this chapter emphasize the importance of identification to the nonessentialist Western. They unsettle the genre's underlying assumptions about race and national identity by focusing on alternatives to the colonial practice of dividing subjectivities into us and them. The films reconsider the status of the Western as historical epic, relocating its conventions and repopulating its landscapes in order to lay bare the way its logic of radical individualism and colonial conquest depend upon essentialist identities.

CONCLUSION

Film Identification and Postmodern Identity Politics

Throughout this book, I have analyzed the ways that Irish and African American films between 1980 and 2000 challenged essentialist discourses of gender, sexual, racial, and national identity. I have argued that these films articulate the problems and possibilities of postmodern identities-in-progress through identification, a process whereby characters attempt to get out of themselves and engage with or perform otherness. I have also suggested that there are political ramifications stemming from the depiction of these character identifications, which decenter and undermine traditional Irish and African American identities.

These analyses suggest that, although characters may come to acknowledge the fluidity of identity, their identifications with otherness and performances of identity do not in themselves allow them to transcend their specific historical situations. Those situations are, in many cases, scenarios of violence and social marginalization. Characters' identifications often shed light on the institutional structures in which the characters function and, as such, serve as critique. But, even when characters enact their identities as postmodern performances, moments of heteropathic identification do little to effect lasting, structural change.

Musical identification may serve as a useful metaphor for the shifting subject positions of postmodernity, but even those acts of identification and performance rarely provide a basis for intervention in the material circumstances of the characters' lives. For example, in *Danny Boy*, Danny eventually comes to identify with both victims and killers, but the violent acts he undertakes are orchestrated by other, more powerful actors committed to exploiting the Irish national conflict. The music of the African American jazz tradition invites Bleek and Shadow to perform the music of others (for others) and make it their own. Although experiences of musical virtuosity that permit characters to suspend themselves temporarily may generate aesthetic breakthroughs, they do not provide the tools to alter the social grammar of *us* and *them*, of racial difference, or of gender-marked childhood and adulthood (in the case of Troy).

In most of the films discussed in this book, narratives center on character growth and development. Despite the political undercurrent informing Irish and African American cinemas, these narratives channel political solutions through individual, personal experiences. This is unsurprising, given the popular audiences these films seek. The films in chapter 3 depict women who challenge maternal identifications through their problem pregnancies. While the women defy the essentialism implicit in those maternal myths, their acts of defiance reach a limited on-screen audience and remain, for the most part, individual gestures.

In chapter 4, paternal identifications dominate the process of masculine identity formation within the gang community. These films reject fraternal bonding, with its promise of egalitarianism and democratic, rather than hierarchical, relations, in favor of paternal bonding because, they imply, brotherhood inevitably devolves into competitive rivalry. *Cal* and *The Crying Game* explore the radical potential of cross gender identifications, yet both films consign their protagonists to physical, if not psychological, incarceration. In the contemporary Western, the contest of self versus other and of winners versus losers is challenged as both historical record and cultural mythology. But, with the exception of the highly self-conscious *Posse*, a film that takes pains to link its hero to various diverse communities, the films depict the changes induced by characters' multiple identifications as individual or family matters.

The significance of these patterns of character identification extends beyond their textual function. These films tell stories about identity crises, about people who feel estranged from their communities, yet also trapped by their cultural location. They seek to remedy the problem by taking on the attributes of another person, believing that they have the ability to inhabit and understand all forms of otherness. The characters succeed to the extent that they may develop a more sophisticated analysis of their own situation; the films succeed to the extent that they expose the strengths and limitations of both of the models of identity that the characters encounter: essentialism and postmodern performance.

What most of the films reveal is the absence of a political context that would harness these desires to identify with, and as, others. In other words, the postmodern perspective on identity that the characters adopt is itself constrained. "There is something disingenuous about the polarized choice offered by postmodern theory," writes R. Radhakirshnan, "[between] essentialism or a pure subjectless process" (2003 19). These films tend to shore up the duality. They reinforce the notion that inhabiting otherness will not only contribute to redefining difference, renegotiating the divide between subject and object, and reconsidering the boundaries between self and other but also function as politics. Engaging in such gestures of identification is only the first step, however, and these films rarely bring these experiences of identification into a public, political context.

Postmodern identity politics have privileged the anti-essentialism that these films rely upon as a central narrative element. Radhakrishnan cautions, however, that such a stance cannot be effective politically, precisely because it only operates as critique. "The postmodern 'turn' taking shape exclusively as critique would have us believe that a critique is subjectless and that identity is a bad essentialist habit to be discarded by a hardheaded theory" Radhakrishnan contends (13). The alternative position, represented by Marxist counter arguments, views "postmodern pleasure [as] nothing but the most abject form of mystification by the commodity form" (13).

These films carve out a middle ground, using the pleasures that popular culture has to offer its audiences to convey an anti-essentialist critique of race, nation, and gender. Characters question traditional models of identity and explore what it means to perform their identities, yet performances alone are inadequate to the project of enacting a new identity politics. In an era increasingly defined by the dissolution of national identities, it makes sense that individual acts that deconstruct identity might be seen as the only recourse for characters trapped by violence, by lingering colonialist discourses, and by existential ennui. Yet the shifting politics of identity are enacted in these films only as critique; characters too often experience paralysis, not progressive change.

An important conclusion that emerges from the study of these contemporary film cultures is that certain dilemmas posed by postmodern theories of identity—and, in particular, the difficulty of organizing coherent, or at least effective, political activities—are shared conundrums. The troubling implications of postmodernity's emphasis on deconstruction for group politics are central questions in Irish and African American films made between 1980 and 2000. Fragmentation and paralysis bedevil the characters in these films even while they attempt to propel themselves into otherness through acts of identification.

NOTES

INTRODUCTION

This book engages in dialogue with, and is indebted to, scholars in Irish film—a field mapped out by Anthony Slide, Luke Gibbons, John Hill, Martin McLoone, Kevin Rockett, Elizabeth Butler Cullingford, Cheryl Herr, Ruth Barton, Brian McIlroy, Diane Negra, and Lance Pettit, among others—and African American cinema—an area illuminated by the work of Thomas Cripps, Ed Guerrero, Mark Reid, Manthia Diawara, Valerie Smith, Ronald Green, Paula Massood, Jane Gaines, Melvin Donalson, William R. Grant IV, and Wahneema Lubiano, among others.

1. The importance of a few prominent directors in securing recognition for a national cinema can be seen in the example of Australia (Peter Weir, Gillian Armstrong, Peter Jackson, and Jane Campion), Iran (Abbas Kiarostami, Mohsen Makhmalbaf, and Dariush Mehruji), and even, arguably, in the case of the New American Cinema of the 1970s (Arthur Penn, Robert Altman, Francis Ford Coppola, and Martin Scorsese).

2. *Imagined Communities: Reflections on the Origins and Spread of Nationalism* (London: Verso, 1982).

3. See Robert Burgoyne's *Film Nation: Hollywood Looks at U.S. History* (Minneapolis: U Minnesota P, 1997). Also see Susan Hayward's "Framing National Cinemas." *Cinema and Nation.* Eds. M. Pais and S. Mackenzie (London and New York: Routledge, 2001) 88–102.

4. Both the novel and film are surprisingly experimental for works that enjoyed mainstream success. Almost a concert documentary, Parker's film is a series of full-length performances punctuated by scenes of the band's internal dis-

putes. The novel relies almost entirely upon Dublin vernacular, transliterated song lyrics, short sentences, and choppy paragraphs. The privileging of dialogue to the near exclusion of all else runs throughout Doyle's novels. For a discussion of the "oral bias" in Irish writing, see David Lloyd's *Anomalous States: Irish Writing and the Postcolonial Moment* (Durham, NC: Duke UP, 1993).

5. This manner of representing working-class Dublin speech is reminiscent of Southern American and African American "dialect" or vernacular transcriptions in poetry and fiction by both white and black American authors. The representation of vernacular may be an attempt at authenticity but can also depict those who use it in a demeaning manner. For a discussion of Ireland as a bilingual culture and Irish English as a hybrid form of English, see John Cronin's *The Anglo-Irish Novel, Volume 1: The Nineteenth Century* (Belfast: Appletree Press, 1980).

6. For a discussion of black musical forms and their relationship to material circumstances, see Andre Craddock-Willis, "Rap Music and the Black Musical Tradition: A Critical Assessment," *Radical America* 23.4 (1989): 29–38, and Tricia Rose's response to it in *Black Noise: Rap Music and Black Culture in Contemporary America* (Hanover and London: Wesleyan UP/UP of New England, 1994) 23–26. Jazz musician Miles Davis famously repudiated the notion that the blues and jazz represent the music of the downtrodden or are expressive of black angst, arguing for their aesthetic rather than political character.

7. See Eric Lott, *Love and Theft: Blackface Minstrelsy and the American Working Class* (New York and Oxford: Oxford UP, 1993).

8. Seamus Heaney, "The Tollund Man," *Selected Poems, 1966–1987* (New York: Farrar, Straus and Giroux, 1990) 39–40.

9. Lauren Onkey, "Celtic Soul Brothers," *Éire-Ireland: A Journal of Irish Studies* 28.3 (1993): 147–58.

10. An ethno-musicologist might point out that bluegrass and country music developed in part from the music played by Irish and Scottish immigrants who settled in the Appalachian region.

11. James McKelly discusses the relation between Caine and Cain at length in "Raising Caine in a Down Eden: *Menace II Society* and the death of Signifyin (g)," *Screen* 39.1 (Spring 1998): 36–52.

12. The term was coined by Richard Corliss in "Boyz of New Black City," *Time* 17 June 1991 137.24: 64–68 to refer to the work of Spike Lee, Bill Duke, Michael Schultz, John Singleton, Matty Rich, and Mario Van Peebles.

13. Jacquie Jones, "The New Ghetto Aesthetic," *Wide Angle* 13.3–4 (1991): 32–43. The films Jones gathers under this rubric include: *New Jack City* (Mario Van Peebles 1991); *Boyz N the Hood* (Singleton 1991); *Straight Out of Brooklyn* (Matty Rich 1991); and *A Rage in Harlem* (Bill Duke 1991).

14. See Edward Mitchell's "Apes and Essences: Some Sources of Significance in the American Gangster Film." *Film Genre Reader.* Ed. Barry Keith Grant (Austin: U Texas P, 1986) 159–68.

15. For an excellent dissection of capitalism's contradictions in Capra's *It's A Wonderful Life*, see Patrick McGee's *Cinema, Theory, and Political Responsibility in Contemporary Culture* (Cambridge: Cambridge UP, 1997) 7–15.

16. For a study of the early-twentieth-century urban gangster, see David Ruth's *Inventing the Public Enemy: The Gangster in American Culture* (Chicago & London: U Chicago P, 1996).

17. Fatimah Tobing Rony, *The Third Eye: Race, Cinema and Ethnographic Spectacle* (Durham and London: Duke UP, 1996). E. Ann Kaplan, *Looking for the Other: Feminism, Film and the Imperial Gaze* (New York and London: Routledge, 1997). Diane Negra, *Off-White Hollywood: American Culture and Ethnic Female Stardom* (London and New York: Routledge, 2001). Gwendolyn Audrey Foster, *Performing Whiteness* (Albany, NY: SUNY P, 2003).

18. Kaja Silverman, *Threshold of the Visible World* (London and New York: Routledge, 1996).

CHAPTER ONE. IDENTIFYING OTHERS

1. Within nationalism studies, Benedict Anderson's now-famous model of nation as "imagined community" received a great deal of critical attention because of its insistence upon the constructed character of national identity. In an important addendum to Anderson, Philip Spencer and Howard Wollman point out in that the historical and political context for imagining community is important. "Blood and Sacrifice: Politics Versus Culture in the Construction of Nationalism," *Nationalisms Old and New*, ed. Kevin Behony and Naz Rassool (London and New York: MacMillan/St. Martin's, 1999) 87–124. Similarly, the context and means of deconstructing national communities, a process the films I write about are engaged with, is also important.

2. The term "marvelous realism" comes from Haitian writer Jacques Stéphen Alexis. See Michael Dash's "Marvellous Realism: The Way Out of Négritude," *Caribbean Studies* 13.4 (1973): 57–70. Irish travelers, also referred to (pejoratively) as *tinkers* or *Irish gypsies*, are a nomadic indigenous Irish minority group, estimated at about 25,000 to 35,000 individuals (some 5,000 families).

3. The film may be making reference to the 1890 attempt to establish an all-black state in western Oklahoma; in citing the Nicodemus story, it also references Nicodemus, Kansas. See chapter 5 for further discussion.

4. For a discussion of this process in U.S. films about American history, see Robert Burgoyne's *Film Nation: Hollywood Looks at U.S. History* (Minneapolis and London: U Minnesota P, 1997).

5. See Fintan O'Toole's "Going Native: The Irish as Black Indians," *The Lie of the Land: Irish Identities* (London and New York: Verso, 1997) 18–30. Also see Noel Ignatiev's "White Negroes and Smoked Irish," *How the Irish Became White* (New York and London: Routledge, 1995) 34–59. Also consult Luke Gibbons's "Synge, Country and Western: the Myth of the West in Irish and American Culture," *Transformations in Irish Culture* (Cork: Cork University Press, 1996) 23–35. Ireland's anti-colonial struggle has been aimed at the establishment of a nation-state; uprisings since 1798 indicate a legacy of resistance to English colonialism (with assistance from Spain and France) and demands for an Irish nation-state. Those demands have been forwarded by a variety of diverse political and militant organizations, although the culmination of colonial resistance in the early twentieth century coincided with the increasing power and authority of the Catholic Church. The establishment of the Irish Free State in 1922 did not end anticolonial activism because partition divided the island. In African American history, calls for establishing a social, economic, and sometimes geographically separate culture have also assumed state-based forms, relying both on re-claiming particular geographical territories (in Africa and in the United States) or civic spaces (full U.S. citizenship).

6. See L. P. Curtis, *Apes and Angels: The Irishman in Victorian Caricature* (Washington: Smithsonian Institution, 1996).

7. Brian Dooley, *Black and Green: The Fight for Civil Rights in Northern Ireland and Black America* (London and Chicago: Pluto Press, 1998) 1.

8. His book was entitled *Races of Britain* (1862). Dooley, 2.

9. L. P. Curtis, *Anglo-Saxons and Celts: A Study of Anti-Irish Prejudice in Victorian England* (New York: Conference on British Studies and U Bridgeport, 1974) 84.

10. See his Introduction to Tracy Mishkin's *The Irish and Harlem Renaissances* (Gainesville: U Florida P, 1998).

11. Catholic emancipation was aimed at eliminating the last of the Penal Laws, sixty-one statutes passed by the Protestant Irish Parliament between 1691 and 1760. They restricted Catholic rights of land ownership, participation in government, and practice of religion, although historians disagree about the degree of enforcement among peasants as opposed to the Catholic aristocracy. M. Patricia Schaffer, whose Web site contains the text of these laws, writes, "By deliberately defining the haves and the have-nots, the politically powerful and the oppressed, on the basis of religion, these statutes had a profound effect, not only

on the eighteenth century, but on the subsequent history of Ireland to the present day." (http://www.law.umn.edu/irishlaw/intro.html) The Catholic Emancipation Act of 1829 eliminated the last of these laws by allowing Daniel O'Connell, a Catholic, to assume the seat in the English Parliament to which he had been elected.

12. The Act of Union dissolved the Irish Parliament and brought Ireland under the aegis of the English Parliament. In 1845 the potato blight ravaged the crop. By fall it was apparent that famine was imminent. See Marjorie Bloy, http://65.107.211.206/victorian/history/famine.html.

13. Dooley, 20–22.

14. The conflict between Irish Catholics and Protestants is generally referred to as a sectarian conflict. It does not equate with racial division, although it bears certain similarities because these sectarian divisions are lingering traces of the English racialization of the Irish. With the establishment of the Irish Free State and partition, the focal point for that conflict became Northern Ireland, whose population is majority Protestant. Whereas British penal laws had prohibited Catholics from owning property and holding office well into the nineteenth century, contemporary forms of discrimination in Northern Ireland excluded Catholics from jobs, housing, and the political process.

15. The anchoring texts for the 1991 conference that led to Caughie's essay were: Derek Jarman's *The Tempest* (1979); Jean-Luc Godard's *Passion* (1982); Claire Denis's *Chocolat* (1988); Pedro Almodovar's *Women on the Verge of a Nervous Breakdown* (1988), Emir Kusturica's *Time of the Gypsies* (1988), and Isaac Julien's *Young Soul Rebels* (1991). A later summer conference entitled "Borderlines: Films in Europe" included one Irish film, Margo Harkin's *Hush-A-Bye Baby* (1989), which is characterized in the introduction to the collection as a Celtic periphery film (5).

16. One example is Fintan O'Toole's account of the changing character of Irish identifications with Native Americans and African Americans in the twentieth century. He draws an important distinction between historical periods; identification undergoes a semantic transformation from "racial slur" to ironic subversion:

> In Ireland, at the turn of the [twentieth] century, the identification with blacks or Indians was still a real racial slur, still a tool of colonial oppression. . . . For [later] writers who grew up with Hollywood Westerns and black-inspired rock and roll music, Indians and blacks were available images that had both the texture of contemporary pop culture and an ironic subconscious prehistory in the most useful aspects of the Irish past, the Irish past that happened in America. (28–29)

O'Toole argues that such identifications function in a postmodern context as "a way of replacing history with irony, identity with a mongrel freedom, post-colonial angst with jokey doubleness" (33). *The Lie of the Land: Irish Identities* (London and New York: Verso, 1997).

17. See the work of Carol Clover, *Men Women and Chainsaws* (Princeton: Princeton UP 1993); Anne Friedberg, *Window Shopping* (Berkeley: U California Press 1994); and Alexander Doty, *Making Things Perfectly Queer* (Minneapolis: U Minnesota 1993). Also see Dick Hebdige, *Subculture: The Meaning of Style* (London: Routledge 1981), Jacqueline Bobo, *Black Women as Cultural Readers* (New York: Columbia 1995), and Angela McRobbie, *In the Culture Society: Art, Fashion, and Popular Music* (London and New York: Routledge, 1999).

18. Silverman's review of film theory and identification is well worth serious consideration. She examines Brecht's *Verfremdungseffekt* aesthetic as being more interested in making the strange familiar than the familiar strange (87) and distinguishes her idea of excorporative or heteropathic identification from models that posit the spectator's "introjective assimilation" (Friedberg, Doane, Metz), psychic transport (Belazs, Wallon), or "identity at a distance" (Kracauer).

19. Paul Gilroy has written about the "fragmentation of national unity and its recomposition along new economic and regional axes" as one factor affecting the political efficacy of the "language of patriotism" within black nationalism in Britain. *There Ain't No Black in the Union Jack: The Cultural Politics of Race and Nation* (Chicago: University of Chicago, 1991) 68. He argues that in many ways black cultural nationalism inverts and reiterates nationalist ideology and may biologize culture in the same way that conservative right political discourse does.

CHAPTER TWO. SAMPLING BLACKNESS

1. Krin Gabbard attributes this term to Steven Elworth. See Chapter Four, "Representing the Jazz Trumpeter," and p305 n4 in *Jammin' at the Margins: Jazz and the American Cinema* (Chicago and London: U Chicago P, 1996).

2. In *The Souls of Black Folk*, W. E. B. DuBois writes in an oft-quoted passage of a "second sight." "It is a peculiar sensation, this double-consciousness, this sense of always looking at oneself through the eyes of others . . . [o]ne ever feels his twoness—an American, a Negro . . ." (New York: Penguin Books, 1982) 45.

3. The most prominent example is Laura Mulvey's "Visual Pleasure and Narrative Cinema." [1975] *Film Theory and Criticism*, sixth edition, eds. Leo Braudy and Marshall Cohen (London and New York: Oxford UP, 2004) 837–48. Steven Neale and many others have taken up the discussion of spectacle as that which stops the flow of narrative.

4. See Richard Kearney's "Avenging Angel: An Analysis of Neil Jordan's First Irish Feature Film," *Studies: An Irish Quarterly Review* 71.283, Autumn 1982: 296–303, and "Nationalism and Irish Cinema," in his book *Transitions* (Manchester: Manchester UP, 1988) 173–92.

5. The reference to Getz, a white jazz musician, makes Jordan's associations with African American jazz nonexclusive. However, Getz can be distinguished from bop guru Charlie Parker, the focus of "A Night in Tunisia," by the fact that he was an extremely popular, rather than esoteric performer. Thus, Jordan may be highlighting the popular, watered-down version of bop Danny's pop/jazz band plays.

6. Jordan's character's hero-worship of Parker must be distinguished from Roddy Doyle's character Joey's disdain: "The biggest regret of my life is that I wasn't born black . . . Charlie Parker was born black. A beautiful shiny, bluey sort of black.—And he could play. He could play alright. But he abused it, spat on it. He turned his back on his people so he could entertain hip honky brats and intellectuals" (*The Commitments* 109).

7. Parker is "[t]he supreme example of the art of the soloist," according to Brian Priestly in *Jazz: The Rough Guide* (London: Penguin, 1995) 492.

8. Consider, for example, Parker's "Famous Alto Break" from a 28 March 1946 Dial recording of "Night in Tunisia." In a Hollywood, recording session with Miles Davis (trumpet), Lucky Thompson (tenor saxophone), Dodo Marmarosa (piano), Victor McMillan (string bass), Roy Porter (drums), and Arvin Garrison (electric guitar), Parker, according to Mark Gardner, writing for *The Blackwell Guide to Recorded Jazz*, "felt he would be unable to reproduce the soaring spontaneity in subsequent efforts" and thus released the fragment of the song as the "Famous Alto Break" (221). Whether this is the solo identified by Jordan in the story is unclear; a number of versions of Parker playing "Night in Tunisia" exist, including two complete takes from that 28 March 1946 recording session in Hollywood. See *The Blackwell Guide to Recorded Jazz, second edition*, ed. Barry Kernfeld (Cambridge: Basil Blackwell, 1995): 217–25.

9. This reversed order—play performed decades after the film release—echoes that of *The Playboys*, discussed in chapter 3, in which the film version of *Gone With the Wind* (1939) is reenacted on stage in an Irish village the 1950s.

10. Jordan frequently uses the photographic image in symbolic ways. Jordan's novel *The Past* deals with a man trying to reconstruct his ancestry from a series of photographs taken in 1914. And the photograph of Jody and Dil that Jody shows to Fergus while in captivity in *The Crying Game* (1993) establishes Fergus's positions of desire and/or identification in relation to Jody and Dil.

11. *Vertigo* (1958), and its interest in the overinvestment in and loss of the female erotic object, informs several Jordan films, including *The Miracle, The Crying Game*, and *In Dreams* (1999). Hitchcock's interest in women's purses (and

the guilty secrets contained therein) may be most evident in *Rear Window* (1954), *Psycho* (1960), and *Marnie* (1964).

12. For Jordan, the film highlights the gender divide in Ireland.

> It deals with a specifically Irish kind of failure to understand women on the parts of men. It grapples with the inarticulacy that the male character needs in order to keep going (qtd. in O'Dea)

Jordan's treatment of the maternal body as locus of social rupture is related to the social events of the 1980s, discussed more fully in chapter 3. Those events, which initiated debates about gender and sexuality, include referenda on divorce and abortion, along with highly publicized cases such as the Kerry Babies, in which pregnant girls and women gave birth alone and in secret to avoid shame and stigma, but who died or had babies that died. The reverence and the revulsion associated with female sexuality that one senses in this film resonates with Irish history, Catholic orthodoxy, and the public discussions of the 1980s and 1990s.

13. In *Black Film/White Money*, Jesse Algernon Rhines discusses the continuing problem of black participation behind the camera in chapter 9, "The Struggle Continues Behind the Camera" (New Brunswick, NJ: Rutgers UP, 1996).

14. The interest in the paternal figure has caused reviewers to see the jazz musicians in *Mo' Better Blues* and *Crooklyn* as drawn from Lee's own biography. Lee's father, Bill Lee, is a jazz bassist and composer who has scored a number of his son's films.

15. Philip Brian Harper and Tricia Rose have argued that rap became an "American" musical form once its "crossover" appeal was certified in the mid-1980s. Harper underlines the importance of the Run-D.M.C. "Walk This Way" video (1986) as a vehicle for rap's "crossover," arguing that the popular music industry has always viewed white rock as a coherent tradition whereas it saw black music as "just the latest thing" (79). *Are We Not Men? Masculine Anxiety and the Problem of African American Identity* (New York and London: Oxford UP, 1996). Rose notes that early rap, including that of Run-D.M.C., had always drawn upon a range of music, including samples from rock, although ultimately the collaboration with white rock stars was treated as a maturing of rap music itself.

CHAPTER THREE. "IT'S A WISE CHILD THAT KNOWS HIS OWN FATHER"

1. For discussions of the maternal melodrama in classical Hollywood cinema, see Lucy Fischer, *Cinematernity* (Princeton: Princeton UP, 1996) and E. Ann Kaplan's *Motherhood and Representation: The Mother in Popular Culture and Melodrama* (New York and London: Routledge, 1992). See also Kaplan's article

"The Case of the Missing Mother: Maternal Issues in Vidor's *Stella Dallas*." *Issues in Feminist Film Criticism*. Ed. Patricia Erens (Bloomington: Indiana UP, 1990) 126–36. Also see Linda Williams's "'Something Else besides a Mother': *Stella Dallas* and Maternal Melodrama," in Erens, 137–162.

2. Joanne Hayes was accused of and confessed to giving birth to a baby who was washed up on the beach in Kerry, but it was later discovered through DNA testing that she was not the infant's mother. She was then accused of killing that infant and her own child, who died shortly after birth. Ann Lovett, pregnant at fourteen, gave birth to a child that died at the statue of the Virgin Mary in Granard. X was the internationally famous case of the fourteen-year-old girl who was raped and sought an abortion in England but was prevented from doing so by the Irish High Court. The decision was subsequently overturned by the Supreme Court, which interpreted the constitutional ban on abortion (approved by referendum in 1983) to permit abortion in a case where the pregnant woman was suicidal. This decision ultimately led to the second abortion referendum. For further discussion, see Emily O'Reilly's *Masterminds of the Right* (Dublin: Attic Press, 1988). Also see Ailbhe Smyth's collection, *The Abortion Papers Ireland.* Dublin: Attic Press, 1992. Another useful source is Nell McCafferty's *A Woman to Blame: The Kerry Babies Case* (Dublin: Attic Press, 1985).

3. The First Programme for Economic Expansion, implemented by Taoiseach (President) Sean Lemass is credited with opening the economy to foreign investment after decades of Irish Free State policies of economic independence and wartime neutrality. In addition, membership in the UN (1956), application for EEC membership (1961), and the Second Vatican Council "were seen by many as ushering in a welcome, outward-looking attitude in Irish life" according to Luke Gibbons. *Transformations in Irish Culture* (Cork: Cork UP, 1996) 77. John Cooney calls the 1960s a "watershed" in Irish history. He considers Irish television (Radio Telefis Eireann or RTE), chartered in 1961, to be as "a focus and stimulator of much of this new revolution" (83). *The Crozier and the Dail: Church and State 1922–1986* (Cork and Dublin: The Mercier Press Ltd., 1986).

4. Ireland's postfamine demography was unique and its pattern persisted well into the twentieth century. A low marriage rate, a late age at marriage, high marital fertility, and a high percentage of never-married men and women were its distinguishing features. The high rate of migration—and the high rate of single female emigrants—is generally considered a response to the constraints of familism, wherein economic considerations reigned supreme. First-born sons inherited but married late; families with several daughters often could provide only one dowry.

5. For an account of the Republic of Ireland's insularity during WWII, see Donal ó Drisceoil's *Censorship in Ireland, 1939–45: Neutrality, Politics and Society* (Cork: Cork UP, 1996). Chapter 2, "'Neutral at the Pictures,'' discusses the amendment of the 1923 and 1930 Censorship of Films Acts by Article 52 of the

Emergency Powers Order of 1939, which broadened significantly the censor's latitude in rejecting a film. For example, the official film censor James Montgomery required so many scenes cut from *Gone With the Wind* (Fleming 1939) that would-be exhibitors withdrew it; Charlie Chaplin's *The Great Dictator* (1940) was banned by his replacement, Dr. Richard Hayes (Drisceoil 35–36).

6. Ibid, 35.

7. There is a history of Irish agrarian resistance societies adopting female dress, including the Ribbonmen and Whiteboys. The latter group's members dressed in white smocks. See Luke Gibbons's "Identity Without a Centre," in *Transformations in Irish Culture*, 134–47.

8. Finney's character is based on Michael MacLiammoir, an English-born actor, writer, and stage designer born Alfred Willmore who was associated with the Gate Theatre in Dublin from the 1930s to the 1970s. He was also a publicly acknowledged gay man who interpreted Oscar Wilde in a one-man show entitled "The Importance of Being Oscar" (1963) and discussed personal and professional connections between himself and Wilde in a memoir entitled *An Oscar of No Importance* (1968). See Éibhear Walshe's "Sex, Nation and Dissent," (150–69) in *Sex, Nation and Dissent in Irish Writing*. Ed. É. Walshe (New York: St. Martin's, 1996). According to Walshe, MacLiammoir "kept his beauty alive (Dorian-like) with paint and powder, and his face was a familiar, exotic sight on the streets of Dublin . . . [a]s he grew older, his ever more persistent attempts to remain glamorous and star-like were remarkably successful and helped him to achieve the status of a public figure" (11). MacLiammoir and his lover, Hilton Edwards, founded the Gate Theatre in 1928 and staged the first Irish production of Wilde's *Salome* (Walshe 12).

9. It may or may not be coincidental that the use of the term "virginity" in *The Moon Is Blue* (Otto Preminger 1953) is often considered the beginning of the end for the Hollywood Production Code.

10. Between 1975 and 1986, more than 30,000 arrests were made by the British army under the Emergency Provisions Act. Close to 75,000 arrests were made between 1971 and 1986. Anthony Jennings, *Justice Under Fire: The Abuse of Civil Liberties in Northern Ireland* (London: Pluto Press, 1990).

11. Terry Byrne reads the scene as indicating a miscarriage. *Power in the Eye* (London: Scarecrow, 1997) 177–79.

CHAPTER FOUR. CULTURING VIOLENCE

1. Those who claimed responsibility for the Guildford Bombing were the Balcombe Street Four: Martin O'Connell, Eddie Butler, Harry Duggan, and

Hugh O'Doherty. See Tim Pat Coogan's *The Ira: A History* (Niwot, CO: Roberts Rinehart Publishers, 1994) 294–98.

2. In this fictionalized version of actual events, the IRA man has claimed responsibility for the Guildford bombings after being arrested on another charge. This composite character is partly based on Martin O'Connell, one of the Balcombe Street group, an active service IRA unit operating in England. When arrested for other bombings, O'Connell publicly refused to answer the charges because they did not include the Guildford pub bombing. During the trial of the Balcombe Street group, it became increasingly clear that the Guildford Four were not associated with the Balcombe Street group; nevertheless, a 1977 appeal by Conlon and the others was rejected. Shane Docherty, an IRA member who was interned at Wormwood Scrubs when Conlon was there, is another model for this character.

3. Many British and American films about the IRA employ the conventions of the gangster genre, which often serves to dilute political questions. See John Hill's "Images of Violence," *Cinema and Ireland*, eds. Luke Gibbons, John Hill, and Kevin Rockett (Syracuse: Syracuse UP, 1988) 147–93. Black action films from the 1960s through the 1990s make clear references to the gangster genre; the most prominent examples are *Black Caesar* (Cohen 1973) and *New Jack City* (Van Peebles 1991).

4. Certainly there are exceptions to the heroic combat film, such as *Jacob's Ladder* (Adrian Lyne 1990). However, combat films are generally recognized for their representation of individual sacrifice and group solidarity in the face of a foreign threat (*Saving Private Ryan* [Steven Spielberg 1998]). Gangster films are concerned with antisocial behavior. In action films, heroes are typically associated with the greater social good, as agents of government law enforcement, as in the *Lethal Weapon*; *Men in Black*, and *Bad Boys* franchises, or as representatives of a nation struggling with an unjust government, as in the *Terminator* and *Rambo* series.

5 . An apocryphal story about one of the genre's seminal films reveals the gangster's longstanding obsession with image and, particularly, film images. *Scarface* (Howard Hawks 1932) is a sensational chronicle of real underworld figure Al Capone's misadventures. Capone reportedly sent his crony George Raft to audition for the film so that he could obtain information about the production. Raft impressed producer Howard Hughes and earned a featured role as coin-flipping Guido Rinaldo, a character parodied in Vincente Minnelli's *An American in Paris* (1952) and, by Raft himself, as Spats Columbo in Billy Wilder's *Some Like It Hot* (1956).

6. Kevin Rockett points out that while the Irish gangster was a familiar figure in the silent era he came into his own in the sound era. He also writes that

"While *The Public Enemy* is often remembered solely for Cagney's infamous pushing of half a grapefruit into the face of his mistress, played by Mae Clarke, it does contain a theme which has recurred in both Irish-American literature and in earlier silent films: the centrality of the family to the Irish, and of the mother within that family" (1994a 179).

7. I refer here to the well-known parallel editing sequence where Michael becomes godfather to his nephew while his henchmen carry out several murders of rival dons.

8. Conlon discusses most of these events in his autobiography, *In the Name of the Father* (New York: Penguin, 1993); the film does rewrite certain details (the commune is fictional, for example), the chronology of events, and the proximity of those events to his arrest. That the commune is called "Xanadu" is a reference both to the 1960s drug culture—which Conlon dabbled in—and to film history through Orson Welles's *Citizen Kane* (1941).

9. Conlon, Hill, Armstrong, and Richardson are the Guildford Four. Each was sentenced to thirty years and served fifteen years.

10. In the book, Conlon describes their look in terms of sexually ambivalent British popular culture figures: "We walked—or rather we tottered—out of the shop, probably thinking we looked like a couple of rock stars—imitations of Marc Bolan and Gary Glitter" (59).

11. See Martin McLoone's "The Abused Child of History: Neil Jordan's *The Butcher Boy*." *Cineaste* 23.4 (1998): 32–36 and Diane Negra's "Irishness, Innocence, and American Identity Politics Before and After September 11," *Keeping it Real: Irish Film and Television*, eds. Ruth Barton and Harvey O'Brien (London: Wallflower Press, 2004) 54–68.

12. According to Gerry Conlon, Irish language and history were not taught to all students, which had implications for their political education as well. He writes: "part of the curriculum in classes 1A, 1B, and 1C was learning French and more importantly Irish. The history was also very Irish oriented and if I had stayed in that class I would probably have had a greater awareness when the troubles started. . . . Perhaps if I had stayed in 1C, I would have had a more defined Republican attitude at a very early age . . . the vast majority of people who ended up in the IRA had been taught Irish history and Gaelic" (18).

13. In a telling phrase that conflates legal and spiritual realms, Conlon refers to the arrest and incarceration of the Guildford Four and his family members as "an almighty miscarriage of justice" (168).

14. *Boyz* has grossed $57 million, plus $26 million in video rentals. Forest Whitaker's *Waiting to Exhale* (1995), based on Terry McMillan's novel, eclipsed *Boyz*, earning $66 million and $33 million in rentals.

15. The most recent and relevant example of gang-like policing was the LAPD's Rampart Division scandal of the late 1990s.

16. Charles Dutton's fame as an ex-convict-turned-actor on the television show "Roc" suggests his extratextual importance as an officially sanctioned role model for young black men. In another example of the interpenetration of real and fictional gangster worlds, the videotape release of *Menace II Society* is preceded by a public service announcement by Dutton, who encourages young black men and women to stay in school and get an education.

17. See Terrence Rafferty's "Dead End," *The New Yorker*, 31 March 1993.

18. In what may or may not be a coincidence, the internationally famous IRA hunger striker and Member of Parliament, Bobby Sands, used "Marcella" as a pen name on communiquès while in the Maze prison; it was the name of one of his sisters.

19. Elsewhere, I have examined the way these identifications elicit bisexual reading strategies. See "Straddling the Screen: Bisexual Spectatorship and Contemporary Narrative Film," *Representing BiSexualities: Subjects and Cultures of Fluid Desire*, eds. Donald E. Hall and Maria Pramaggiore (New York: NYU Press, 1996) 272–97.

CHAPTER FIVE. "BOTH SIDES OF THE EPIC"

1. John Ford's Irish ancestry also is invoked as a crucial element in his oeuvre. A number of critics observe that Ford's emphasis on agrarian community and his sentimental use of music derive from his Irish Catholic heritage. In Liam O'Leary's *Cinema Ireland 1896–1950* (Dublin: National Library of Ireland, 1990), Ford is characterized as a "distinguished film personality of Irish origin" and his photograph is sweetly captioned: "maker of beautiful westerns" (24).

2. Seamus Heaney's poem "Bogland" compares the horizontality of the American prairie to the vertical depths of the bog as the sedimentation of memory. The poem begins with the line "We have no prairies/To slice a big sun at evening—/Everywhere the eye concedes to/Encroaching horizon,/Is wooed into the cyclops' eye/Of a tarn." *Selected Poems, 1966–1987* (New York: Farrar, Straus and Giroux, 1990) 22.

3. The tension in the closing images has been a source of much discussion and speculation. At the "Irish Film and Genre" conference sponsored by Brian McIlroy at University of British Columbia in March 2005, Cheryl Herr commented that she reads this moment as disturbing rather than transcendent.

4. In addition to playing a central role in African American folk tales, the term "good bad man" was associated with early Western film star Gilbert Ander-

son and his popular character Bronco Billy. Douglas Pye, "Introduction," *The Book of Westerns*, eds. Ian Cameron and Douglas Pye (New York: Continuum, 1996).

5. A professional football player for the Los Angeles Rams in the 1940s and for the Canadian league, Strode crossed any number of color lines in his several careers. His best-known role may be in John Ford's *Sergeant Rutledge* (1960), in which he played an officer falsely accused of rape.

WORKS CONSULTED

Abel, Richard. "'Our Country'/Whose Country? The 'Americanisation' Project of Early Westerns." *Back in the Saddle Again: New Essays on the Western.* Eds. Edward Buscombe and Roberta Pearson. London: BFI, 1998. 77–95.

Altman, Rick. "A Semantic/Syntactic Approach to Film Genre." *Film Genre Reader.* Ed. Barry Keith Grant. Austin: U Texas P, 1986. 26–40.

Anderson, Benedict. *Imagined Communities: Reflections on the Origin and Spread of Nationalism.* London: Verso, 1984.

Anderson, James. "Territorial Sovereignty and Political Identity: National Problems, Transnational Solutions?" *In Search of Ireland: a Cultural Geography.* Ed. Brian Graham. London and New York: Routledge, 1997. 215–35.

Anderson, S. E. "Revolutionary Black Nationalism and the Pan-African Idea." *The Black Seventies.* Ed. Floyd Barbour. Boston: Porter Sargent, 1970. 99–126.

Ang, Ien. "Hegemony-in-Trouble: Nostalgia and the Ideology of the Impossible in European Cinema." *Screening Europe.* Ed. Duncan Petrie. London: British Film Institute, 1992. 21–31.

Appiah, Kwame Anthony. *The Ethics of Identity.* Princeton, NJ: Princeton UP, 2005.

———. "Is the 'Post-' in 'Postcolonial' the 'Post' in 'Postmodern'?" *Dangerous Liaisons: Gender, Nation, and Postcolonial Perspectives.* Eds. Anne McClintock, Aamir Mufti, and Ella Shohat. Minneapolis and London: U Minnesota P, 1997. 420–44.

Armstrong, Gordon. "Cultural Politics and the Irish Theatre: Samuel Beckett and the New Biology." *Theatre Research International* 18. (1993): 215–21.

Arnold, James. "Irish Movies: a Renaissance." *America* 175. 13 (2 Nov. 1996): 16–22.

———. "Bloody politics, daring cinema (interview with Neil Jordan, director of *Michael Collins*)" *Insight on the News* 12. 43 (18 Nov. 1996): 36–37.

Ashcroft, Bill, Gareth Griffiths, and Helen Tiffin. *The Empire Writes Back: Theory and Practice in Post-Colonial Literatures.* London and New York: Routledge, 1989.

Austin, Valerie. "The Céilí and the Public Dance Halls Act, 1935." *Éire-Ireland* 28.3 (Fall 1993): 7–16.

Back, Les. "The 'White Negro' Revisited: Race and masculinities in south London." *Dislocating Masculinity.* Eds. A. Cornwall and N. Lindisfarne. London and New York: Routledge, 1994.

Baird, Robert. "Going Indian: *Dances with Wolves* (1990)." *Hollywood's Indian: The Portrayal of the Native American in Film.* Eds. Peter C. Rollins and John E. O'Connor. Lexington: UP of Kentucky, 1998. 153–69.

Baker, Houston. *Blues, Ideology and Afro-American Literature: A Vernacular Theory.* Chicago: U Chicago P, 1984.

Baldwin, James. "Of the Sorrow Songs: The Cross of Redemption." In *The Picador Book of Blues and Jazz.* London: Picador, 1979. 324–31.

Balibar, Etienne and Immauel Wallerstein. *Race, Nation, Class: Ambiguous Identities.* London and New York: Verso, 1991.

Balio, Tino. "Adjusting to the New Global Economy: Hollywood in the 1990s." *Film Policy: International, National and Regional Perspectives.* Ed. A. Moran. London and New York: Routledge, 1996. 23–38.

Banton, Michael. *Racial Theories*, 2nd ed. Cambridge: Cambridge UP, 1998.

Barbour, Floyd. *The Black Seventies* (Ed.). Boston: Porter Sargent, 1970.

Barker, Chris. *Television, Globalization and Cultural Identities.* Buckingham and Philadelphia: Open UP, 1999.

Barton, Ruth. *Irish National Cinema.* London and New York: Routledge, 2004.

———. "Feisty Colleens and Faithful Sons: Gender in Irish Cinema," *Cineaste* 24. 2–3 (1999): 40–45.

"Basic Tenets of Revolutionary Black Nationalism." *The Black Seventies.* Ed. Floyd Barbour. Boston: Porter Sargent, 1970. 309–10.

Baxter, John. *The Gangster Film.* New York: A.S. Barnes, 1970.

Beale, Jenny. *Women in Ireland: Voices of Change.* Bloomington and Indianapolis: Indiana UP, 1984.

Beaumont, Catriona. "Gender, citizenship and the state in Ireland, 1922–1990," in *Ireland in Proximity: History, Gender, Space.* Eds. Scott Brewster, Virginia Crossman, Fiona Beckett, and David Alderson. London and New York: Routledge, 1999. 94–108.

Beckett, Samuel. *Disjecta: Miscellaneous Writings and a Dramatic Fragment.* Ed. Ruby Cohn. New York: Grove Press, 1984.

Bell, J. Bowyer. *The Gun in Politics: An Analysis of Irish Political Conflict,* 1916–1986. New Brunswick and Oxford: Transaction Books, 1986.

Bell-Metereau, Rebecca. *Hollywood Androgyny.* New York: Columbia, 1993.

Benson, Sheila. "*Blues* Trumpets Lee's Strengths, Weaknesses." *Los Angeles Times,* 1990 F1, col. 2.

Berg, Charles Ramirez. "The Margin as Center: The Multicultural Dynamics of John Ford's Westerns" *John Ford Made Westerns: Filming the Legend in the Sound Era.* Eds. Gaylyn Studlar and Matthew Bernstein. Bloomington: Indiana UP, 2001. 102–29.

Bhabha, Homi K. "Are You a Man or a Mouse." *Constructing Masculinity.* Eds. Maurice Berger, Brian Wallis, and Simon Watson. New York and London: Routledge, 1995. 57–65

———. *The Location of Culture.* London and New York: Routledge, 1994.

———. (1990a) "Introduction: Narrating the Nation." *Nation and Narration.* Ed. Homi K. Bhabha. London and New York: Routledge 1990. 1–7.

———. (1990b) "DissemiNation: Time, Narrative, and the Margins of the Modern Nation." *Nation and Narration.* Ed. Homi K. Bhabha. London and New York: Routledge, 1990 291–322.

"Black Code of Louisiana, 1724." *African American Alamanc.* http://www.toptags.com/aama/docs/lublkcodes.htm.

Blake, Richard. "Choice Cuts." *America* (16 May 1998) 178.17 (1998): 20–21.

Bloy, Marjorie. Irish Famine Web site. http://65.107.211.206/victorian/history/famine.html.

Bobo, Jacqueline. *Black Women Film and Video Artists.* New York: Routledge, 1998.

———. *Black Women as Cultural Readers.* New York: Columbia UP, 1995.

Bogle, Donald. *Bright Boulevards, Bold Dreams: The Story of Black Hollywood.* New York: Ballantine, 2005.

———. *Toms, Coons, Mulattoes, Mammies and Bucks: An Interpretive History of Blacks in American Films.* New York: Continuum, 1992.

Boozer, Jack. "Bending Phallic Patriarchy in *The Crying Game*." *Journal of Popular Film and Television* 22.4 (1995):172–79.

Bowser, Pearl, Jane Gaines, and Charlres Musser (Eds.). *Oscar Micheaux and His Circle: African-American Filmmaking and Race Cinema of the Silent Era.* Bloomington: Indiana UP, 2001.

Breen, Richard, Damian F. Hannan, David B. Rottman, and Christopher T. Whelan. *Understanding Contemporary Ireland: State, Class and Development in the Republic of Ireland.* New York: St. Martin's, 1990.

Brennan, Timothy. "The National Longing for Form." *Nation and Narration.* Ed. Homi K. Bhabha. London and New York: Routledge, 1990. 58–67.

Breskin, David. *Inner Views: Filmmakers in Conversation.* New York: Da Capo Press, 1997.

Browder, Laura. *Slippery Characters: Ethnic Impersonators and American Identities.* Chapel Hill: U North Carolina P, 2000.

Brown, Bill. *Reading the West: an Anthology of Dime Westerns.* New York: Bedford, 1997.

Brown, H. Rap. "A Letter from H. Rap Brown.," *The Black Seventies.* Ed. Floyd Barbour. Boston: Porter Sargent, 1970. 311–13.

Burgoyne, Robert. *Film Nation: Hollywood Looks at U.S. History.* Minneapolis: U Minnesota P, 1997.

Burke, Marina. "Celtic Dreamer" (Neil Jordan interview), *Film Ireland* 34 (April/May 1993): 17–21.

Burns-Bisogno, Louisa. *Censoring Irish Nationalism: The British, Irish and American Suppression of Republican Images in Film and Television, 1909–1995.* Jefferson, NC: McFarland, 1997.

Buscombe, Edward. "Photographing the Indian." *Back in the Saddle Again: New Essays on the Western.* Eds. Edward Buscombe and Roberta E. Pearson. London: BFI, 1998. 29–45.

———. *BFI Companion to the Western* (Ed.). New York: Athenaeum, 1988.

Byrne, Terry. *Power in the Eye: An Introduction to Contemporary Irish Film.* Lanham, MD and London: Scarecrow Press, 1997.

Cairns, David and Shaun Richards. *Writing Ireland: Colonialism, Nationalism and Culture.* New York: St. Martin's, 1988.

Cameron, Ian and Dougles Pye. *The Book of Westerns* (Eds.). New York: Continuum, 1996.

———. "Unforgiven." *The Book of Westerns.* New York: Continuum, 1996. 294–301.

Canby, Vincent. "Spike Lee Riffs about An Artist, Not a Genius." *The New York Times.* August 26, 1990: S2, p. 9, col 1.

Cantrell, James P. "Irish Culture and the War Between the States: *Paddy McGann* and *Gone With the Wind*," *Éire-Ireland: a journal of Irish Studies* 27.2 (1992): 7–15.

Carby, Hazel. "'On the Threshold of the Woman's Era': Lynching, Empire, and Sexuality in Feminist Theory." *Dangerous Liaisons: Gender, Nation and Postcolonial Perspectives.* Eds. Anne McClintock, Aamir Mufti, and Ella Shohat. London and Minneapolis: U Minnesota P, 1997. 330–43.

Carr, Jay. "*He Got Game* Is a Slam-Dunk for Spike Lee." *The Boston Globe*, 1 May 1998, D1.

———. "Lee's *Crooklyn* Is Filled with Convictions," *The Boston Globe*, 13 May 1994: D33.

Carroll, Noel. "The Professional Western: South of the Border." *Back in the Saddle Again: New Essays on the Western.* Eds. Edward Buscombe and Roberta E. Pearson.London: BFI, 1998. 46–62.

Caughie, John. "Becoming European: Art, Cinema, Irony and Identity." In *Screening Europe.* Ed. Duncan Petrie. London: BFI, 1992. 32–44.

Caughie, John with Kevin Rockett. *The Companion to British and Irish Cinema.* London: Cassell and the BFI, 1996.

Cawelti, John. *The Six Gun Mystique.* Bowling Green, OH: Bowling Green State University, 1985.

Chumo, Peter N. II. "*The Crying Game*, Hitchcockian Romance, and the Quest for Identity." *Literature Film Quarterly* 23.4 (1995): 247–53.

Clark, Andrew. *Riffs & Choruses: A New Jazz Anthology* (Ed.). London and New York: Continuum, 2001.

Clark, Mike. "Spike Lee's still on his 'Game': basketball saga wins with passion." *USA Today* 1 May 1998, 11E.

———. "Spike Lee's Surprising Slip: Nostalgia *Crooklyn* Has Heart but Lacks Art." *USA Today*, May 13, 1994: 8D.

———. "Stylish *Mo' Better Blues* Lacks a Story that Flows." *USA Today*, 3 August 1990: Life Section.

Cleary, Joe (Ed.) *The Cambridge Companion to Modern Irish Culture.* Cambridge: Cambridge UP, 2005

———. "'Fork-Tongued on the Border Bit': Partition and the Politics of Form in Contemporary Narratives of the Northern Irish Conflict." *South Atlantic Quarterly* 95.1 (1996) 227–76.

———. "Into Which West?: Irish Modernity and the Maternal Supernatural." *Literature and the Supernatural*. Ed. Brian Cosgrove. Dublin: The Columba Press, 1995. 147–71.

Clifford, James. "Travelling Cultures." *Cultural Studies*. Ed. Lawrence Grossberg. New York and London: Routledge, 1992.

Clover, Carol. *Men, Women and Chainsaws: Gender in the Modern Horror Film.* Princeton, NJ: Princeton UP, 1993.

Comiskey, Ray. "From Script to Screen." *The Irish Times*, 26 March 1985: 10.

———. Interview with Neil Jordan. *Irish Times*, 11 May 1982: 8.

Conlon, Gerry. *In the Name of the Father* [Original Title: *Proved Innocent]*. New York: Plume, 1993.

Coogan, Tim Pat. *The IRA: A History*. Niwot, CO: Roberts Rinehart Publishers, 1994.

Cooney, John. *The Crozier and the Dáil: Church and State in Ireland 1922–1986.* Dublin: The Mercier Press, 1986.

Corliss, Richard. "Boyz of New Black City." *Time*, 137.24 (17 June 1991): 64–68.

Cornell, Stephen and Douglas Hartmann. *Ethnicity and Race: Making Identities in a Changing World*. Thousand Oaks, London, and New Delhi: Pine Forge Press, 1998.

Coyne, Michael. *The Crowded Prairie: American National Identity in the Hollywood Western.* London and New York: I.B. Tauris, 1997.

Craddock-Willis, Andre. "Rap Music and the Black Musical Tradition: A Critical Assessment." *Radical America* 23.4 (1989): 29–38.

Creekmur, Corey K. "Acting Like a Man: Masculine Performance in *My Darling Clementine*." *Out in Culture: Gay, Lesbian and Queer Essays on Popular Culture.* Eds. C. Creekmur and A. Doty. Durham, NC: Duke UP, 1995. 167–82.

Cronin, John. *The Anglo-Irish Novel, Vol. 1: The Nineteenth Century*. Belfast: Appletree, 1980.

Crump, Ian (1996). "A Terrible Beauty Is Born: Irish Literature as a Paradigm for the Formation of Postcolonial Literatures." *English Postcoloniality: Literatures from Around the World*. Eds. Mohanram, R. and G. Rajan. Westport, CT and London: Greenwood, 1996. 31–42.

Cullingford, Elizabeth Butler. "Virgins and Mothers: Sinéad O'Connor, Neil Jordan, and *The Butcher Boy*." *The Yale Journal of Criticism*. 15.1 (Spring 2002). http://muse.jhu.edu/journals/yale_journal_of_criticism/toc/yale15.1.html.

———. *Ireland's Others: Gender and Ethnicity in Irish Literature and Popular Culture.* Notre Dame, IN: U Notre Dame P/Field Day, 2001.

———. "Seamus and Sinead: From "Limbo" to *Saturday Night Live* by way of *Hush-a-Bye Baby*," *Colby Quarterly*, 3(1) (March 1994): 43–62.

Cunningham, Francine. "A Tender Triad Caught in a Small World," *The Irish Times*, 23 November 1990: 14.

Curtis, L. P. *Apes and Angels: The Irishman in Victorian Caricature.* Washington: Smithsonian Institution, 1996.

———. *Anglo Saxons and Celts: A Study of Anti-Irish Prejudice in Victorian England.* New York: Conference on British Studies and University of Bridgeport, 1974.

Dagle, Joan. "Linear Patterns and Ethnic Encounters in the Ford Western." *John Ford Made Westerns: Filming the Legend in the Sound Era.* Eds. Gaylyn Studlar and Matthew Bernstein. Bloomington: Indiana UP, 2001. 102–29.

Dash, Julie, with Toni Cade Bambara and bell hooks. *Daughters of the Dust: The Making of an African-American Woman's Film.* New York: New Press, 1992.

Dash, Michael. "Marvellous Realism: The Way Out of Négritude" *Caribbean Studies* 13. 4 (1973): 57–70.

Dean, Joan. "Screening the IRA," *Film West* 20 (1995): 26–28.

Deane, Seamus. *Strange Country: Modernity and Nationhood in Irish Writing since 1790.* Oxford: Clarendon Press, 1997.

Diamond, Elin. "The Violence of 'We': Politicizing Identification." *Critical Theory and Performance.* Eds. Janelle Reinelt and Joseph Roach. Ann Arbor: U Michigan P, 1992. 390–98.

Diawara, Manthia. "Afro-Kitsch." *Performing Hybridity.* Eds. May Joseph and Jennifer Natalya Fink. Minneapolis: U Minnesota P, 1999. 177–81.

———. "Black American Cinema: The New Realism." *Black American Cinema.* Ed. Manthia Diawara. New York and London: Routledge, 1993. 3–25.

———. "Noir by Noirs: Towards a New Realism in Black Cinema," *African American Review*, 27.4 (Winter 1993): 525–37.

Dirlik, Arif. "The Postcolonial Aura: Third World Criticism in the Age of Global Capitalism." *Dangerous Liaisons: Gender, Nation and Postcolonial Perspectives.* Eds. Anne McLintock, Aamir Mufti, and Ella Shohat. Minneapolis and London: U Minnesota P, 1997. 501–28.

———. "The Global in the Local." *Global/Local: Cultural Production and the Transnational Imaginary.* Eds. Wilson, Rob and Wimal Dissanayake. Durham, NC: Duke UP, 1996. 21–45.

Dollimore, Jonathan. "Desire and Difference: Homosexuality, Race, Masculinity." *Race and the Subject of Masculinities.* Eds. Harry Stecopoulos and Michael Uebel. Durham: Duke UP, 1997.17–44.

Donalson, Melvin. *Black Directors in Hollywood.* Austin: U Texas P, 2003.

Doolan, Leila. "Irish Film Now." *Film Base News* 20 (1990): 13–15.

Dooley, Brian. *Black and Green: The Fight for Civil Rights in Northern Ireland and Black America.* London and Chicago: Pluto Press, 1998.

Doty, Alexander. *Making Things Perfectly Queer.* Minneapolis: U Minnesota P, 1993.

Douglass, Frederick. "Address to Belfast Anti-Slavery Society." 1865. The Papers of Frederick Douglass at the Library of Congress. *http://memory.loc.gov/ammem/doughtml/doughome.html* (accessed on October 29 2005).

Dowell, Pat. "The Mythology of the West: Hollywood Perspectives on Race and Gender in the Nineties." *Cineaste* 21.1–2 (1995): 6–10.

Doyle, Leonard. "Good Reviews for *Eat the Peach* in New York." *The Irish Times,* 20 July 1987: 10.

Doyle, Roddy. *The Barrytown Trilogy: The Commitments, The Snapper and The Van.* New York and London: Penguin Books, 1995.

DuBois, W. E. B. *The Souls of Black Folk* [1903]. New York: Penguin, 1982.

Dwyer, Michael. "Summertime in Bray." *The Irish Times,* 12 April 1991: 10.

Dyer, Richard. *White.* London and New York: Routledge, 1997.

Dyson, Michael Eric. "Between Apocalypse and Redemption: John Singleton's *Boyz N The Hood.*" *Film Theory Goes to the Movies.* Eds. Jim Collins, Hilary Radner, and Ava Preacher Collins. New York:Routledge, 1993. 209–26.

Eagleton, Terry. *Heathcliff and the Great Hunger: Studies in Irish Culture.* London and New York: Verso, 1995.

———, Fredric Jameson and Edward Said (Eds.). *Nationalism, Colonialism and Literature.* Minneapolis: U Minnesota P, 1990.

Edge, Sarah. "Women and the Image." *Film Ireland* 40 (1994): 36–37.

Ellis, Kirk. "On the Warpath: John Ford and the Indians." *Journal of Popular Film and Television* 8.2 (1980): 34–41.

Ellis, Peter Berresford. *Celtic Women: Women in Celtic Society and Literature.* Grand Rapids, MI: William B. Eerdmans Publishing Co., 1995.

Ellis, Trey. "The New Black Aesthetic," *Callaloo* Issue 12, No. 1 (Winter 1989): 233–43.

Elsaesser, Thomas. "Hyper-, Retro-, or Counter-Cinema: European Cinema and Third Cinema between Hollywood and Art Cinema." *Mediating Two Worlds: Cinematic Encounters in the Americas.* Eds. John King, Ana Lopez, and Manuel Alvarado. London: BFI, 1993. 119–35.

Engel, Leonard. "Mythic Space and Monument Valley: Another Look at John Ford's *Stagecoach.*" *Literature Film Quarterly* 22.3 (1994): 174–80.

Eshun, Kodwo. "From Blaxploitation to Rapsploitation." *Celluloid Jukebox: Popular Music and the Movies Since the 50s.* Eds. Jonathan Romney and Adrian Wooten. London: British Film Institute, 1995. 52–59.

Esty, Joshua D. "Excremental Postcolonialism." *Contemporary Literature* 40.1 (Spring 1999): 22–59.

Falcon, Richard. *He Got Game* (review) *Sight and Sound* 8.10 (1998): 44–45.

Farred, Grant. "Feasting on Foreman: The Problematics of Postcolonial Identification," *Camera Obscura* 39 (September 1996): 53–76.

———. "*Menace II Society*: No Way Out for the Boyz in the Hood." *The Movies: Texts, Receptions, Exposures.* Ed. Laurence Goldstein. Ann Arbor: U Michigan P, 1996. 114–30.

Fenton, Steven and Stephen May. "Ethnicity, Nation, and 'Race': Connections and Disjunctures." *Ethnonational Identities.* Eds. Steven Fenton and Stephen May. Houndmills, Basingstoke, and New York: Palgrave Macmillan, 2002. 1–20.

Finney, Angus. *The State of European Cinema: A New Dose of Reality.* London: Cassell, 1996.

Fischer, Lucy. *Cinematernity: Film. Motherhood, Genre.* Princeton, NJ: Princeton UP, 1996.

Floyd, Nigel. "*The Miracle,*" *Monthly Film Bulletin* 58 (1991): 107.

Foreman, James. "The Black Manifesto." [1969] *The Black Seventies.* Ed. Floyd Barbour. Boston: Porter Sargent, 1970. 296–308.

Foster, Gwendolyn Audrey. *Performing Whiteness: Postmodern Reconstructions in the Cinema.* Albany: SUNY P, 2003.

———. *Captive Bodies: Postcolonial Subjectivity in Cinema.* Albany: SUNY P, 1999.

———. *Women Filmmakers of the African and Asian Diaspora: Decolonizing the Gaze, Locating Subjectivity.* Carbondale and Edwardsville: Southern Illinois UP, 1997.

Foster, John Wilson. *Colonial Consequences: Essays in Irish Literature and Culture.* Dublin: The Lilliput Press, 1991.

Frankenberg, Ruth. "Introduction: Local Whitenesses, Localizing Whiteness." *Displacing Whiteness: Essays in Social and Cultural Criticism.* Ed. R. Frankenberg. Durham and London: Duke UP, 1997. 1–33.

Fregoso, Rosa Linda. *The Bronze Screen. Chicana and Chicano Film Culture.* Minneapolis: U Minnesota P, 1993.

Friedberg, Anne. *Window Shopping: Cinema and the Postmodern.* Berkeley: U California Press, 1994.

Fuss, Diana. "Interior Colonies: Frantz Fanon and the Politics of Identification." [1995] *Rethinking Fanon.* Ed. Nigel Gibson. Amherst, NY: Humanity Books, 1999. 294–328.

———. *Essentially Speaking: Feminism, Nature, & Difference.* New York: Routledge, 1990.

———. "White Privilege and Looking Relations: Race and Gender in Feminist Film Theory." *Issues in Feminist Film Criticism.* Ed. P. Erens Bloomington: Indiana UP, 1990. 197–214.

Gabbard, Krin. *Black Magic.* New Brunswick, NJ: Rutgers UP, 2004.

———. *Jammin' at the Margins: Jazz and the American Cinema.* Chicago: U Chicago P, 1996.

Gabriel, Teshome. "Thoughts on Nomadic Aesthetics and the Black Independent Cinema." *Blackframes: Critical Perspectives on Black Independent Cinema.* Ed. Cham Mybe and Claire Watkins. Cambridge, MA: MIT Press, 1988. 62–79.

Gaines, Jane and Charlotte Cornelia Herzog. "The Fantasy of Authenticity in Western Costume." *Back in the Saddle Again: New Essays on the Western.* Eds. Edward Buscombe and Roberta E. Pearson. London: British Film Institute, 1998. 172–81.

Gallagher, Tag. "Shoot-out at the Genre Corral: Problems in the 'Evolution' of the Western." *Film Genre Reader III.* Ed. Barry Keith Grant. Austin: U Texas P, 2003. 262–76.

Gardner, Mark. *The Blackwell Guide to Recorded Jazz, 2nd ed.* Ed. Barry Kernfeld Cambridge, MA: Basil Blackwell, 1995. 217–25.

Gates, Henry Louis, Jr. *The Signifying Monkey: A Theory of African-American Literary Criticism.* New York: Oxford UP, 1988.

Geier, Thom. "One Irish rebel films another." *U.S. News & World Report* 121.15 (14 October 1996): 33.

George, Nelson. *Buppies, B-Boys, Baps, and Bohos: Notes on Post-Soul Black Culture.* New York: Harper Collins, 1992.

George, Rosemary Marangoly. *The Politics of Home: Postcolonial Relocations and Twentieth-Century Fiction.* Cambridge: Cambridge UP, 1996

Geraghty, Christine. "Albert Finney: A Working-Class Hero." *Me Jane: Masculinity, Movies and Women.* Eds. P. Kirkham and J. Thumin. New York: St. Martin's, 1995. 62–71.

Gerber, Leslie. "The Virtuous Terrorist: Stanley Hauerwas and *The Crying Game.*" *Cross Currents* 42. 2 (Summer 1993): 230–35.

Gibbons, Luke. "Projecting the Nation: Cinema and Culture." *The Cambridge Companion to Modern Irish Culture.* Eds. Joe Cleary and Claire Connolly. Cambridge: Cambridge UP, 2005. 206–24.

———. (1996a) *Transformations in Irish Culture.* Cork: Cork UP/Field Day, 1996.

———. (1996b) "Topographies of Terror: Killarney and the Politics of the Sublime," *South Atlantic Quarterly* 95.1 (1996): 23–44.

———. (1996c) "Engendering the State: Narrative, Allegory and *Michael Collins.*" *ÉireIreland* 31.3–4 (Fall/Winter 1996): 261–68.

———. "On the Beach: Luke Gibbons on the Other Ireland." *Artforum International* 31.2 (October 1992), 13.

———. "Fragments in Pictures." *Film Base News,* November/December 1990: 8–11.

Gilles, John R. "Bringing Up Father: British Paternal Identities, 1700 to Present." *masculinities* 3.3 (1995): 1–27.

Gilman, Sander. "Black Bodies, White Bodies: Toward an Iconography of Female Sexuality in Late Nineteenth-Century Art, Medicine, and Literature." '*Race', Culture and Difference.* Eds. James Donald and Ali Rattansi, London and Newbury Park, CA: Sage Publications and The Open UP,1992. 171–97.

Gilroy, Paul. *The Black Atlantic: Modernity and Double Consciousness.* Cambridge, MA: Harvard UP, 1993.

———. *There Ain't No Black in the Union Jack: The Cultural Politics of Race and Nation.* Chicago: U Chicago P, 1991.

Gledhill, Christine and Gillian Swanson (Eds.). *Nationalising Femininity: Culture, Sexuality and British Cinema in the Second World War.* Manchester and New York: Manchester UP, 1996.

Glicksman, Marlaine. "Interview with Neil Jordan." *Film Comment,* 26 January 1990: 9.

Gmelch, George. "Irish Travellers Revisited." *Éire-Ireland: A Journal of Irish Studies* 21 (1986): 22–28.

Gorbman, Claudia. *Unheard Melodies: Narrative Film Music.* Bloomington and Indianapolis: Indiana UP, 1987

Graham, Brian. "The Imagining of Place: Representation and Identity in Contemporary Ireland." *In Search of Ireland: a Cultural Geography.* Ed. Brian Graham. London and New York: Routledge, 1997. 192–212.

Grant, William R., IV. *Post-Soul Black Cinema: Discontinuities, Innovations, and Breakpoints, 1970–1995.* New York and London: Routledge, 2004.

Gray, Michael. "Those Bad-Tempered, Redhaired Celts." *Cineaste* 24.2–3 (1999): 35.

Grayson, Sandra. *Symbolizing the Past: Reading Sankofa, Daughters of the Dust, and Eve's Bayou as Histories.* Lanham, New York, and Oxford: UP of America, 2000.

Greene, Dennis. "Tragically Hip: Hollywood and African-American Cinema." *Cineaste* 20. 4 (1994): 28–33.

Grenier, Richard. "History No Obstacle for Hollywood (*In the Name of the Father*)." *Insight on the News* 10.12 (21 March 1994): 34.

Greskovic, Robert. "*Riverdance, the Show.*" *Dance Magazine* 70.9 (September 1996): 99.

Grist, Leighton. "'It's only a piece of meat.' Gender Ambiguity, Sexuality, and Politics in *The Crying Game* and *M. Butterfly.*" *Cinema Journal* 42.4 (Summer 2003): 3–28.

Gubar, Susan. *Racechanges: White Skin, Black Face in American Culture.* New York and Oxford: Oxford UP, 1997.

Guererro, Ed. (1993a) "Spike Lee and the Fever in the Racial Jungle." *Film Theory Goes to the Movies.* Eds. Jim Collins, Hilary Radner, and Ava Preacher Collins. New York: Routledge, 1993. 170–81.

———. (1993b). *Framing Blackness: The African American Image in Film.* Philadelphia: Temple UP, 1993.

Hall, Stuart (1997a). "The Local and the Global: Globalization and Ethnicity." *Dangerous Liaisons: Gender, Nation and Postcolonial Perspectives.* Eds. Anne McClintock, Aamir Mufti, and Ella Shohat. Minneapolis and London: U Minnesota P, 1997. 173–87.

———. (1997b) "What is this 'Black' in Black Popular Culture?" *Representing Blackness: Issues in Film and Video.* Ed. Valerie Smith. New Brunswick, NJ: Rutgers UP, 1997. 123–33.

———. "European Cinema on the Verge of a Nervous Breakdown." *Screening Europe.* Ed. Duncan Petrie. London: BFI, 1992. 45–53.

Hammonds, Evelynn. "Toward a Genealogy of Black Female Sexuality: The Problematic of Silence." *Feminist Genealogies, Colonial Legacies, Democratic Futures.* Eds. M. J. Alexander and C. Mohanty. London and New York: Routledge, 1997. 170–82.

Hanchard, Michael. "Identity, Meaning and the African-American." *Social Text* 24 (1990): 31–42.

Harper, Phillip Brian. *Are We Not Men? Masculine Anxiety and the Problem of African American Identity.* New York and London: Oxford UP, 1996.

Harrison, William. "European Postcoloniality: *The Saorstát Éireann/Irish Free State Official Handbook,* 1932." *Éire-Ireland* 30.1 (Spring 1995): 35–42.

Harvey, Clodagh Brennan. "Some Irish Women Storytellers and Reflections on the Role of Women in the Storytelling Tradition." *Western Folklore* 48 (1989): 109–28.

Hayden, Joanne. "The Film Institute of Ireland: A Time of Reckoning," *film west,* 32 (1998): 26–28.

Hayward, Susan. "Framing National Cinemas." *Cinema and Nation.* Eds. M. Pais and S. Mackenzie. London and New York: Routledge, 2001. 88–102.

Heaney, Seamus. *Selected Poems, 1966–1987.* New York: Farrar, Straus and Giroux, 1990.

Hebdige, Dick. *Subculture: The Meaning of Style.* London: Routledge, 1981.

Hechter. Michael. *Containing Nationalism.* Oxford: Oxford UP, 2000.

———. *Internal Colonialism: The Celtic Fringe in British National Development 1536–1966.* Berkeley and Los Angeles: U California P, 1967.

Henderson, Brian. "*The Searchers*: An American Dilemma." *Film Quarterly* 34:2 (Winter 1980–1981). 9–23.

Hening, William Walter. *The Statutes at Large; Being a Collection of all the Laws of Virginia, from the First Session of the Legislature in the Year 1619.* New York: RWG Bartow, 1823. Vol. 1. http://www.law.du.edu/russell/lh/alh/docs/virginiaslaverystatutes.html.

Herr, Cheryl. "Re-imagining *Man of Aran.*" *Canadian Journal of Irish Studies.* 29.2 (2003): 11–16.

———. *Critical Regionalism and Cultural Studies: From Ireland to the American Midwest.* Gainesville: U P of Florida, 1996.

———. "The Erotics of Irishness." *Identities.* Eds. K. A. Appiah and H. L.Gates, Jr. Chicago: U Chicago P, 1995. 271–304.

Hill, John. "Filming in the North," *Cineaste* 24.2–3 (1999): 26–27.

———. "Crossing the Water: Hybridity and Ethics in *The Crying Game.*" *Textual Practice* 12.1 (1998): 89–100.

———. "British Film Policy." *Film Policy: International, National and Regional Perspectives.* Ed. A Moran. London and New York: Routledge, 1996. 101–13.

———. "Boxed In." *Film Ireland* 40 (1994): 11–12.

———, Martin McLoone and Paul Hainsworth (Eds.). *Border Crossing: Film in Ireland, Britain and Europe.* Antrim: Institute of Irish Studies, University of Ulster & BFI, 1994.

———. "Images of Violence." *Cinema and Ireland.* Eds. Kevin Rockett, Luke Gibbons, and John Hill. Syracuse: Syracuse UP, 1988. 147–93.

Hoffman, Donald. "Whose Home on the Range? Finding Room for Native Americans, African Americans, and Latino Americans in the Revisionist Western." *MELUS* 22.2 (Summer 1997): 45–59.

hooks, bell. "Sorrowful Black Death Is Not a Hot Ticket," *Sight and Sound* 4 (8) (August 1994): 10–14.

Hopper, Keith. "Brave Hearts and Cute Hoors: Exploitation and the Irish Film Industry." *Film West* 23 (1995): 20–21.

Ignatiev, Noel. *How the Irish Became White.* New York: Routledge, 1995.

Innes, C. L. *Woman and Nation in Irish Literature and Society, 1880–1935.* Athens: U Georgia P, 1993.

"Interview with Eric Leguèbe." In *John Ford Interviews.* Ed. Gerald Peary. Jackson: University Press of Mississippi, 2001 [1965]. 70–74.

"Irish Cinema at the Crossroads: A Filmmakers's Symposium." *Cineaste* 24. 2–3 (1999): 70–73.

James, Joy. "Black Femmes Fatales and Sexual Abuse in Progressive 'White' Cinema; Neil Jordan's *Mona Lisa* and *The Crying Game.*" *Camera Obscura* (September 1995): 33–46.

James, Caryn. "Spike Lee's Middle-Class Jazz Musician." *The New York Times,* 3 August 1990: C1, p. 1, col. 2.

Jeffords, Susan. "The Big Switch: Hollywood Masculinity in the Nineties." *Film Theory Goes to the Movies.* Eds. Jim Collins, Hilary Radner, and Ava Preacher Collins. New York: Routledge, 1993. 196–208.

Jewell, K. Sue. *From Mammy to Miss America and Beyond: Cultural Images and the Shaping of U.S. Policy.* London: Routledge, 1993.

Johnson, Malcolm. Lee Scores with *He Got Game.*" *Hartford Courant,* 1 May 1998, F1.

———. "A Softer Lee in *Crooklyn.*" *The Hartford Courant,* 13 May 1994: B1.

———. "New Group of African-American Directors Sets the Pact for Serious Filmin the '90s." *Hartford Courant,* July 28, 1991: G1.

Johnson, Michael K. "'Try to refrain from that desire': Self-Control and Violent Passion in Oscar Micheaux's African American Western." *African American Review* 38.3 (2004): 361–77.

Johnson, Sterling. *Black Globalism: The International Politics of a Non-State Nation.* Aldershot, England and Brookfield, VT: Ashgate, 1998.

Johnson, Victoria E. "Polyphony and Cultural Expression: Interpreting Musical Traditions in *Do the Right Thing.*" *Film Quarterly* 47.2 (Winter 1993–1994): 18–29.

Johnston, Dillon. "Cross-Currencies in the Culture Market: Arnold, Yeats, Joyce." *South Atlantic Quarterly* 95.1(1996): 45–77.

Jones, Jacquie. "The Accusatory Space." *Black Popular Culture.* Ed. G. Dent. Seattle: Bay Press, 1992. 95–98.

———. "The New Ghetto Aesthetic." *Wide Angle* 13.3–4 (1991): 32–43.

Jordan, Neil. "Tally ho! Mr. Harris." *The Irish Times on the web* (front page) 23 October 1996.

———. (1993) *A Neil Jordan Reader.* New York: Vintage International, 1993.

Kamiya, Gary ."*He Got Game.*" Salon.com. April 20, 1998.

Kaplan, E. Ann. *Looking for the Other: Feminism, Film and the Imperial Gaze.* New York and London: Routledge, 1997.

———. *Motherhood and Representation: The Mother in Popular Culture and Melodrama.* New York: Routledge. 1992.

Kaplan, Elaine Bell. *Not Our Kind of Girl: Unraveling the Myths of Black Teenage Motherhood.* Berkeley: U California P, 1997.

———. *The Lure of Motherhood: A Study of Black Teen-age Mothers.* PhD dissertation, University of California at Berkeley, 1988.

Kasdan, Margo and Susan Tavernetti. "Native Americans in a Revisionist Western: *Little Big Man* (1970)." *Hollywood's Indian: The Portrayal of Native Americans in Film.* Lexington: U P of Kentucky, 1998. 121–36.

Kearney, Richard. *Strangers, Gods, and Monsters: Interpreting Otherness.* London and New York: Routledge, 2004.

———. *Postnationalist Ireland: Politics, Culture, Philosophy.* London and New York: Routledge, 1997.

———. *Transitions: Narratives in Modern Irish Culture.* Manchester: Manchester UP, 1988.

———. (Ed.) *Across the Frontiers: Ireland in the 1990s.* Dublin: Wolfhound Press, 1988.

———. (Ed.) *The Irish Mind: Exploring Intellectual Traditions.* Dublin: Wolfhound Press, 1985.

———. "Film Notes: The Iphigenia Complex in Recent Irish Cinema," *Studies: An Irish Quarterly Review* 73.289 (1984): 67–69.

———. "Avenging Angel: An Analysis of Neil Jordan's First Irish Feature Film." *Studies: an Irish Quarterly Review* 71.283 (1982): 296–303.

Keller, Alexandra. "Historical Discourse and American Identity in Westerns since the Reagan Era." *Hollywood's West: The American Frontier in Film, Television and History.* Eds. Peter C. Rollins and John E. O'Connor. Lexington: UP of Kentucky, 2004. 239–60.

———. "Generic Subversion as Counterhistory: Mario Van Peebles's *Posse.*" *The Western Through History.* Ed. Janet Walker. London and New York: Routledge, 2001. 27–46.

Kenneally, Michael (Ed.). *Cultural Contexts and Literary Idioms in Contemporary Irish Literature.* Gerrards Cross, Great Britain: Colin Smythe Press, 1988.

Kennedy, Brian P. "The Arts in Ireland, 1990." *Éire-Ireland: A Journal of Irish Studies* 25.4 (1990): 111–19.

Kennedy, Harlan. "Shamrocks and Shillelaghs: Idyll and Ideology in Irish Cinema." *Film Comment* 30. 3 (1994): 24–28.

Kennedy, Kieran A. (Ed). *Ireland in Transition: Economic and Social Change Since 1960.* Cork and Dublin: The Mercier Press, 1986.

Kermode, Mark. "The American Connection." *Sight and Sound* 2.2 (1992): 29.

———. "*December Bride.*" *Monthly Film Bulletin* 38 (1991): 43.

Kiberd, Declan. (1996a) "The Periphery and the Center." *South Atlantic Quarterly* 95.1 (1996): 5–21.

———. (1996b) "White Skins, Black Masks?: Celticism and *Négritude.*" *Éire-Ireland: A Journal of Irish Studies* 31.1–2 (Spring/Summer 1996): 163–75.

———. *Inventing Ireland: The Literature of the Modern Nation.* Cambridge, MA: Harvard UP, 1995.

———. "Irish Literature and Irish History." *The Oxford Illustrated History of Ireland.* Ed. R. F. Foster. New York and Oxford: Oxford UP, 1989. 275–337.

Kirkland, Richard. "Gender, nation, excess: reading *Hush-a-Bye-Baby.*" *Ireland in Proximity: History, Gender, Space.* Eds. Scott Brewster, Virginia Crossman, Fiona Becket, and David Alderson. London and New York: Routledge, 1999. 109–21.

Kofsky, Frank. *John Coltrane and the Jazz Revolution.* New York: Pathfinder, 1998.

Kolodny, Annette. "Among the Indians: The Uses of Captivity." *New York Times Book Review,* 31 January 1993: 1, 26–29.

Kotsopoulos, Aspasia and Josephine Mills. "*The Crying Game*: Gender, Genre and 'Postfeminism'" *Jump Cut* 39 (1994): 15–24.

Larkin, Emmett. "The Devotional Revolution in Ireland, 1850–1875." *American Historical Review* 77.3 (June 1972): 625–52.

Lee, J. J. "Continuity and Change in Ireland, 1945–70." *Ireland 1945–70.* Ed. J. J. Lee. New York: Barnes and Noble, 1979. 166–77.

Lenihan, John. H. *Showdown: Confronting Modern America in the Western Film.* Urbana, Chicago, and London: U Illinois P, 1980.

Lev, Peter. *The Euro-American Cinema.* Austin: U Texas P, 1993.

Liddy, Kevin. "*December Bride.* " *Film Base News* 17 (1991): 21–22.

Linehan, Hugh. "Myth, Mammon and Mediocrity: The Trouble with Recent Irish Cinema." *Cineaste* 24.2–3 (1999): 46–49.

———. "Family Man." *Film Ireland* 41 (1994): 11–13.

Lloyd, David. *Anomalous States: Irish Writing and the Post-Colonial Moment.* Durham: Duke UP, 1993.

Loomba, Ania. *Colonialism/Postcolonialism.* London and New York: Routledge, 1998.

Lott, Eric. "All the King's Men: Elvis Impersonators and White Working-Class Masculinity." *Race and the Subject of Masculinities.* Eds. Harry Stecopoulos and Michael Uebel. Durham, NC: Duke UP, 1997. 192–227.

———. *Love and Theft: Blackface Minstrelsy and the American Working Class.* New York and Oxford: Oxford UP, 1993.

Loy, R. Philip. *Westerns in a Changing America, 1955–2000.* Jefferson, NC: McFarland, 2004.

Lubiano, Wahneema. "Shuckin' Off the African-American Native Other: What's 'Po-Mo' Got to Do With It?" *Dangerous Liaisons: Gender, Nation, and Postcolonial Perspectives.* Eds. Anne McClintock, Aamir Mufti, and Ella Shohat. Minneapolis and London: U Minnesota P, 1997. 204–29.

———. "But Compared to What?: Reading Realism, Representation and Essentialism in *School Daze, Do the Right Thing,* and the Spike Lee Discourse." *Representing Blackness: Issues in Film and Video.* Ed. Valerie Smith. New Brunswick, NJ: Rutgers UP, 1997. 97–122.

Lugowski, David. "Genre Conventions and Visual Style in *The Crying Game.*" *Cineaste* 20.1 (1993): 32–34.

Luker, Kristin. *Dubious Conceptions: The Politics of Teenage Pregnancy.* Cambridge: Harvard UP, 1996.

Lupak, Barbara Tepa. *Literary Adaptations in Black American Cinema: From Micheaux to Morrison.* Rochester, NY: Rochester UP, 2002.

Lusted, David. *The Western.* Essex, UK: Pearson, 2003.

MacKillop, James. "Introduction." *Contemporary Irish Cinema: From The Quiet Man to Dancing at Lughnasa.* Ed. Kames MacKillop. Syracuse: Syracuse UP, 1999.

———. "Ireland and the movies: From the Volta Cinema to RTÉ." *Éire-Ireland: A Journal of Irish Studies* 19.2 (1984): 7–22.

MacLaverty, Bernard. *Cal.* New York: Norton, 1995.

Maher, Kevin. "From Angel to Vampire." *Film Ireland* 45 (February/March 1995): 16–18.

Mahony, Christina Hunt. "Poetry in Modern Ireland: Where Postcolonial and Postmodern Part Ways." *The Comparatist* 20 (1996): 82–92.

Mailer, Norman. *The White Negro.* San Francisco: City Lights Books, 1957.

Malik, Kenan. *The Meaning of Race: Race, History and Culture in Western Society.* New York: New York UP, 1996.

Maslin, Janet. "A Spike Lee Explosion Roams All Over the Court," *The New York Times,* 1 May 1998, Section E, Part 1, p. 16; col. 1.

———. "A Tender Domestic Drama From, No Joke, Spike Lee," *The New York Times,* 13 May 1994: 5C, col. 1

Massood, Paula. *Black City Cinema: African American Urban Experiences in Film.* Philadelphia: Temple UP, 2003.

McAleer, Gráinne. "Imagining Irish film." *Film Ireland* 37 (1993): 12.

McArthur, Colin. *Underworld U.S.A.* New York: The Viking Press, 1972.

McCarty, John. *Bullets Over Hollywood: The American Gangster Picture from the Silents to "The Sopranos."* New York: Da Capo, 2004.

McCartney, John. *Black Power Ideologies: An Essay in African-American Political Thought.* Philadelphia: Temple UP, 1992.

McClintock, Anne. "No Longer in a Future Heaven: Gender, Race, and Nationalism." *Dangerous Liaisons: Gender, Nation and Postcolonial Perspectives.* Eds. Anne McClintock, Aamir Mufti, and Ella Shohat. London and Minneapolis: U Minnesota P, 1997. 89–112.

———. *Imperial Leather: Race, Gender and Sexuality in the Colonial Contest.* New York: Routledge, 1995.

McCracken, Donal. "'Fenians and Dutch Carpetbaggers': Irish and Afrikaner Nationalisms, 1877–1930." *Éire-Ireland* 29.3 (Fall 1994): 109–25.

McDowell, Deborah. "Pecs and Reps: Muscling in on Race and the Subject of Masculinities." *Race and the Subject of Masculinities.* Ed. Harry Stecopoulos and Michael Uebel. Durham and London: Duke UP, 1997. 361–85.

McFarlane, Brian. *Australian Cinema 1970–1985.* London: Secker and Warburg, 1987.

McGarry, John. "Globalization, European Integration, and the Northern Ireland Conflict," in *Minority Nationalism and the Changing International Order.* Eds. Michael Keating and John McGarry. Oxford: Oxford UP, 2001. 295–324.

McGarry, Patrick. "A Different Voice: Ireland's Growing Film Industry." *Commonweal* 122.6 (24 March 1995): 17–18.

McGee, Patrick. *Cinema, Theory and Political Responsibility in Contemporary Culture.* Cambridge: Cambridge UP, 1997.

McIlroy, Brian. "Exodus, Arrival, and Return: The Generic Discourse of Irish Diasporic and Exilic Narrative Films." *Keeping It Real: Irish Film and Television.* Eds. Ruth Barton and Harvey O'Brien. London and New York: Wallflower Press, 2004. 66–77.

———. *Shooting to Kill: Filmmaking and the "Troubles" in Northern Ireland.* Richmond, BC: Steveston Press, 2001.

———. "Challenges and Problems in Contemporary Irish Cinema: The Protestants." *Cineaste* 24.2–3 (1999): 56–60.

———. *World Cinema 4: Ireland.* Trowbridge, Wiltshire: Flicks Books, 1989.

McKelly, James. "Raising Caine in a Down Eden: *Menace II Society* and the Death of Signifyin(g)." *Screen* 39.1 (Spring 1998): 36–52.

McLaverty, Bernard. *Cal.* New York: WW Norton, 1983.

McLoone, Martin. *Irish Film: The Emergence of a Contemporary Cinema.* London: BFI, 2000.

———. "Reimagining the Nation: Themes and Issues in Irish Cinema." *Cineaste* 24.2–3 (1999): 28–34.

———. "The Abused Child of History: Neil Jordan's *The Butcher Boy.*" *Cineaste* 23.4 (1998): 32–36.

———. "National Cinema and Cultural Identity: Ireland and Europe." *Border Crossing: Film in Ireland, Britain and Europe.* Eds. John Hill, Martin McLoone, and Paul Hainsworth. Antrim: Institute of Irish Studies, University of Ulster & BFI, 1994. 146–73.

———. "Funding an Identity Crisis." *Film Ireland* 30 (1992): 12–13.

———. "Cinema Irish Style." *Studies: An Irish Quarterly Review* 74.294 (1985): 220–224.

McLoughlin, Tim. "Settler Instability: Edgeworth's Irish Novels and Settler Writing from Zimbabwe." *Irish and Postcolonial Writing: History, Theory, Practice.* Eds. Glenn Hooper and Colin Graham Houndmills. Basingstoke: Palgrave Macmillan, 2002. 89–108.

McMillan, Liz. "Lifting the Veil from Whiteness: Growing Body of Scholarship Challenges a Racial 'Norm.'" *The Chronicle of Higher Education* 42.2 (8 September 1995): A23.

McNally, Patrick. "'The Whole People of Ireland: Patriotism, National Identity, and Nationalism in Eighteenth-Century Ireland." *Ireland in Proximity: History, Gender, Space.* Eds. Scott Brewster, Virginia Crossman, Fiona Becket, and David Alderson. London and New York: Routledge, 1999. 28–41.

McRobbie, Angela. *In the Culture Society: Art, Fashion and Popular Music.* London and New York: Routledge, 1999.

McSwiney, Séamus. "From Hollywood Barracks to Hollywood Boulevard," *Film West* 25 (1996): 10–17.

Merod, Jim. "A World Without Whole Notes: The Intellectual Subtext of Spike Lee's *Blues*," *boundary 2* 18.2 (1990): 238–51.

Michel, Frann. "Racial and Sexual Politics in *The Crying Game*," *Cineaste* 20.1 (1993): 30.

Mietkiewicz, Henry. "*Mo' Better Blues* Would've Been Better Without Spike's Prickly Screenplay." *Toronto Star.* August 3, 1990: E14

Millar, Jeff. "A Labor of Love from Spike Lee." *Houston Chronicle.* 13 May 1994: Weekend Preview Section, p. 1.

"Miracle Worker." *Film Industry*, 4 March 1991, 7–8.

Mishkin, Tracy. *The Harlem and Irish Renaissances.* Gainesville: UP of Florida, 1998.

Mitchell, Edward [1976]. "Apes and Essences: Some Sources of Significance in the American Gangster Film." *Film Genre Reader.* Eds. Barry Keith Grant. Austin: U Texas P, 1986. 159–68.

Monrahan, Radhika and Gita Rajan. "Introduction: The Concept of English Postoloniality." *English Postcoloniality: Literatures from around the World.* Eds. R. Mohanram and G. Rajan. Westport, CT, and London: Greenwood, 1996. 3–18.

Moon, Spencer. *Reel Black Talk: A Sourcebook of 50 America Filmmakers.* Westport, CT, and London: Greenwood, 1997.

Morgan, Jack. "The Irish in John Ford's Seventh Cavalry Trilogy—Victor McLaglen's Stooge-Irish Caricature." *MELUS* 22.2 (Summer 1997): 33–44.

Morrison, Toni. *Playing in the Dark: Whiteness and the Literary Imagination.* Cambridge, MA, and London: Harvard UP, 1992.

Mulkerns, Helena. "Film in the Fifth Province," *Cineaste* 24.2–3 (1999): 50–55.

Mulvey, Laura. "Visual Pleasure and Narrative Cinema." [1975] *Film Theory and Criticism*, sixth ed. Eds. Leo Braudy and Marshall Cohen. London and New York: Oxford UP, 2004. 837–48.

Murphy, Patsy. "Hush-A-Bye Baby." *Film Base News* 16 (1990): 8–10.

Naficy, Hamid. "Phobic Spaces and Liminal Panics: Independent Transnational Film Genre." *Global/Local: Cultural Production and the Transnational Imaginary*. Eds. Rob Wilson and Wimal Dissanayake. Durham: Duke UP, 1996. 119–44.

Nash, Catherine. "Embodied Irishness: Gender, Sexuality and Irish Identities." *In Search of Ireland: a Cultural Geography*. Eds. Brian Graham. London and New York: Routledge, 1997. 108–27.

Neal, Larry. "New Space/The Growth of Black Consciousness in the Sixties." *The Black Seventies*. Ed. Floyd Barbour. Boston: Porter Sargent, 1970. 9–31.

Neal, Mark Anthony. *What the Music Said: Black Popular Music and Black Public Culture*. New York and London: Routledge, 1999.

Neale, Steven. "Vanishing Americans: Racial and Ethnic Issues in the Interpretation and Context of Post-war 'Pro-Indian' Westerns." *Back in the Saddle Again: New Essays on the Western*. Eds. Edward Buscome and Roberta E. Pearson. London: BFI, 1998. 8–28.

Negra, Diane. "Irishness, Innocence, and American Identity Politics Before and After September 11." *Keeping It Real: Irish Film and Television*. Eds. Ruth Barton and Harvey O'Brien. London: Wallflower Press, 2004. 54–68.

———. *Off-White Hollywood.: American Culture and Ethnic Female Stardom*. London and New York: Routledge, 2001.

Nesbit, Molly. "Apart without a Face: *Orlando* and *The Crying Game*." *Artforum* 31.1 (1993): 92–94.

Nic Suibhne, Fionnuala. "'On the Straw' and Other Aspects of Pregnancy and Childbirth from the Oral Tradition of Women in Ulster." *Ulster Folklife* 38 (1992): 12–24.

Nolley, Ken. "The Representation of Conquest: John Ford and the Hollywood Indian (1939–1964)." *Hollywood's Indian: The Portrayal of the Native American in Film*. Eds. Peter C. Rollins and John E. O'Connor. Lexington: UP of Kentucky, 1998. 73–90.

O'Brien, Harvey. *The Real Ireland: The Evolution of Ireland in Documentary Film*. Manchester: Manchester UP, 2004.

———. "Documenting Ireland," *Cineaste* 24.2–3 (1999): 64–68.

O'Connell Dióg. "Women on the Verge." *Film Ireland* 32 (1992): 22–23.

O'Connor, Pat. "Defining Irish Women: Dominant Discourses and Sites of Resistance." *Éire-Ireland* 30.3 (Fall 1995): 177–87.

O'Day, Alan. "Revising the Diaspora." *The Making of Modern Irish History: Revisionism and the Revisionist Controversy.* Eds. D. G. Boyce and A. O'Day. London: Routledge, 1996.

O'Dea, Tom. "Miracle Worker." *Irish Independent* 3 April 1991.

O'Donnell, Eamonn. "The Miracle" *Film Base News* 24 (1991): 21–22.

O'Dowd, Liam. "British Nationalism and the Northern Ireland 'Peace Process.'" *Nationalisms Old and New.* Eds. Kevin Brehony and Naz Rassool. London and New York: MacMillan/St. Martin's, 1999. 174–93.

Ó Drisceoil, Donal. *Censorship in Ireland, 1939–1945: Neutrality, Politics and Society.* Cork: Cork UP, 1996.

O'Leary, Liam. *Cinema Ireland, 1896–1950: From the Liam O'Leary Archives.* Dublin: National Library of Ireland and Liam O'Leary Film Archives, 1990.

Onkey, Lauren. "A Melee and Curtain." *Jouvert: a journal of postcolonial studies* 4:1 (Fall 1999): http://social.chass.ncsu.edu/jouvert/v4i1/onkey.htm.

———. "Celtic Soul Brothers." *Éire-Ireland: A Journal of Irish Studies* 28.3 (1993): 147–58.

Oppenheimer, Jean. "Revolutionary Images." *American Cinematographer* 77.10 (1996): 80–85.

O'Regan, Tom. *Australian National Cinema.* New York and London: Routledge, 1996.

O'Reilly, Emily. *Masterminds of the Right.* Dublin: Attic Press, 1992.

Orr, Stanley. "Genres and Geographies: Cultural Decolonization in Mike Newell's *Into the West,*" *Jouvert: a journal of postcolonial studies* 4:1 (Fall 1999): *http://social.chass.ncsu.edu/jouvert/v4i1/orr.htm.*

O'Sullivan, Patrick. "Introduction to Volume 3: the creative migrant." *The Creative Migrant,* vol. 3. Irish World Wide History, Heritage, Identity Series. Ed. P. O'Sullivan. New York: St Martin's, 1999.1–27

O'Toole, Fintan. *White Savage: William Johnson and the Invention of America.* London: Faber, 2005.

———. "Working-Class Dublin on Screen: The Roddy Doyle Films," *Cineaste* 24.2–3 (1999): 36–39.

———. *The Lie of the Land: Irish Identities.* London and New York: Verso, 1997.

———. "Going Native." In *Black Hole, Green Card: The Disappearance of Ireland.* Dublin: New Island Books, 1994.

Palmer, Ian. "In the Border Country." *Film Base News* 24 (1991): 21.

———. "Paddle your own Canoe." *Film Base News* 28 (1992): 16–17.

Palmer, R. Barton. "A Masculinist Reading of Two Western Films: *High Noon* and *Rio Grande*." *Journal of Popular Film and Television* 12.4 (Winter 1984/5): 156–62.

Pareles, Jon. "In the Movies, Jazz Musicians Are Destined to Die Young." *The New York Times*, 12 August 1990: S2, p. 22, col. 3.

Parry, Benita. "Resistance Theory/Theorizing Resistance or Two Cheers for Nativism." *Rethinking Fanon*. Ed. Nigel Gibson. Amherst, NY: Humanity Books, 1999. 215–50.

Payne, Robert M. "*The Crying Game*: Crossed Lines." *Jump Cut* 39 (1994): 7–14.

Peary, Gerald (Ed.). *John Ford Interviews*. Jackson: University Press of Mississippi, 2001.

Petrie, Duncan (Ed.). *Screening Europe: Image and Identity in Contemporary European Cinema*. London: BFI, 1992.

———. "Introduction: Change and Cinematic Representation in Modern Europe." *Screening Europe*. Ed. Duncan Petrie. London: BFI, 1992. 1–8.

Pettit, Lance. *Screening Ireland: Film and Television Representation*. Manchester: Manchester UP, 2000.

———. (1999) "A Construction Site Queered: 'Gay' Images in New Irish Cinema." *Cineaste* 24.2–3 (1999): 61–63.

———. "G(ay)uinness Is Good for You." *South Atlantic Quarterly* 95.1 (1996): 205–12.

Pfeil, Fred. *White Guys: Studies in Postmodern Domination and Difference*. London and New York: Verso, 1995.

Phelan, Peggy. *Unmarked: The Politics of Performance*. London and New York: Routledge, 1993.

Pieterse, Jan. *White on Black: Images of Africa and Blacks in Western Popular Culture*. New Haven and London: Yale UP, 1992.

Pinkney, Alphonso. *Red, Black, and Green: Black Nationalism in the United States*. Cambridge: Cambridge UP, 1976.

Poole. Michael. "In Search of Ethnicity in Ireland." *In Search of Ireland: A Cultural Geography*. Ed. Brian Graham. London and New York: Routledge, 1997. 128–47.

Power, Paul. "The Irish are Rising Again," *Cineaste* 24.2–3 (1999): 74–75.

———. "Actors Fight for Eire." *Variety* 370.10 (20 April 1998): 16.

Priestly, Brian. *Jazz: The Rough Guide*. London: Penguin, 1995.

Pye, Douglas. "Double Vision: Miscegenation and Point of View in *The Searchers*," in *The Book of Westerns*. Eds. Ian Cameron and Douglas Pye. New York: Continuum, 1996. 229–35.

———. "Genre and History: *Fort Apache* and *The Man Who Shot Liberty Valence*," in *The Book of Westerns*. Eds. Ian Cameron and Douglas Pye. New York: Continuum, 1996. 111–22.

Radhakrishnan, R. *Theory in an Uneven World*. Malden, MA, and Oxford: Blackwell, 2003.

———. *Diasporic Meditations: Between Home and Location*. Minneapolis: U Minnesota P, 1996.

Rafferty, Terence. "Dead End." *New Yorker*. 31 March 1993.

Rancière, Jacques. "Politics, Identification, and Subjectivization." *The Identity in Question*. Ed. John Rajchman. New York: Routledge, 1995. 63–72.

Ray, Robert. *A Certain Tendency of the Hollywood Cinema, 1930–1980*. Princeton: Princeton UP, 1985.

Redlich, Patricia. "Women and the Family." *Women in Irish Society: The Historical Dimension*. Eds. MacCurtain, M. and D. Ó Corráin. Westport, CT: Greenwood, 1979. 82–91.

Reed, Adolph, Jr. *Stirrings in the Jug: Black Politics in the Post-Segregation Era*. London and Minneapolis: U Minnesota P, 1999.

Regester, Charlene. "Oscar Micheaux's Multifaceted Portrayals of the African-American Male: The Good, the Bad and the Ugly." *Me Jane: Masculinity, Movies, and Women*. Eds. Pat Kirkham, and Janet Thumin. New York: St. Martin's, 1995.166–83.

Reid, Mark. *Black Lenses, Black Voices: African American Film Now*. Lanham, Boulder, Toronto, and Oxford: Rowman and Littlefield, 2005.

———. *PostNegritude Visual and Literary Culture*. Albany: SUNY P, 1997.

———. *Redefining Black Film*. Berkeley: U California P, 1993.

Reizbaum, Marilyn. "Not a Crying Game: The Feminist Appeal: Nationalism, Feminism and the Contemporary Literatures of Scotland and Ireland." *Scotlands* 2 (1994): 24–31.

"Report of the Film Industry Committee" (1968). Dublin: The Stationery Office (Prl 145).

Rhines, Jesse Algernon. *Black Film/White Money*. New Brunswick, NJ: Rutgers UP, 1996.

Robinson, Mary T. W. "Women and the New Irish State." *Women in Irish Society: The Historical Dimension*. Eds. M. MacCurtain and D. Ó Corráin. Westport, CT: Greenwood, 1979. 58–70.

Rocchio, Vincent F. *Reel Racism: Confronting Hollywood's Construction of Afro-American Culture.* Boulder, CO: Westview, 2000.

Rockett, Kevin and Emer Rockett. *Neil Jordan: Exploring Boundaries.* Dublin: Liffey Press, 2003.

———. "Irish Cinema: The National in the International," *Cineaste* 24.2–3 (1999): 23–25.

———. *Still Irish: A Century of the Irish in Film.* Dublin: Red Mountain Press, 1995.

———. (1994a) "The Irish Migrant and Film." *The Creative Migrant,* vol. 3. The Irish World Wide History, Heritage, Identity Series. Ed. P. O'Sullivan. New York: St. Martin's, 1994. 170–91.

———. (1994b) "Culture, Industry and Irish Cinema." *Border Crossing: Film in Ireland, Britain and Europe.* Eds. John Hill, Martin McLoone, and Paul Hainsworth. Antrim: Institute of Irish Studies and British Film Institute, 1994. 126–39.

———. (1994c). "Phases of the Moon: A Short History of Cinema in Ireland." *Film Comment* 30.3 (May–June 1994): 25–28.

———. (1992a) "From Atlanta to Dublin," *Sight and Sound* 2.2 (1992): 26–28, 29.

———. (1992b) "Points of View: What Is an Irish Film?" *Film West* 14 (1992): 6–7.

———. (1988). "An Irish Film Studio." *Cinema and Ireland.* Eds. Luke Gibbons and John Hill. Syracuse: Syracuse UP, 1988. 95–126.

Rogers, Deborah. "Rockabye Lady: Pregnancy as Punishment in Popular Culture." *Journal of American Studies* 26.1 (1992): 81–83.

Rony, Fatimah Tobing. *The Third Eye: Race, Cinema and Ethnographic Spectacle.* Durham and London: Duke UP, 1996.

Rose, Tricia. *Black Noise: Rap Music and Black Culture in Contemporary America.* Hanover and London: Wesleyan UP/UP of New England, 1994.

Rosenthal, David H. *Hard Bop: Jazz and Black Music 1955–1965.* New York and Oxford: Oxford UP, 1992.

Roth, Marty. "'Yes, My Darling Daughter': Gender, Miscegenation, and Generation in John Ford's *The Searchers.*" *New Orleans Review* 18.4 (Winter 1991): 65–73.

Rueschman, Eva. "Introduction." *Moving Pictures, Migrating Identities.* Ed. Eva Rueschman. Jackson: UP of Mississippi, 2003. ix–xxx.

Russell, Hawley. "Crossing Games: Reading Black Transvestism at the Movies." *Critical Matrix* 8.1 (1994): 109–25.

Ruth, David. *Inventing the Public Enemy: The Gangster in American Culture.* Chicago and London: U Chicago P, 1996.

Sawyer, Roger. *"We Are But Women": Women in Ireland's History.* London and New York: Routledge, 1993

Scallan, Anne. "Non Places: Irish Cinema from Another Perspective," *film west* 32 (1998), 22–24.

Schaeffer, Patricia. Text of Penal Laws. http://www.law.umn.edu/irishlaw/intro.html.

Schickel, Richard. "Childhood Nightmares." *Time* 151.13 (6 April 1998): 70.

Schneider, Tassilo. "Finding a New Heimat in the Wile West: Karl May and the German Western of the 1960s." *Back in the Saddle Again: New Essays on the Western.* Eds. Edward Buscombe and Roberta E. Pearson. London: BFI, 1998. 141–59.

Severin, Laura. "Distant Resonances: Contemporary Scottish Women Poets and African-American Music." *Mosaic* 39.1 (March 2006): 45–59.

Sheehy, Tim. *The Butcher Boy* (interview with Neil Jordan). *Film Ireland* 63 (March 1998): 14–15.

Shohat, Ella. "Post-Third-Worldist Culture: Gender, Nation and the Cinema." *Rethinking Third Cinema.* Eds. Anthony R. Guneratne and Wimal Dissanayake. London and New York: Routledge, 2004. 51–78.

——— and Robert Stam. *Unthinking Eurocentrism Multiculturalism and the Media.* London and New York: Routledge, 1994.

Silverman, Kaja. *The Threshold of the Visible World.* New York and London: Routledge, 1996.

Skerry, Philip J. "What Makes a Man to Wander? Ethan Edwards of John Ford's *The Searchers.*" *New Orleans Review* 18.4 (Winter 1991): 86–91.

———. "The Western Film: A Sense of an Ending." *New Orleans Review* 17.3 (Fall 1990): 13–17.

Slide, Anthony. *Cinema and Ireland.* Jefferson, NC: McFarland, 1988.

Slotkin, Richard. *Gunfighter Nation.* New York: Athenaeum, 1992.

Smith, Jeff. *The Sounds of Commerce: Marketing Popular Film Music.* New York: Columbia UP, 1998.

Smith, Murray. *Engaging Characters: Fiction, Emotion, and the Cinema.* Oxford and New York: Clarendon Press/Oxford UP, 1995.

Smyth, Ailbhe. *The Abortion Papers Ireland.* Dublin: Attic Press, 1992.

Snead, James. *White Screens: Black Images.* Eds. Colin McCabe and Cornel West. New York and London: Routledge, 1994.

———. (1990) "European Pedigrees/African Contagions: Nationality, Narrative, and Communality in Tutuola, Achebe, and Reed." *Nation and Narration.* Ed. Homi K. Bhabha. London and New York: Routledge. 231–49.

Spencer, Philip and Howard Wollman. "Blood and Sacrifice: Politics Versus Culture in the Construction of Nationalism." *Nationalisms Old and New.* Eds. Kevin Brehony and Naz Rassool. London and New York: MacMillan/St. Martin's, 1999. 87–124.

Spillers, Hortense. "Mama's Baby, Papa's Maybe: An American Grammar Book." *Diacritics* 17.2 (1987): 65–81.

Stam, Robert. (1997a) *Tropical Multiculturalism: A Comparative History of Race in Brazilian Cinema and Culture.* Durham and London: Duke UP, 1997.

———. (1997b) "Multiculturalism and Neoconservatives." *Dangerous Liaisons: Gender, Nation and Postcolonial Perspectives.* Eds. Anne McClintock, Aamir Mufti, and Ella Shohat. Minneapolis and London: U Minnesota P, 1997. 188–203.

———. "Cross-Cultural Dialogisms: Race and Multiculturalism in Brazilian Cinema." *Mediating Two Worlds: Cinematic Encounters in the Americas.* Eds. John King, Ana Lopez, and Manuel Alvarado. London: BFI, 1993. 175–91.

Stanfield, Peter. "Dixie Cowboys and Blue Yodels: The Strange History of the Singing Cowboy." *Back in the Saddle Again: New Essays on the Western.* Eds. Edward Buscombe and Roberta E. Pearson. London: BFI, 1998. 96–118.

Staunton, Denis. "Neil Jordan's New Film a Hit in Berlin." *The Irish Times* 22 February 1991: 10.

Stephens, Michael L. *Gangster Films: A Comprehensive, Illustrated Reference to People, Film and Terms.* Jefferson, NC, and London: McFarland, 1996.

Sterrit, David. "Freeze Frame." Review of *Eat the Peach. Christian Science Monitor* 24 July 1987. http://www.csmonitor.com/cgi-bin/wit_article.pl?tape/86/lff24.

Stoler, Ann Laura. *Race and the Education of Desire: Foucault's History of Sexuality and the Colonial Order of Things.* Durham, NC: Duke UP, 1995

Studlar, Gaylyn. "Sacred Duties, Poetic Passions: John Ford and the Issue of Femininity in the Western." *John Ford Made Westerns: Filming the Legend in the Sound Era.* Eds. Gaylyn Studlar and Matthew Bernstein. Bloomington: Indiana UP 2001. 43–74.

Sullivan, Megan. *Women in Northern Ireland: Cultural Studies and Material Conditions.* Gainesville: UP of Florida, 1999.

Taylor, Clyde. "New U.S. Black Cinema." *Movies and Mass Culture.* Ed. J. Belton. New Brunswick, NJ: Rutgers UP, 1996. 231–46.

Thomas, Rebecca. "There's a Whole Lot o' Color in the 'White Man's" Blues: Country Music's Selective Memory and the Challenge of Identity." *The Midwest Quarterly* 38.1 (1996): 73–89.

Tompkins, Jane. *West of Everything: The Inner Life of Westerns.* New York and Oxford: Oxford UP, 1992.

Toop, David. "Rock Musicians and Film Soundtracks." *Celluloid Jukebox: Popular Music and the Movies Since the 50s.* Eds. Jonathan Romney and Adrian Wooten. London: British Film Institute, 1995. 72–81.

Trachsel, Mary. "Oral and Literate Constructs of 'Authentic' Irish Music." *Éire-Ireland* 30.3 (Fall 1995): 27–46.

Turan, Kenneth. "A Warm and Fuzzy Spike Lee: The Cinematic Polemicist Strolls Down Memory Lane in *Crooklyn.*" *Los Angeles Times* 13 May 1994: F1, col. 2

Tuska, Jon. *The American West in Film: Critical Approaches to the Western.* Westport, CT: Greenwood, 1985.

Walker, Michael. "Dances with Wolves." *The Book of Westerns.* Eds. Ian Cameron and Dougles Pye. New York: Continuum, 1996. 284–93.

Wallace, Michele. "*Boyz N the Hood* and *Jungle Fever.*" *Black Popular Culture.* Ed. Gina Dent. Bay Press: Seattle, 1992.

Walsh, Orla. "Abortion and Censorship" *Film Base News* 16 (1990): 13.

Walshe, Èibhear (Ed.). *Sex, Nation and Dissent in Irish Writing.* Cork: Cork UP, 1997.

Ward, Catherine. "Wake Homes: Four Modern Novels of the Irish-American Family." *Éire-Ireland: a Journal of Irish Studies* 26.2 (1991): 78–91.

Ware, Vron. "Island Racism: Gender, Place and White Power." *Displacing Whiteness: Essays in Social and Cultural Criticism.* Ed. R. Frankenberg. Durham and London: Duke UP, 1997. 283–310.

Watkins, S. Craig. *Representing: Hip Hop Culture and the Production of Black Cinema.* Chicago and London: U Chicago P, 1998.

Watt, Stephen. "The Politics of Bernard MacLaverty's *Cal.*" *Éire-Ireland* 28.3 (Fall 1993): 130–46.

Wellman, David. "Minstrel Shows, Affirmative Action Talk, and Angry White Men: Marking Racial Otherness in the 1990s." *Displacing Whiteness: Essays in Social and Cultural Criticism.* Ed. R. Frankenberg. Durham and London: Duke UP, 1997. 311–31.

Welsh, James W. "*The Crying Game.*" *Films in Review* 44 (1993): 188–89.

Wexman, Virginia Wright. "The Family on the Land: Race and Nationhood in Silent Westerns." *The Birth of Whiteness: Race and the Emergence of U.S. Cinema.* Ed. Daniel Bernardi. New Brunswick, NJ: Rutgers UP, 1996. 129–69.

Wiegman, Robyn. "Fiedler and Sons." *Race and the Subject of Masculinities.* Eds. Harry Stecopoulos and Micharl Uebel. Durham, NC: Duke UP, 1997. 45–68.

———. "Feminism, 'The Boyz,' and Other Matters Regarding the Male." *Screening the Male: Exploring Masculinities in Hollywood Cinema.* Eds. Ina Rae Hark and Steven Cohen. London and New York: Routledge, 1993. 173–93.

———. "Black Bodies/American Commodities: Gender, Race and the Bourgeois Ideal in Contemporary Film." *Unspeakable Images: Ethnicity and the American Cinema.* Ed. L. Friedman. Urbana: U Illinois P, 1991. 308–28.

Willeman, Paul. "The Third Cinema Question: Notes and Reflections." *Questions of Third Cinema.* Eds. Jim Pines and Paul Willeman. London: BFI, 1989. 1–29.

Wills, Clair. "Joyce, Prostitution and the City," *South Atlantic Quarterly* 95.1 (1996): 79–95.

Wright, Michelle. *Becoming Black: Creating Identity in the African Diaspora.* Durham, NC: Duke UP, 2004.

Wyatt, Justin. *High Concept: Movies and Marketing in Hollywood.* Austin: U Texas P, 1994.

Yearwood, Gladstone. *Black Film as Signifying Practice: Cinema, Narration, and the African-American Aesthetic Tradition.* Trenton, NJ, and Asmara, Ethiopia: African World Press, 2000.

Young, Lola. *Fear of the Dark: 'Race,' Gender and Sexuality in the Cinema.* London and New York: Routledge, 1996.

———. "'Nothing Is As It Seems': Re-viewing *The Crying Game.*" *Me Jane: Masculinity, Movies and Women.* Eds. P. Kirkham and J. Thuman. New York: St. Martin's, 1995. 273–85.

Young, Robert. *Colonial Desire: Hybridity in Theory, Culture and Race.* London and New York: Routledge, 1995.

Zillax, Amy. "The Scorpion and the Frog: Agency and Identity in Neil Jordan's *The Crying Game.*" *Camera Obscura* 35 (May 1995): 25–51.

INDEX